Constitutional Precedent in US Supreme Court Reasoning

For Margaret and Frederick

Constitutional Precedent in US Supreme Court Reasoning

David Schultz

Distinguished University Professor of Political Science, Legal Studies, and Environmental Studies, Hamline University, Saint Paul, Minnesota, USA, Professor of Law, University of Minnesota and Saint Thomas Schools of Law, Minneapolis, Minnesota, USA

Edward Elgar
PUBLISHING

Cheltenham, UK • Northampton, MA, USA

Published by
Edward Elgar Publishing Limited
The Lypiatts
15 Lansdown Road
Cheltenham
Glos GL50 2JA
UK

Edward Elgar Publishing, Inc.
William Pratt House
9 Dewey Court
Northampton
Massachusetts 01060
USA

Paperback edition 2023

A catalogue record for this book
is available from the British Library

Library of Congress Control Number: 2022931149

This book is available electronically in the **Elgar**online
Law subject collection
http://dx.doi.org/10.4337/9781839103131

ISBN 978 1 83910 312 4 (cased)
ISBN 978 1 83910 313 1 (eBook)
ISBN 978 1 0353 1556 7 (paperback)

Printed and bound by CPI Group (UK) Ltd, Croydon, CR0 4YY

Contents

Acknowledgements

I want to thank all my law students over a long and productive teaching career whose terrific questions on legal reasoning, analysis, and precedent formed the basis of this book and the reasons for why I wrote it.

Introduction: The nature of legal precedent in American law

I   INTRODUCTION

Chief Justice John Marshall famously declared in *Marbury v. Madison* that "It is emphatically the province and duty of the judicial department to say what the law is."[1] But what if the Court got it wrong? What if, after declaring in one case what the law means, especially when it comes to an interpretation of the US Constitution, the current Court, or a later one, decided that the original decision was no longer correct. Should it continue to accept the original decision as binding, or should it overrule it and declare a new rule? Addressing the question of when previous decisions are precedent—that is, binding and should be followed, and when and under what circumstances they should no longer be viewed as such—is among the most central questions of American law and legal reasoning. The enigma of constitutional precedent is also central to major disputes in American politics.

Consider the case of *Roe v. Wade*,[2] the landmark US Supreme Court decision declaring that women have a constitutionally protected right to terminate their pregnancies, especially during the first two trimesters. From practically the day it was decided it was a controversial decision, producing a political and legal backlash among conservative religious followers and scholars. For the former, *Roe* went against their beliefs that "life began at conception" or that the fetus was a person deserving legal protection. For the latter, the Court's decision was an example of legislating from the branch, grounding abortion rights not in any justifiable legal principle or argument but simply in politics. *Roe* launched a massive political and legal countermobilization to overturn it; the detailed story is not able to be told here.

But over time there were many situations in court or in Supreme Court Justice confirmation hearings where the status of *Roe v. Wade* was central. After a series of Supreme Court decisions post-1973, where it upheld some restrictions on *Roe* or where it appeared several Justices had questioned it,

---

[1]   Marbury v. Madison 5 U.S. 137, 177 (1803).
[2]   410 U.S. 113 (1973).

in *Planned Parenthood v. Casey*[3] many thought the decision would be overturned. This was especially the case because the appointments of Sandra Day O'Connor, Anthony Kennedy, and David Souter by Republican presidents seemed to place mostly conservatives on the Court. But alas these three Justices wrote the plurality opinion in *Planned Parenthood*, affirming its central holding, and explaining why it should retain its precedential status. Additionally, during the confirmation hearings in 1986 for Robert Bork and 1993 for Ruth Bader Ginsburg, they were asked about their views on the case. In 2005 Senator Arlen Specter asked then nominee John Roberts whether *Roe* was a "super precedent," presumably implying that it was a decision that could or should not be overruled. Perhaps it was a foundational decision, such as *Marbury v. Madison*, a decision really no one thinks will be overturned.[4] Again in 2020, when Donald Trump nominated Amy Coney Barrett to replace Ginsburg on the Court, the status of *Roe* again re-emerged, as the former was quizzed about her views on the case and the role of constitutional precedent. Barrett's confirmation hearing and placement on the Supreme Court again raised the possibility that the days for *Roe v. Wade* were numbered and short.

Why should a current American court, be it the US Supreme Court or any other, care about previous rulings or decisions issued? Should not cases simply be decided based on the facts and law presented before it, and not be influenced by previous decisions which have nothing to do with the present dispute? If one is a constitutional originalist, such as Justices Antonin Scalia or Clarence Thomas, precedent should not matter. One should simply interpret the Constitution in terms of the intent of the framers, disregarding precedent, especially if it is wrong. What if a previous court simply misread the plain language of the text: should one defer to the decision or would overruling it be permissible, if not obligatory? These are the questions that precedent raises.

II   TYPE OF LEGAL SYSTEMS

There are many ways to classify legal systems across the world. For our purposes, one distinction is between civil and common law systems. Civil law systems constitute most legal systems in the world. While all legal systems, by definition, begin with constitutions, laws, or other legal texts, how judges in civil and common law systems approach and interpret them is different. Simplified, in civil law systems the task of legal interpretation places premium on the legal text or provision. It is the task of the judge when interpreting the law to apply the facts to it and render a decision based on what the former says.

---

3   505 U.S. 833 (1992).
4   Gerhardt, Michael J. 2006. *Super Precedent*, 90 Minn. L. Rev. 1204.

In rendering such a decision, judges do not look to previous decisions they have issued as a guide to how they should interpret in this case. Each case is decided on its own merits and facts considering what the law says, and other decisions, no matter how factually close they are to the present dispute, are not supposed to be cited as authority.

Civil law systems stand in contrast to common law systems. England is the origin of common law legal systems, influencing other countries such as the United States, Canada, Australia, and New Zealand. Precedent is central to legal reasoning and argumentation. Here courts again try to decide a case by applying the facts to the law. Judges seek to understand legal texts initially via a variety of legal techniques, including perhaps plain language or intent of the framers or the authors. But that is not the sum of techniques. Judges will also consult previous decisions rendered by it, a superior court, or perhaps even by a parallel court. The goal will be to determine if another case factually similar in relevant ways was decided and, if so, that decision should perhaps also bind the judgment in this case. That previous decision might well guide the decision in the current case and be consulted along with the language of the law or legal text and other interpretive techniques to render a decision. Here the previous decision is perhaps a weak precedent, serving as only one factor in guiding a decision. Or perhaps it is a strong precedent, providing definitive guidance to the court, and binding its decision in the present case.

In common law systems, a decided case should in part be guided by past court decisions, and it should also serve as a guide for future courts. Once a court has rendered an interpretation of a text, its interpretation for all future and similar fact patterns is precedent and theoretically binding upon it and future courts, especially if it is a court of last instance, and on all lower courts within its jurisdiction. If the facts in the present case of *Smith v. Jones* are arguably identical or similar enough to a previous *Doe v. Roe* decision, the former should be decided the same or like the latter. At least this is the text-book answer for a common law system. But determining whether two cases are factually similar and how a previous decision needs to be reconciled with the legal text, among other issues, renders the real answer more complex.

The important role of previous court decisions to guide present and future interpretations and decisions is unique to the history of common law systems. Its origin is in England. English law simply evolved over time. It evolved because of a series of historical accidents and events, such as the signing of the Magna Carta in 1215, or with the adoption of the English Bill of Rights in 1689. Both events or documents were efforts to limit royal power. But British law also was unwritten. Rights that individuals had to property, for example, were a product of unwritten custom or practice. Questions about duties individuals had to others became the basis of contract and tort law. There were no clearly promulgated and written rules. Judges perhaps had some basic principles of law to guide them, but in the absence of clear legal texts that specified the law and duties for individuals, they were placed in a position of having to ascertain what exactly the law said and meant in a particular situation. Judges, looking for guidance regarding how to decide a present case, often turned to past decisions to provide some direction. Judges thus, in interpreting the law, effectively were making law or at least deciding what the law meant or said. Once they had consulted previous decisions as direction for the current case, the latter would become a guide for a future judge regarding how to decide. Common law thus created a space for judge-made law, for the role of past decisions to influence or guide the future.

Such a system of judge-made law thus became a fixture or component of common law. It did so perhaps out of necessity when there were no codified rules, when rights were evolving, and when judges needed help in deciding cases. Looking to past decisions to assist judges resolve disputes appealed to the concepts of efficiency, fairness (like cases decided alike), and predictability. Knowing that how a past case was decided would bind or influence a future case helped litigants predict what would happen, and it was a good rule of thumb or shorthand for deciding a case.

Case law, or precedents, thus became an important feature of British common law. It especially became easier for this to occur when past court decisions were published. Court reporters, collections of past decisions, even if only summarized, facilitated the ability of past decisions to guide judges in their work. Legal research thus gradually included looking at collections of past decisions, seeking out one that would be similar enough to bind or instruct a judge in a present dispute. Precedent in common law England was a product of historical accident and necessity, but it also addressed the problem of the open texture of language.

Some language philosophers may assert that words are clear in their meaning. In Lewis Carroll's *Alice in Wonderland*, the March Hare implores Alice that she should "say what you mean," only for the latter to retort "I mean what I say." Words are not always clear, and meanings are often elusive. Almost every 1L law school student is treated to the classic problem of a law that says, "No vehicles are allowed in the park." Lacking a clear definition of what a vehicle is, one does not know whether it includes bicycles, skateboards, golf carts, or what. Judges faced with an open meaning to what constitutes a vehicle need to interpret the law. Once an initial judge has decided or not that a bicycle is a vehicle, it makes no sense for every judge to recreate the initial inquiry. Instead, if one judge has said a bicycle is a vehicle, unless there is good reason to think that decision was wrong or something has changed, defer to that decision and let it guide the decision in this dispute and in all future cases.

The often indeterminacy of legal texts and language renders past judicial interpretations important. It allows one judge or court simply to defer to someone else or another court an explanation and interpretation that is persuasive. It solves the problem of indeterminacy for all by letting one person resolve it and then encouraging or compelling others to follow it. Of course, the open texture of the law is also a problem in civil law systems. But in them legal culture and tradition did not allow judges to have the degree of freedom they did in common law systems to act. In English history this power of judges was a byproduct in part of the struggles between the Crown and Parliament for supremacy, as well as by political arguments by individuals such as John Locke for there to be a separation of powers to check and limit governmental authority, especially that of the king or queen.

The importance of cases or judge-made law in England was exported to the colonies of the British Empire, including eventually the United States. Thus, by the time of independence in 1776, common law and precedent were central to the American legal system. Thus, by the time Chief Justice John Marshall declared in *Marbury v. Madison* that "It is emphatically the province and duty of the judicial department to say what the law is," on one level he was no more than stating a legal truism that judges make law by way of issuing decisions that serve as legal precedent.

III   WHAT ARE PRECEDENTS AND WHY DO WE HAVE THEM?

Precedent is a central feature of common law legal systems such as the United States. But what exactly is a precedent and when does a court case or decision turn into one?

Consider several possible definitions.

> Precedents, we said, are prior decisions that function as models for later decisions. Authoritative precedents are prior decisions that for some reason one ought to use as governing models for later decisions.[5]
> A decided case that furnishes a basis for determining later cases involving similar facts or issues.[6]
> An action of official decision that can be used for support for later actions or decisions; esp., a decided case that furnishes a basis for determining later cases involving similar facts or issues.[7]
> A precedent is a past event—in law the event is nearly always a decision—which serves as a guide for present action. Not all past events are precedents.[8]

These four definitions tell us that precedents are court decisions, but not necessarily all decisions. They are of a certain character such that they serve as a guide for future decisions. They are meant, in part, to restrict the decision-making or discretion of judges, providing a roadmap for how to decide a present or future fact pattern or controversy.

The concept of precedent is from the Latin phrase *stare decisis*, literally translated from the Latin as "stand by things decided." *Stare decisis* means that if something was decided a particular way in the past, the current dispute should also be decided that way. *Stare decisis* or precedent is different from another legal concept, *res judicata*, which says that once an issue has been decided, if it comes up again, the prior decision controls. By that, if I sue you for contract damages and win and if there is then another lawsuit arising out of the same set of facts, *res judicata* demands that this decision control here.

Precedent involves different controversies. It is a situation asking whether the facts in a case *Smith v. Jones* where the court ruled thus should be binding upon a new case with different parties or litigants involved. Precedent asks whether the factual disputes between the two cases are similar enough that the decision in the first case controls the second. On one level, precedent arises out of a concept of justice or fairness that says similar cases or issues should be decided similarly. Precedents perhaps simply reflect shared understandings of what strikes many of us as fair or reasonable by treating things the same if they are the same.

---

[5] MacCormick, D. Neil and Robert S. Summers, "Introduction," In MacCormick, D. Neil, and Robert S. Summers. 1997. *Interpreting Precedents*. New York: Routledge, 1, 2.

[6] Garner, Bryan A. 2016. *The Law of Judicial Precedent*. Saint Paul, MN: Thomson Reuters, 22.

[7] *Id.* at 801.

[8] Duxbury, Neil. 2008. *The Nature and Authority of Precedent.* New York: Cambridge, 1.

There are several types of precedent. Precedents may initiate within a court which has a prior decision factually similar to a present dispute. Here a past decision by a specific court binds it in a present dispute. There is then the concept of a vertical precedent.[9] A court of higher authority decides a case and therefore inferior courts within its jurisdiction are compelled to follow it. In the United States, Article VI, Section Two of the Constitution, referred to as the Supremacy Clause, binds lower courts to follow the decisions of the US Supreme Court.[10] There is then also the concept of horizontal precedent, where a court decides to follow a decision by another court of parallel authority.[11] This could be one court of appeals in the US, such as the Second Circuit, deciding to follow a similar decision rendered by the Eleventh Circuit. Another scenario is where a supreme court in one state decides to follow the logic of a supreme court in another state. Strictly speaking, the former is not really within the same jurisdiction as the latter, but the latter nonetheless finds the logic of the former compelling enough to follow. Finally, a state's highest court in interpreting its own constitution might look to decisions by the US Supreme Court or courts in other states to help them decide a case. In the first scenario, precedent is binding, and the lower court must follow what the higher-level court said. In the other situations the precedent is persuasive or compelling, providing guidance or justification for a decision, even if not specifically legally binding.

Note in all these scenarios there are commonalities of language, indicating that precedents are important because they are binding, compelling, or persuasive. All this is significant because they capture the essence of what precedential authority is all about. Why follow precedent? There are a cluster of reasons for this.

On one level, following past precedent adheres with Western conceptions of justice that go back to Aristotle that similar things should be treated similarly. All things being equal, two individuals or disputes that are relevant in all material or important ways should be decided the same. This is the concept of equality, or what philosopher John Rawls would call justice as fairness. Neil Duxbury sees precedent as a heuristic, that is, a cognitive tool employed so that we do not have to rethink every decision—it provides a ready-made decision or answers for a judge.[12] Duxbury also contends that following precedent appeals to judicial economy, saving time and resources for a judge and not having to come up with a new decision *ab initio*. There is a sense of law and

---

[9]   Garner at 801.
[10]   *Id.*
[11]   *Id.*
[12]   Duxbury at 94.

economies reasoning here. Following precedent also ensures certainty and predictability in the law, something important to litigants and disputants who want
to have some sense of what the law requires before they act.[13] Schauer sees
a cluster of values, including fairness, predictability, efficiency, institutional
strengthening, and stability, being promoted by generally following precedent.[14] Former Supreme Court Justice Robert Jackson argued that stability
alone was not value in itself, but needed to be considered along with the need
of legal evolution and change.[15]

Aleksander Peczenik reinforces these points.[16] He sees *stare decisis* as
appeal to the concepts of uniformity,[17] equality,[18] and efficiency.[19] Following
precedent helps avoid disputes and controversies, by theoretically providing
clear answers or guidance in terms of how disputes, such as the interpretation
of a legal document, should be resolved, or what are my obligations to another
person in a possible tort or contract dispute.[20] Others argue that following precedent allows for a passing down of wisdom from one generation to another.[21]
Following precedent allows for the incremental building of knowledge; it is
a form of judicial minimalism[22] that allows for refinement and development of
the law one step at a time.[23] Following precedent contains judicial discretion
so that it does not look like judges are simply politicians with robes, issuing
opinions based on policy preferences and not via some neutral principles of
law.[24] Precedent is part of legal doctrine, a body of rules to constrain judging.[25] Former US Supreme Court Justice Benjamin Cardozo saw following
precedent as a way of bringing finality or closure to issues so that they are not

---

[13]   Duxbury at 116.

[14]   Schauer, Frederick. 1987. *Precedent*, 39 Stan. L. Rev. 571.

[15]   Jackson, Robert. 1944. *Decisional Law and Stare Decisis*, 30 A. B. A. J. 334.

[16]   Peczenik, Aleksander, "The Binding Force of Precedent," In MacCormick, D.
Neil, and Robert S. Summers. 1997. *Interpreting Precedents*. New York: Routledge,
461.

[17]   *Id.* at 486.

[18]   *Id.* at 487.

[19]   *Id.* at 490.

[20]   *Id.* at 490.

[21]   Easterbrook, Frank H. 1988. *Stability and Reliability in Judicial Decisions*, 73
Cornell Law Review, 422, 422–23.

[22]   Sunstein, Cass R. 2001. *One Case at a Time: Judicial Minimalism on the
Supreme Court*. Cambridge: Harvard University Press.

[23]   Lieber, Francis. 1883. *On Civil Liberty and Self Government*, 223; Raz, Joseph.
2009. *The Authority of Law: Essays on Law and Morality*, 196.

[24]   Sunstein, Cass R. 1993. *On Analogical Reasoning*, 106 Harvard Law Review,
741, 782.

[25]   Schlag, Pierre, and Amy J. Griffin. 2020. *How to Do Things with Legal Doctrine.*
Chicago: University of Chicago Press, 23.

constantly reopened or relitigated.[26] Following precedent respects reliance or settled expectations on interests in the law, ensuring that investments of time, money, or simply choices in life are not made in vain and that it is possible to plan for the future.[27] Some have argued, though, that there are different types of reliance interests that deserve more or less respect.[28] Finally, one can argue that following precedent promotes democracy, ensuring judges act within their realm and not encroach upon the authority of other branches.

All these reasons are practical grounds for precedent. There too are legal grounds. As noted above, the Supremacy Clause and the concept of vertical precedent means lower courts should follow the direction of higher-level courts within their jurisdiction. Precedent should also be followed because such decisions are in fact law. How are they law? We return again to the concept of the open texture of the law.

A basic task of judges and perhaps attorneys is interpreting legal texts. Texts include constitutions, bills of rights, statutes, contracts, and perhaps other documents. Yet the words used in them are not always clear. What does due process of law or equal protection mean? What are privileges or immunities, or what constitutes cruel and unusual punishment, or what counts as speech for the purposes of the First Amendment? All of these are good questions. A judge facing a controversy may have to interpret the language of these or other clauses. How does that occur? There are many theories of legal interpretation, and they will not be reviewed here. But initially perhaps one should try to read the plain language of the text and ascertain what the rules mean. One can also try to look at the intent of the authors of the documents. These are valid techniques, but they may not yield definitive answers. Words are not always clear, and intent may be hard to ascertain, especially if there are multiple authors. This is where precedents become helpful.

What happens is that, when a court or judge first examines a legal text, let us say to determine what due process means, that court will do its best to find an answer. Its answer will be subject to review by higher courts which profit from the initial reading. A court of last resort, such as the Supreme Court, then issues its opinion about what the clause means. Its opinion becomes law. The original text, along with its understanding of it, constitutes the law. Over time subsequent courts review this decision, refine it, apply it, perhaps modify it to new situations. All these opinions form the law on this clause. Think of court precedents as being incorporated into the text to form the body of law or

---

[26]   Cardozo, Benjamin N. 1991. *The Nature of the Judicial Process*, 149.
[27]   Holmes, Oliver Wendell, Jr. 1897. *The Path of Law*, 10 Harvard Law Review, 457, 457.
[28]   Kozel, Randy J. 2013. *Precedent and Reliance*, 62 Emory L.J. 1459.

jurisprudence for it. Ronald Dworkin, a famous legal philosopher, suggested that the law be thought of as a big chain novel written by multiple authors.[29] Elsewhere he suggested that law was an effort at creating a larger and more coherent theory about a subject or issue.[30] Or even elsewhere he contended in his debates against another legal philosopher, H.L.A. Hart, that the law does contain some legal principles or values that help define it.[31] His point with all of these is that there is not necessarily a clean line separating or defining a legal text; there may be other components to it that together define or make up the law. This is precedent.

Precedent is law, at least in common law systems such as the United States. They are as binding as the original text. They define it, give it meaning, apply it to specific situations, and connect a specific ruling, both to previous interpretations of the law and prospectively to future interpretations. Precedents are part of the chain novel of law; the last precedent or pronouncement dictates decisions in the next case, assuming similar fact patterns. This is no different than how the last sentence in a novel sets the stage for the next sentence. The text of a legal document plus subsequent court interpretations form the law; they define the context for future decisions requiring courts to react by following, distinguishing, or rejecting the precedent's applicability. Of course, the difficulty in using precedent as an interpretive technique is that it may conflict with the rule of (written) law[32] or originalism.[33]

Simply put, for all the practical reasons why precedent makes sense, these ideas are incorporated into the law to make them something that is binding on future courts or judges, or at least persuasive enough to make them feel like they have to follow them.

IV   THE BASIS OF LEGAL REASONING

Where do precedents fit into legal reasoning and why and how are they binding or persuasive?

Edward Levi's *An Introduction to Legal Reasoning* is a classic discussion on the topic on what it means to do legal analysis or thinking. Legal reasoning

---

[29]   Dworkin, Ronald. 1986. *Law's Empire*. Cambridge: Harvard University Press.

[30]   Dworkin, Ronald. 1985. *A Matter of Principle*. Cambridge: Harvard University Press.

[31]   Dworkin, Ronald M. 1967. *The Model of Rules*, 35 University of Chicago Law Review, Iss. 1, Article 3, 14.

[32]   Farber, Daniel A. 2006. *The Rule of Law and the Law of Precedents*, 90 Minn. L. Rev. 1173.

[33]   Markman, Stephen. 2011. *Originalism and Stare Decisis*,

is part of the process of interpretation and argumentation in the law, and use of precedent is critical to both. According to Levi:

> The basic pattern of legal reasoning is reasoning by example. It is reasoning from case to case. It is a three-step process described by the doctrine of precedent in which a proposition descriptive of the first case is made into a rule of law and then applied to the next similar situation. The steps are these: similarity is seen between cases; next the rule of law inherent in the first case is announced; then the rule of law is made applicable to the second case.[34]

Legal reasoning is using cases to abstract the law or principle in it and then applied to another case, assuming the latter is similar enough factually to the first case. What facts are material or operative to determining whether two cases are similar enough to apply the law in the first case to the second is key, and this is the task of the interpreter, such as a lawyer or judge.[35]

The art or key to legal reasoning is persuading one or others regarding the similarity of facts. When does a difference make a difference, or not? Consider a case such as *United States v. Nixon*,[36] where the Supreme Court ruled that the Constitution embodies a concept of executive privilege grounded in the concept of separation of powers. However, executive privilege did not insulate the president from having to deliver the recordings of White House conversations that were sought for a grand jury investigation into possible criminal activity there, perhaps even involving the president. The Court here noted that in this case the president was not asserting that there were sensitive national security reasons for refusing to deliver the tapes. But what if there is a future case where a subpoena is issued to a president?

Does *Nixon* stand for the proposition that the president can withhold such recordings or documents, or must he or she turn them over? In *In re Grand Jury Subpoena Duces Tecum*,[37] President Clinton originally wished to argue that *Nixon* supported his ability to refuse to turn over certain White House conversations to the Special Prosecutor Kenneth Starr as part of the latter's investigations into possible criminal activity. Eventually Clinton dropped the use of that case as precedent, perhaps conceding that it would not support their argument or case. *Nixon* might stand for the proposition that presidents cannot withhold materials under executive privilege from grand jury criminal inquiries, but throw in a question of national security as grounds for refusal, or even make it a congressional inquiry, and the answer may be different. Thus,

---

[34] Levi, Edward H. 1949. *An Introduction to Legal Reasoning*. Chicago: University of Chicago Press, 1–2.
[35] *Id.* at 2.
[36] 418 U.S. 683 (1974).
[37] 112 F. 3d 910 (8th Cir. 1997).

in *Trump v. Mazars*[38] the Supreme Court ruled that President Trump did not have to turn over his tax records to Congress as part of their investigation, but in *Trump v. Vance*,[39] he had to turn them over to a grand jury, or eventually the courts ruled he did have to. The change or turn of one fact produces a different decision. *Nixon* is precedent in the latter but not the former.

Precedent is thus critical to legal reasoning and analysis, but how do we determine when a precedent is correctly applied and when it should govern? Here is where the concept of judicial review fits in, as well as a determination of the weight or persuasiveness of a precedent.[40] Both of these points are related.

Assume a trial court issues a decision. It does so based on the facts in the case, the law, and it also references other cases that serve as precedent to guide and support its decision. If either party to the case believes the judge has erred, perhaps misapplying precedents, they can appeal. Appellate review might affirm, correct, or reject the decision and the deployment of the precedents used. This court might use its own selected case law as precedents to support its decision. This decision too might arguably be appealed, and the process repeats itself. In the course of this specific vertical review of cases, judicial and appellate review serve as correction mechanisms. Additionally, how this decision is then viewed by other courts and other decisions might also serve as other vertical and horizontal checks. This collective process of judicial review serves to refine or clarify when a precedent is properly involved, especially after the US Supreme Court has spoken on a matter.

Second, how much weight should be applied to a precedent? It would be great if there were a way to construct a mathematical formula, a multifactor regression analysis, or some algorithm that does that. For example, when the Supreme Court in *Planned Parenthood v. Casey* decided to affirm the central holding and precedent of *Roe v. Wade* that the Constitution protects a woman's right to terminate a pregnancy, what weight should the Court have given to *Roe*? Currently, as many speculate the Supreme Court is perhaps looking to overturn that decision and perhaps *Planned Parenthood*, what factors weigh in favor of retaining the precedent? Some of these factors have already been discussed in terms of issues of predictability, consistency, preservation of reliance interests, and checking judicial discretion. But there are other factors one can point to.

---

[38]   US (2020).
[39]   US (2020).
[40]   Schauer, Frederick. 1987. *Precedent*, 39 Stan. L. Rev. 571.

For example, Duxbury argues that the "weight" a precedent has relied in part on which court or judge or justice wrote the opinion.[41] Was the opinion unanimous? Was the specific legal point or matter well reasoned or reasoned in depth versus the topic or issue being given more perfunctory discussion?[42] Additionally, was the opinion a published or unpublished one? How generalizable are the facts in this case to other fact patterns, or are the issues here unique? Additionally, when we are discussing a case as precedent, are we referring to the facts serving as precedent, the holding,[43] the dicta,[44] or the reasoning (*ratio decidendi*)?[45] All can be cited as precedent or support for a decision.

Finally, perhaps, how many other times has the precedent been cited by other courts such that it has become firmly embedded in law? For example, some have argued that *Marbury v. Madison* is a super precedent because so many subsequent decisions have been based on it. Others may reference cases such as *Brown v. Board of Education* or *Griswold v. Connecticut* as cases that have been cited so many times that they are beyond ability to reject them, perhaps even overruling them. Overall, a host of factors, both formal and informal, determine the weight of a precedent.[46]

In sum, there are several factors that internally determine how weighty a precedent is, as just noted. These factors then impact how weighty they will appear to other and future courts. The question now is when is a precedent no longer weighty, or weighty enough, such that another or future court can reject or overturn it?

V   OVERTURNING PRECEDENT

Given the centrality of precedent to common law legal systems such as the United States, at what point, if ever, and when should precedent be overruled? Again, there is no mechanical answer that is mathematical that tells us when a precedent is no longer weighty or persuasive enough to deserve preference. However, over time, legal writers and the Supreme Court have offered a variety of reasons and explanations justifying departure from or overruling precedent.

At one point law legal reasoning was viewed almost in a mathematical or geometry sense. By that, law was seen as a self-contained and almost sealed set of rules and principles from which one could deduce the correct answer. This

---

[41]   Duxbury at 62.
[42]   Peczenik at 477–478.
[43]   Marshall, Geoffrey. 2016. In MacCormick, D. Neil, and Robert S. Summers. 1997. *Interpreting Precedents*. New York: Routledge, 503, 504–514.
[44]   Garner at 44–92.
[45]   Duxbury at 83.
[46]   Peczenik, at 461, 477.

was the concept of legal formalism or legal positivism. The idea here is that the task of judging or legal interpretation was basic use of logic or analogy. There was belief in a single correct answer. Within this world, precedent served a role in the deductive process. Precedents were to be honored, and finding the right one led one to the correct legal answer. Under this view, law was slow to change, if at all, with respect for precedent serving as a constant pull to decide cases the way they had been decided in the past.

However, such a view of the law was criticized as abstract and divorced from the rest of the world. Law in this guise did not reflect what was happening in the world; it ignored the empirical conditions from which the law originated. Changes in society did not drive changes in the law; only factors internal to the legal system or rules allowed for that.

Oliver Wendell Holmes, Jr. was one of the first to criticize this model of law. In his 1881 *Common Law* Holmes famously declares:

> The life of the law has not been logic: it has been experience. The felt necessities of the time, the prevalent moral and political theories, intuitions of public policy, avowed or unconscious, even the prejudices which judges share with their fellow-men, have had a good deal more to do than the syllogism in determining the rules by which men should be governed. The law embodies the story of a nation's development through many centuries, and it cannot be dealt with as if it contained only the axioms and corollaries of a book of mathematics. In order to know what it is, we must know what it has been, and what it tends to become. We must alternately consult history and existing theories of legislation. But the most difficult labor will be to understand the combination of the two into new products at every stage. The substance of the law at any given time pretty nearly corresponds, so far as it goes, with what is then understood to be convenient; but its form and machinery, and the degree to which it is able to work out desired results, depend very much upon its past.[47]

Holmes contends that laws are a product of their times. Laws change to reflect evolution in society. "Experience" refers to a host of variables outside of the mathematical model of law that can impact how we think about the law. Law has an empirical basis. So too, then, do precedents. Court decisions are a product of their times. They are of course based on the facts in a particular case. But these facts reside within a broader social, economic, and political context. Court decisions reflect philosophies about justice, fairness, and perhaps other variables. The same is true for court decisions that become precedents. They are based on specific facts at hand and they too reflect assumptions about the world at the time the court rendered an opinion. But what happens if the world has changed? By that, what if the empirical condi-

---

[47]   Holmes, Oliver Wendell, Jr. 1881. *The Common Law*. Boston: Little Brown, 5.

tions under which the precedent was decided have changed or eroded, or what if the beliefs or assumptions behind it have changed? For example, in *Plessy v. Ferguson*,[48] the Court enunciated the "separate but equal" doctrine when it came to race. More specifically, the Equal Protect clause was not found to be violated if the law mandated that races could be segregated. Or consider a line of cases from *Bradwell v. State of Illinois*[49] to *Hoyt v. Florida*.[50] These cases addressed sex or gender discrimination and collectively one could argue that they reflected a sociological view that women could be treated differently from and inferior to men. The constitutional presumption was in favor of different treatment. As Justice Bradley said in his concurrence in *Bradwell*:

> On the contrary, the civil law, as well as nature herself, has always recognized a wide difference in the respective spheres and destinies of man and woman. Man is, or should be, woman's protector and defender. The natural and proper timidity and delicacy which belongs to the female sex evidently unfits it for many of the occupations of civil life. The constitution of the family organization, which is founded in the divine ordinance, as well as in the nature of things, indicates the domestic sphere as that which properly belongs to the domain and functions of womanhood.[51]

Or consider *Bowers v. Hardwick*,[52] where the Court framed a holding declaring that homosexuals did not have a constitutional right to engage in sodomy.[53] In these cases, the decisions were based upon or reflected then held societal views on race, women, and homosexuality. But what if societal views changed? Is a change in society views an operative fact that can or should influence a decision of a court later on when it comes to reconsider that continued viability of that precedent?

Benjamin Cardozo's 1921 *The Nature of the Judicial Process* addresses these points.

> In these days, there is a good deal of discussion whether the rule of adherence to precedent ought to be abandoned altogether. I would not go so far myself. I think adherence to precedent should be the rule and not the exception. I have already had occasion to dwell upon some of the considerations that sustain it. To these I may add that the labor of judges would be increased almost to the breaking point if every past decision could be reopened in every case, and one could not lay one's own

---

[48]   163 U.S. 537 (1896).
[49]   83 U.S. 130 (1873).
[50]   368 U.S. 57 (1961).
[51]   83 U.S. at 141.
[52]   478 U.S. 186 (1986).
[53]   *Id.* at 190–191.

course of bricks on the secure foundation of the courses laid by others who had gone before him...

... The situation would, however, be intolerable if the weekly changes in the composition of the court were accompanied by changes in its rulings. In such circumstances there is nothing to do except to stand by the errors of our brethren of the week before, whether we relish them or not. But I am ready to concede that the rule of adherence to precedent, though it ought not to be abandoned, ought to be in some degree relaxed. I think that when a rule, after it has been duly tested by experience, has been found to be inconsistent with the sense of justice or with the social welfare, there should be less hesitation in frank avowal and full abandonment.[54]

Cardozo articulates several factors weighing in against adherence to precedent. One, implicitly referencing Holmes, he says that precedents tested by experience may be abandoned if the conditions under which they were pronounced have so changed that they are no longer viable. Or holding to precedent will lead to inconsistencies in the law or they fail to reflect a sense of justice. Cardozo does not think rejection of precedent should occur easily or because a court thinks that the previous decision was wrong, and they want to change it. As Amy Coney Barrett argues, rejection of precedent must come with a justification, not simply disagreement.[55] Summers and Eng contend that the justification could be that the precedent is obsolete, no longer workable, or that there are no longer reliance interests supporting it. Overemphasizing precedent produces rigidity in the law.[56] There are thus discretionary and mandatory reasons for rejecting precedent, but simple disagreement is not enough.[57] The question is whether the law should be settled or settled correctly, with the presumption being the former unless good reasoning and justification compels the latter.[58]

In addition to thinking about constitutional versus statutory precedent, there is the issue of ignoring, distinguishing, versus overturning precedent.

One way to deal with a precedent, especially if deemed bad, is simply to ignore or distinguish it. By that, strictly defined, a case is only a precedent if it is factually similar to a present controversy. Rarely if at all are two cases

---

[54]   Cardozo, Benjamin. 1969. *The Nature of the Judicial Process*. New Haven: Yale University Press, 149–151.

[55]   Barrett, Amy Coney. 2013. *Precedent and Jurisprudential Disagreement*, 91 Texas Law Review, 1711, 1722.

[56]   Bankowski, Zenon, D. Neil MacCormick, Lech Morawski, and Alfonso Ruiz. 1997. "Rationales for Precedent." In MacCormick, D. Neil, and Robert S. Summers. *Interpreting Precedents*. New York: Routledge, 481, 491.

[57]   Summers, Robert S. and Svein Eng. "Departures from Precedent." In MacCormick, D. Neil, and Robert S. Summers. 1997. *Interpreting Precedents*. New York: Routledge, 519, 526.

[58]   *Id.* at 1714.

identical to the last detail. Precedents are authority when there is a parallel in facts that are material. It is theoretically always possible to simply distinguish the facts from a precedent or prior case to a present one.

Consider *Gibbons v. Ogden*,[59] which was a John Marshall era case declaring broad authority of Congress to regulate interstate commerce. At issue was whether an act of Congress granting a person a license to operate ships between two states preempts a state from granting a private individual the exclusive right to operate ships in its waters. The Court held yes, but in doing so established broad federal authority to regulate commerce, almost to the point of excluding state authority. Yet in *Cooley v. Board of Wardens*,[60] the issue before the Court was whether the Pennsylvania state legislature might pass a law which authorizes ships of a certain size or bound to/from a foreign port or a port outside of the Delaware River, to make use of a pilot, or pay a fee for such a service to the Board of Wardens. On one level both cases involved navigation and questions about federal and state regulation. *Gibbons* could have easily dictated the result in *Cooley* and the Court could have struck down the Pennsylvania law. However, there were enough factual differences in the cases to allow the latter Court under Chief Justice Taney to distinguish the matter from being controlled by *Gibbons*.

There are many other situations where on the face a prior case as precedent should be controlling, yet the Court has managed to distinguish and explain why there is a difference. Classic examples in constitutional law classes would include *Dartmouth College v. Woodward*[61] compared with *Charles River Bridge v. Warren Bridge*[62] as ways the Court used factual differences in cases to modify Contract Clause doctrine, or *Schechter Poultry v. United States*[63] and *Carter v. Carter Coal*[64] compared with *National Labor Relations Board v. Jones and Laughlin Steel*[65] and *Wickard v. Filburn*[66] when it comes to the scope of federal authority under the Commerce Clause to regulate interstate commerce. Specifically, these cases divide over the scope of power when it comes to direct versus indirect effects on commerce, and cumulative effects.

---

[59]   22 U.S. 1 (1824).

[60]   53 U.S. 299 (1852).

[61]   17 U.S. 518 (1819) (state changes to articles of incorporation for a college).

[62]   36 U.S. 420 (1837) (state changes to an exclusive right to build a bridge across a river).

[63]   295 U.S. 495 (1935) (federal regulation of agriculture and poultry industry that included codes of commercial conduct).

[64]   298 U.S. 238 (1936) (federal regulation of the coal industry and the setting of minimum prices for coal).

[65]   301 U.S. 1 (1937) (federal regulation of commercial and labor practices).

[66]   317 U.S. 111 (1942) (regulation of agricultural market including quotas and prices for wheat).

Again, while there are enough factual differences in the cases to distinguish the first cases from the second (and the Court did distinguish them), many also see the Court in the latter repudiating the holdings in the First Deal decisions after Franklin Roosevelt's 1936 reelection and issuance of his famous Court-packing speech and plan. The Court reversed earlier decisions, although not explicitly saying so.

Yet blindly following precedent for the sake of precedent is not good lawyering or judging for Holmes, Cardozo, or Barrett. As the US Supreme Court has declared, *stare decisis* is not an "inexorable command;"[67] sometimes it can be rejected. In thinking about deference to precedent, there are at least two types: constitutional and statutory precedent. Levi argues that the courts are freer to depart from precedents based on constitutional as opposed to statutory grounds.[68] In the case of a court rendering a decision on statutory grounds, an appropriate legislative body can pass a law to overrule the decision. This error correction is consistent with the concept of checks and balances. But a decision rendered on constitutional grounds requires a constitutional amendment, a much more difficult checks and balances process. Thus, the argument is that the Supreme Court should give more deference to statutory precedents than constitutional ones.[69] Of course, at a time when the American politics process is polarized and passing legislation is difficult, perhaps this distinction is contestable.

Yet distinguishing statutory from constitutional precedent and the courts giving greater weight to the former versus the other calls into question the concept of super precedents, which have become almost a fashionable theory in politics since the time of Chief Justice John Roberts' confirmation. With there being so much concern or controversy surrounding the viability of *Roe v. Wade* as a constitutional precedent, especially since the confirmation of Justice Barrett and the emergence of a 6–3 conservative majority as of 2021, what does it mean to say something is a super precedent? If the concept of checks and balances makes sense, on one hand the Court should give less deference to a constitutional precedent and feel freer to overturn *Roe* because of the relative inability of Congress to overturn it with a constitutional amendment.

But there is still another option beyond distinguishing, narrowing, or ignoring a precedent. This is overturning it—declaring the precedent is no longer good law. Perhaps there are times that a precedent must be overturned. For someone like Ronald Dworkin, embedded principles in the law or an evolving political morality might compel that, not merely make it optional. Overturning

---

[67] Payne v. Tennessee, 501 U.S. 808, 827–28 (1991).
[68] Levi, *An Introduction to Legal Reasoning* at 7.
[69] Levi at 58–59; Barrett at 1713.

precedent must be compelling, even for constitutional decisions. Even Barrett acknowledges that simply disagreement with a decision is not enough justification to overturn it.

One must weigh the competing factors of checks and balances and the ability of Congress and the political process to correct a constitutional decision it thinks is in error against factors that support retaining precedent, including reliance interests, predictability, and stability. One might also add the idea of principle and institutional integrity. By that, several legal scholars have argued that the essence of judicial decision-making is basing decisions on principle and not political considerations.[70] Should the Court abandon principle, it would be acting no more than simply like another political institution, essentially making the Justices nine politicians wearing robes. If this were to occur, the other problem emerges—does the public lose support for the judiciary, no longer seeing it as a neutral or apolitical institution that the American constitutional Framers, such as Alexander Hamilton, hoped for, as described in *Federalist Paper* number 78.

VI   TAKING PRECEDENT SERIOUSLY

There are basically two approaches to studying constitutional law: a legal analysis and a political science perspective.

The legal analysis perspective is the one thus far described in this book. It is an approach that takes the law seriously. It is the one that emphasizes that judges and Justices make decisions, render opinions, and interpret text primarily if not exclusively based on legal factors and principles. It is an approach that says that judges are constrained in their decision-making by the law, that texts matter, and that for our purposes, legal precedents serve as limits on what courts cannot do.[71] Precedents, according to a legal analysis approach, are binding and constraining. Judges and Justices do not have full autonomy or free rein to disregard them. Precedents are internal to the legal reasoning process, and they impose internal or external restraints on decision-making. Making decisions subject to the constraints of legal principles and precedents is supposedly what distinguishes legal analysis from political decision-making. It is the belief that law controls politics, or that law controls the discretion of at least judges. It prevents judges from engaging in policy-making or using their personal political preferences as factors in rendering court opinions.

---

[70]   Wechsler, Herbert. 1959. *Toward Neutral Principles of Constitutional Law*, Harvard Law Review, 73(1), 1–35; Bork, Robert H. 1971. *Neutral Principles and Some First Amendment Problems*, 47 Ind. L. J. 1–35; Bickel, Alexander. 1962. *The Least Dangerous Branch*. Indianapolis: Bobbs-Merrill.
[71]   Schauer, Frederick. 1987. *Precedent*, 39 Stan. L. Rev. 571.

Law school approaches to teaching legal analysis emphasize this approach. When students are urged to "think like a lawyer," the focus is on ascertaining legal reasons for why a court, judge, or justice rendered a specific opinion. One is supposed to find legal reasons for why cases are distinguished or how a specific case serves as a precedent controlled a decision or dictated a result. It would be a failure of legal reasoning to contend or argue that judges decided the way they did because they were politically liberal or conservative, or that they voted the way they did because they were a member of a specific political party. The story of the law school or legal analysis method is one of legal neutrality and rationality, similar to the model that Justice Holmes described and criticized earlier in this chapter.

But there is another model which we will call the political science approach. It looks to extra-legal factors to explain judicial decision-making. Over time various schools of thought, whether it be legal realism,[72] sociological jurisprudence,[73] or the attitudinal model,[74] have looked at personal, social, or political factors to explain why judges and justices decide the way they do. These models offer powerful empirical evidence to support their claims, finding that political actors engage in strategic thinking in order to translate their preferences into judicial outputs such as case selection for review or in deciding cases.[75] While not necessarily going as far as arguing that judges are policy-makers wearing robes, these models come close to that assertion. Generally according to these models, legal analysis and appeals to precedents are of lesser if not little constraint upon judges. Judges and Justices learn how to navigate the law, including precedents, in order to achieve the outputs they desire.

Setting up these two models is critical to thinking about precedent. A law school or legal analysis model treats precedents seriously. It sees them as real constraints upon judges who are forced to follow them or provide justifications, as described so far in this book, to depart from them. The political science model sees the decision to follow or reject precedent as more strategic. Precedents are not real constraints on decision-making; the choice to follow or reject is calculated, whether conscious or not, and their use is simply a means of getting to the preferred outcome.

---

[72]   Frank, Jerome. 1963. *Law and the Modern Mind.* New York: Anchor Books.
[73]   Pound, Roscoe. 2014. *The Spirit of the Common Law.* Charleston, SC: Nabu Press.
[74]   Segel, Jeffrey A., and Harold J. Spaeth. 2002. *The Supreme Court and the Attitudinal Model Revisited.* New York: Cambridge University Press.
[75]   Murphy, Walter F. 1963. *Elements of Judicial Strategy.* Chicago: University of Chicago Press.

In some ways this book tests these two models of law. Do precedents matter such that they constrain judicial opinions? This is one of the questions readers should ask as they look at the opinions here where mostly constitutional precedent was rejected (although there are some cases included where precedent is followed). One will find that very few constitutional precedents have been reversed over time and that in some cases specific Justices have upheld precedents that one would have expected they would have rejected. Perhaps that speaks to the fact that precedent does constrain in some way, even if not to the extent that the law school model dictates.

VII   CONSTITUTIONAL PRECEDENT IN AMERICAN LAW

This is a casebook that examines the role of constitutional precedent in US Supreme Court reasoning. Its aim is several-fold. One, it seeks simply to understand how the Supreme Court has approached the topic of constitutional precedent when it decides to overturn it. By that, what factors or considerations, as discussed above, has it actually applied when deciding to overturn precedent? Second, the book serves as a teaching tool. One of the most difficult tasks in law school when one is learning how to "think or reason like a lawyer" is the issue of applying or rejecting precedent. If legal reasoning in part is based on analogies—when two cases are factually similar enough to be treated the same—students and lawyers their entire life or career grapple with the issue of how to distinguish or use prior decisions to help them in a present case.

A third purpose for this book is somewhat judicial politics or political science in focus. By that, during the 1960s at the height of the Warren Court, there were allegations that it was simply overturning precedent based on political preferences, and that its reasoning was far from principled, or at least it was doing so for reasons that were inconsistent with what legal theory suggested it should be. Similar criticisms are now being raised with the Roberts Court, with claims that it is cavalier in its respect for precedent and that it is going after decisions it does not like with alacrity. Perhaps these propositions have some merit, but to answer them one needs to examine how the Court has approached constitutional precedent over time. By that, how many times has the Court overturned constitutional precedent? Are there some Courts with a greater propensity to rejecting precedent? Have the reasons for overturning precedent changed over time? These are all good questions, and this book aims to provide analysis to help clarify answers.

One of the first tasks is identifying all the cases where the US Supreme Court has overturned constitutional precedent. This is not an easy task. According to the Supreme Court database located at the University of Washington, St.

Louis Law School, from 1788 until 2020 the Supreme Court has issued 26,544 judgments and opinions that were orally argued. Searching among all those cases for those that overturned constitutional precedent would be the figurative searching for a needle in a haystack. Reading all those opinions would be impossible. Two, it is not always clear if the Court is overturning precedent. By that, there are some cases where the Supreme Court has explicitly said something to the effect that "This Court overturns X case as no longer good precedent." Yet such explicit statements are rare. Often the Court is more subtle or less direct. Sometimes determining whether the Court has overturned a precedent is a contested matter of legal judgment. Finally, it also is nearly impossible to ascertain all of the cases where the Court had a constitutional issue posed before it where it was asked then to affirm or overturn the precedent. Having such a number or list of cases would give one a truer or perhaps the most accurate picture regarding the Court's approach to constitutional precedent.

Having recognized all the above, the Congressional Research Service in 2018 produced a table of cases and decisions it thought constituted an overruling of precedent.[76] In amassing its list, the CRS used as its criteria:

> The table was compiled by searching the LEXIS database for all Supreme Court decisions that use the word "overrule" in the headnotes, syllabus, or text of the Court's opinion. Decisions supported by a majority of the Court that expressly overruled an earlier decision were listed in the table. The listed cases include decisions identified by the search terms in which the Court partially overruled or otherwise qualified a prior case. These findings were also cross-checked with other sources to ensure that the search had captured any relevant results.[77]

The analysis the CRS did produced 141 Supreme Court decisions that overturned its constitutional precedents. The CRS study was inclusive to decisions through 2018. This book updated the analysis through the end of the 2020 Supreme Court term, adding four more cases where the Roberts Court overturned its own precedent. This gives us a total of 145 decisions identified as rejecting or overturning precedent over time. Take this 145 and divide it by 26,544 judgments and opinions issued after oral arguments, and one finds over time that the Supreme Court has overturned constitutional precedent in 0.005% of its decisions—an infinitely small or infrequent amount of the time. Again, if we knew how many times the Court was asked to overturn a precedent and it did or did not, perhaps that would be a better measure.

---

[76] Murrill, Brandon J. 2018. *The Supreme Court's Overruling of Constitutional Precedent*. Washington, D.C.: Congressional Research Service.

[77] *Id.* at 23.

Table I.1   Supreme Court constitutional precedent reversals

Judgment and opinion orally argued		Court	Constitutional Reversals	
1	1789-1795	Jay	0	0
11	1796-1800	Ellsworth	0	0
1154	1801-1835	Marshall	0	0
1642	1836-1864	Taney	1	0.0006
1362	1864-1873	Chase	1	0.0007
3639	1874-1888	Waite	2	0.0005
4927	1888-1910	Fuller	0	0
2422	1910-1921	White	3	0.001
1584	1921-1930	Taft	3	0.001
1784	1930-1941	Hughes	12	0.006
718	1941-1945	Stone	7	0.009
729	1946-1953	Vinson	7	0.009
1538	1953-1969	Warren	32	0.02
2235	1969-1986	Burger	32	0.014
1802	1986-2005	Rehnquist	30	0.016
996	2005-2020	Roberts	15	0.015
26544		total*	145	0.005

* As of October 16, 2020

Additionally, using the Supreme Court database, we can break down the overturning of constitutional precedent by Court. Specifically, we can look at which Court under which Chief Justice has overturned the most Supreme Court decisions and what percentage of their decisions have overturned constitutional precedents. This information is found in Tables I.1 and I.2. Here we find that for the Jay, Ellsworth, Marshall, and Fuller Courts, there are no identified constitutional precedents that were overturned. For the first two Courts there is no real surprise. Under the Jay and Ellsworth Courts there were but 12 decisions and the Court was just beginning to issue opinions and there were no prior ones to overturn. Also, the status of judicial review was uncertain and just not clear what role the Court had in constitutional adjudication until the 1803 *Marbury v. Madison* decision asserted this authority.

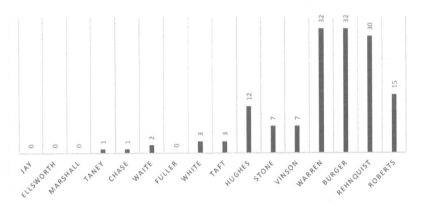

Table I.2   Supreme Court constitutional precedent reversals

The Marshall Court issued 1,154 decisions, and one would have thought there would have been an overruling there. But since this Court, and especially Chief Justice John Marshall, was in the process of building the law and the Constitution, it is no real surprise that it did not change its mind when it came to the Constitution. It is more of a surprise that the Fuller Court, having issued nearly 5,000 decisions, did not overturn any constitutional precedents. The first recorded constitutional precedent overturned as identified by the CRS was under the Taney Court in 1851, *The Genesee Chief*,[78] addressing issues of admiralty law and the Constitution arising out of a boat collision on Lake Ontario. Subsequent to that decision there were only nine more decisions overturning constitutional precedent until one reaches the Hughes Court. This is when the New Deal is enacted, and the Court is confronted with constitutional challenges to it. From the Hughes Court on is really the period when one sees it confronting constitutional issues and overturning past precedents.

As we see from Table I.1, up until 2020, the Warren Court did overturn the greatest number of precedents at 32, but it was tied with the Burger Court for that number and the Rehnquist Court was close behind at 30. Through 2020, the Roberts Court was at 15. In terms of a percentage of its decisions overturning constitutional precedent, the Warren Court had the highest at 0.02, still a very small percentage. The Burger, Rehnquist, and Roberts Courts are very close to one another in terms of their overruling percentages.

Table I.3 presents the percentage of all constitutional precedents overturned by the Court. The Warren and Burger Courts account each for approximately 22% of all precedents overturned, followed by the Rehnquist Court at 20.7%.

---

[78]   53 U.S. 443 (1851).

Table I.3   Supreme Court constitutional precedent per Court,
              1789-2020

Table Three: Supreme Court Constitutional		
Precedent Per Court: 1789-2020		
Court	**Reversals**	**% Total**
Jay	0	0%
Ellsworth	0	0%
Marshall	0	0%
Taney	1	0.69%
Chase	1	0.69%
Waite	2	1.38%
Fuller	0	0%
White	3	2.68%
Taft	3	2.68%
Hughes	12	8.27%
Stone	7	4.82%
Vinson	7	4.82%
Warren	32	22.06%
Burger	32	22.06%
Rehnquist	30	20.69%
Roberts	15	9.65%
total*	145	100%

Through 2020, the Roberts Court was less than 10%. Several observations are possible here. Most of the overruling constitutional precedent decisions have taken place since the Warren Court, with the last four Courts accounting for nearly 75% of these decisions. Perhaps this reflects the increased ideological disagreement on the Court. What we are seeing simply are that Justices disagree more frequently with past decisions rendered by Courts they disagree with as a result of ideological differences. Rarely do we see one Court reversing itself on constitutional precedent, although as we shall see, the Burger Court did do that several times. Conversely, these reversals could be the product of simply that times have changed, that old precedents do not work anymore and that the conditions under which the old precedents were issued are no longer applicable. The first explanations are more of a judicial process or political science answer, the latter more traditional legal.

Another observation is that the entire Court does not change over when Chief Justices do. There are clear holdovers that impact how a Court decides. When Earl Warren was replaced by Warren Burger in 1969, many of the former Court Justices, such as Thurgood Marshall and William Brennan, stayed on for years, still tilting the decisions in one direction. Gradually Presidents Nixon and Reagan replaced many of these holdovers with their appointees, thereby influencing how the Court decided. The point here is that using as a unit of analysis a Chief Justice's tenure on the Court as markers for examining overturning of precedents may be crude, and perhaps we should be looking at how specific groupings of Justices approached precedent. This is a fair critique and perhaps a subject for future study. However, since so much emphasis is placed on looking at the Marshall, Hughes, or Warren Courts, for example, this unit of analysis is reasonable and useful.

Finally, can we discern a changing pattern of grounds for reversal of constitutional precedent? By that, over time have different Courts offered the same or different reasons for rejection of precedent? To answer that this casebook has excerpted a selection of cases from all the Courts where constitutional precedent was overturned. It would be impossible to produce a casebook with all 145 cases in it as they would prove to be a much larger text than is envisioned here. Consider this text a sample of cases which excerpt the main passages and discussion, mostly by the majority or plurality opinion, regarding the reasons for overturning precedent in that case. The focus has also been on cases that often are referenced as notable precedents or decisions by the Court. Based on the cases selected, several patterns are discernable. One is that until the Rehnquist Court, it appeared that error correction was the most frequent reason for constitutional precedent being overturned. In many cases the Court thought the previous decision was simply wrong in that it was badly reasoned. With that, note how many of the decisions in overturning precedent discussed how the original precedent had proved unworkable or that conditions had changed, rendering the previous precedent as no longer binding. In these pre-Rehnquist Court decisions there also is no significant theoretical discussion or theory of precedent. The approach to precedent, if not strictly ad hoc or one case at a time, was close to that. The closest one has to an annunciation of any approach to constitutional issues is in *Ashwander v. Tennessee Valley Authority*,[79] where the Court lists a set of rules for how it approaches constitutional adjudication and its goal in terms of seeking to render opinions on constitutional matters if at all possible.

---

[79]   297 U.S. 288 (1936).

During the Rehnquist Court the approach to precedent changes. Beginning in *Payne v. Tennessee*,[80] the Court begins a more self-conscious discussion of constitutional precedent and the grounds under which it may be overturned. Here the Court refers to many of the factors discussed earlier in this chapter. It is almost like the Court is seeking to construct a theory of precedent for itself. *Payne v. Tennessee* became somewhat a precedent for how the Court approaches precedent. After it, the Court cites the case repeatedly in cases where it is asked to overturn constitutional precedent. Whether this reflects the force of precedent constraining the Court or the discussion is a camouflage for ideology or policy preferences is a question to ask.

As you read these cases, ask yourself a series of questions:

- Did the Court actually overturn precedent?
- What reasons did the Court give for overturning the precedent?
- Were you persuaded by the reasons for overturning the precedent?
- Do you think the decision for overturning the precedent was made on legal or more political or policy grounds?
- Do you see any patterns in terms of how different Courts or eras have approached precedent?
- Do different Courts or Justices give different reasons for overturning precedent?
- How does the Court or do specific Justices weigh contending factors when they are determining whether to follow or overturn constitutional precedent?
- To what extent do you see precedent as binding or limiting judicial decision-making?
- Does the legal analysis or political science model offer a better explanation on how the Court approaches precedent?

REFERENCES

Bankowski, Zenon, D. Neil MacCormick, Lech Morawski, and Alfonso Ruiz. 1997. "Rationales for Precedent." In MacCormick, D. Neil, and Robert S. Summers. *Interpreting Precedents*. New York: Routledge, 481.

Barrett, Amy Coney. 2013. *Precedent and Jurisprudential Disagreement*, 91 Texas Law Review, 1711.

Bickel, Alexander. 1962. *The Least Dangerous Branch*. Indianapolis: Bobbs-Merrill.

Bork, Robert H. 1971. *Neutral Principles and Some First Amendment Problems*, 47 Ind. L. J. 1–35.

Cardozo, Benjamin N. 1991. *The Nature of the Judicial Process*. New Haven: Yale University Press.

---

[80]   501 U.S. 808 (1991).

Duxbury, Neil. 2008. *The Nature and Authority of Precedent.* New York: Cambridge.
Dworkin, Ronald M. 1967. *The Model of Rules,* 35 University of Chicago Law Review
   Iss. 1, Article 3, 14.
Dworkin, Ronald. 1985. *A Matter of Principle.* Cambridge, MA: Harvard University
   Press.
Dworkin, Ronald. 1986. *Law's Empire.* Cambridge, MA: Harvard University Press.
Dworkin, Ronald. 1977. *Taking Rights Seriously.* Cambridge, MA: Harvard University
   Press.
Farber, Daniel A. 2006. *The Rule of Law and the Law of Precedents,* 90 Minn. L. Rev.
   1173.
Frank, Jerome. 1963. *Law and the Modern Mind.* New York: Anchor Books.
Garner, Bryan A. 2016. *The Law of Judicial Precedent.* Saint Paul, MN: Thomson
   Reuters.
Gerhardt, Michael J. 2006. *Super Precedent,* 90 Minn. L. Rev. 1204.
Holmes, Oliver Wendell, Jr. 1897. "The Path of Law." 10 Harvard Law Review, 457.
Holmes, Oliver Wendell, Jr. 1881. *The Common Law.* Boston: Little Brown.
Jackson, Robert. 1944. *Decisional Law and Stare Decisis,* 30 A. B. A. J. 334.
Kozel, Randy J. 2013. *Precedent and Reliance,* 62 Emory L.J. 1459.
Levi, Edward H. 1949. *An Introduction to Legal Reasoning.* Chicago: University of
   Chicago Press.
Lieber, Francis. 1883. *On Civil Liberty and Self Government.* Philadelphia: J.B.
   Lippincott & Co.
MacCormick, D. Neil, and Robert S. Summers. 1997. *Interpreting Precedents.* New
   York: Routledge.
Markman, Stephen. 2011. *Originalism and Stare Decisis,* 34 Harv. J.L. & Pub. Pol'y
   111.
Monaghan, Henry Paul. 1988. *Stare Decisis and Constitutional Adjudication,* 88
   Colum. L. Rev. 723.
Murphy, Walter F. 1963. *Elements of Judicial Strategy.* Chicago: University of
   Chicago Press.
Murrill, Brandon J. 2018. *The Supreme Court's Overruling of Constitutional Precedent.*
   Washington, D.C.: Congressional Research Service.
Pound, Roscoe. 2014. *The Spirit of the Common Law.* Charleston, SC: Nabu Press.
Powell, Lewis F. Jr. 1990. *Stare Decisis and Judicial Restraint,* 47 Wash. & Lee L.
   Rev. 281.
Raz, Joseph. 2009. *The Authority of Law: Essays on Law and Morality.* New York:
   Oxford University Press.
Schauer, Frederick. 1987. *Precedent,* 39 Stan. L. Rev. 571.
Schlag, Pierre, and Amy J. Griffin. 2020. *How to Do Things with Legal Doctrine.*
   Chicago: University of Chicago Press.
Segel, Jeffrey A., and Harold J. Spaeth. 2002. *The Supreme Court and the Attitudinal
   Model Revisited.* New York: Cambridge University Press.
Summers, Robert S. and Svein Eng. "Departures from Precedent." In MacCormick, D.
   Neil, and Robert S. Summers. 1997. *Interpreting Precedents.* New York: Routledge,
   519.

Sunstein, Cass R. 1993. *On Analogical Reasoning*, 106 Harvard Law Review, 741, 782.

Sunstein, Cass R. 2001. *One Case at a Time: Judicial Minimalism on the Supreme Court.* Cambridge, MA: Harvard University Press.

Supreme Court Database. 2020. Located at http://scdb.wustl.edu/ (Site last visited on July 13, 2021).

Wechsler, Herbert. 1959. *Toward Neutral Principles of Constitutional Law*, Harvard Law Review, 73(1), 1–35.

1. Jay to Vinson Courts

INTRODUCTION

The Framers wrote the US Constitution in 1787, and with ratification that year, George Washington took the Oath of Office the following year. The task that befell the new president was organizing a new government, literally from scratch. While there may have been English legal principles and precedents to guide a new nation and regime, to a large extent Washington, his administration—which included Thomas Jefferson and Alexander Hamilton—along with Congress, were operating with a somewhat blank slate. The words of the constitutional text did exist, but they were words on paper that had to be given meaning and operationalized. Words do not have inherent meaning but need to be interpreted and understood in terms of their use, as language philosopher Ludwig Wittgenstein said.[1] The task that befell the new government was ascertaining what the text of the Constitution meant and how to apply it.

The complication in doing the above was twofold. One, James Madison, who was the recording secretary at the Constitutional Convention, did not make public his notes on it until 1840, four years after he died. Thus, if in fact one accepts the ideas that the Constitution should be interpreted in light of the intent of the Framers, direct evidence of their thoughts or deliberations was absent, at least for many years. Two, this meant the first elected leaders were on their own to ascertain meaning. In some cases, those involved in setting up the first government were among the Constitutional Framers, and they did not always agree on what the text meant, much in the same way that Madison's and Max Farrand's[2] notes on the Convention revealed. The Framers were not of one mind in their debates over the Constitution, and they produced a document born of compromise. The simple point here is that from a historical perspective, there was no clear intent of the Framers or simple understanding regarding what different clauses of the Constitution meant.

---

[1]   Wittgenstein, Ludwig. 1953. *Philosophical Investigations*. New York: Macmillan Publishing Company.
[2]   Farrand, Max. 1911. *The Records of the Federal Convention of 1787.* New Haven, CT: Yale University Press.

This lack of clarity extended to the three vesting clauses of the Constitution—Article I, Section 1; Article II, Section 1; and Article III, Section 1. These are the three clauses, respectively, that vest legislative, executive, and judicial power in Congress, the president, and the Supreme Court (and lower courts as Congress may create). In the case of Congress, there are many clauses outlining their authority and powers, and the same is true for the president. But still, getting clarity to what these powers mean, such as how broad or how far they extend, or how to reconcile congressional power with the president, or state with national power, were questions that needed to be addressed. But with the judicial branch, Article III's brevity left a lot to the imagination, or at least to clarification.

The story is well known about the scope of judicial power and the Supreme Court. It need not be detailed here. However, come 1789 the power and prestige of the Supreme Court is negligible, or at least debatable. The first Chief Justice, John Jay (1789–1795), left the Court to become governor of New York. During his tenure there was only one case orally argued before it with an opinion issued. The second Chief Justice, John Rutledge (1795), was nominated by George Washington, served 138 days, and then resigned after failing to secure Senate confirmation. There were no opinions issued during his tenure. The third Chief Justice, Oliver Ellsworth (1796–1800), served for four years, during which there were merely 11 orally argued cases that resulted in opinions issued.

The point of this story is that in its first decade or so, the Supreme Court was an insignificant player in American politics—it truly was the "least dangerous branch," as Alexander Hamilton described it in *Federalist Paper* number 78. All of that changed with Chief Justice John Marshall (1801–1835). Marshall is credited with several important points when it comes to the judiciary and American politics. He was an ardent nationalist who used his Court opinions to create broad national power. Two, he used the cases he heard and the decisions he issued to transform the Court into a serious player in American government and politics. Most famously he did that in *Marbury v. Madison*, where he declared that "It is emphatically the province and duty of the judicial department to say what the law is."[3] Marshall is credited with asserting that the federal courts have the power of judicial review or the ability to declare laws void if they conflict with the Constitution. There is a historical debate over whether Marshall asserted this power contrary to the intent of the Framers, the text of the Constitution, or history. The origins of judicial review need not concern us here. Instead, in Marshall's hands and under his Supreme Court, he used the power of judicial review to interpret both federal laws and the text of

---

[3]   Marbury v. Madison 5 U.S. 137, 177 (1803).

the Constitution. In the Introduction we outlined and noted some of the greatest hits or decisions issued under the Marshall Court.

What all this suggests it that under the Jay, Rutledge, Ellsworth, and most especially the Marshall Court, the Justices were establishing constitutional precedent. They were expounding upon what they thought the Constitution meant, thereby establishing an initial gloss on the document. Future decisions or Courts would have to react to these initial opinions, either agreeing or disagreeing with them—in effect, upholding or reversing constitutional precedent. In the case of the first three Justices (two if one excludes Rutledge), there were so few opinions issued there almost seemed to be no chance that the Court could have reversed precedent or changed its mind. When it came to the Marshall Court, what is remarkable is that of the 1,154 opinions issued, the Court never looked back. It never reversed any early decision, conceding or saying that it got it initially wrong and then reversed itself.

The story of reversal begins with the Taney Court. Here the narrative is that Chief Justice Roger Taney (1836–1864) was appointed to the Supreme Court by President Andrew Jackson in 1836. If Marshall was a nationalist, Taney was a states' rights person. His legacy is damaged by his *Dred Scott v. Sanford*[4] opinion, which declared slaves to be mere property and incapable of becoming citizens. Yet he also issued important decisions such as *Cooley v. Board of Wardens*,[5] which narrowed the scope of US commerce authority and created a space for state regulation. But it is also the Taney Court in 1851 in *The Genesee Chief*[6] that the Supreme Court records the first instance of the Supreme Court reversing a constitutional precedent. That would be the only Supreme Court constitutional precedent reversal by the Taney Court. In fact, the next one would not come until 20 years later in the *Legal Tender Cases*[7] in the Chase Court (1864–1873), and then two under the Waite Court (1874–1888), none for Fuller (1888–1910), and then three each for White (1910–1921) and Taft (1921–1930). In fact, under the first nine Courts, encompassing 132 years, there were only 10 Supreme Court constitutional precedent reversals. Then came the Hughes Court with 12.

What is remarkable for the Waite, Fuller, and White Courts is that they covered the period that legal historians would refer to as the substantive due process or liberty of contract era, where the Supreme Court undertook essentially pro-business and conservative positions regarding economic regulation and individual rights. It was often called the *Lochner* era, referring to the

---

4   60 U.S. 393 (1857).
5   53 U.S. 299 (1852).
6   53 U.S. 443 (1851).
7   79 U.S. 457 (1870).

famous case after which it was named where the Court questioned the constitutionality of workplace regulations.[8] One would have presumed that perhaps at a time when the Court was prone to second-guessing legislation it would have also perhaps been more likely to overturn past constitutional precedent. That did increase, but certainly not dramatically. Among the few cases during this era when a constitutional precedent was overturned was *Kilbourn v. Thompson*[9] under the Waite Court. It is an unusual opinion regarding congressional contempt of power. The original precedent upholding such authority was based on English law, and the decision to overturn it was also based on English precedent.

During the White, Taft, and Hughes Courts, too, one might have expected increases in overturning constitutional precedent. This was the period during which the Progressive Era economic and political reforms were being adopted and the national government, especially post-World War I, were challenging the status quo, especially when it came to business regulation. Yet even during the first two Courts there were few major cases overturning precedent, at least ones that history books or constitutional scholars might have considered notable. Look at a case such as *Terral v. Burke Construction Company*.[10] It is a dry technical case regarding state authority to revoke a license of a foreign corporation. The decision to reject precedent here came as a result of cases after the original precedent in *Doyle v. Continental Insurance Company* that eroded the original case's status.[11]

The legal history story then changes with the Supreme Court under Chief Justice Charles Evans Hughes (1930–1941). Under Hughes, 12 constitutional precedents are overturned, more in total than the 10 for the entire prior history of the United States. The Hughes Court is the one confronting the Depression that began with the Black Friday stock market crash on October 24, 1929, and it continues through the election of President Franklin Roosevelt in 1932, the New Deal, and up to the edge of World War II. Roosevelt's effort to transform the US economy and provide more federal intervention led to the first New Deal cases, such as *Schechter Poultry Corp. v. United States*,[12] where the Court invalided much of what Roosevelt and Congress tried to do. That was followed by Roosevelt's 1936 landslide presidential election, and then his 1937 speech calling for expansion of the Court's number of Justices, often referred to as the "Court Packing Plan." While the plan failed, the Court did eventually reverse course, and often constitutional doctrine and precedent.

---

[8]   Lochner v. New York, 198 U.S. 45 (1905).
[9]   103 U.S. 168 (1880)
[10]   257 U.S. 529 (1922).
[11]   94 U.S. 535 (1876).
[12]   295 U.S. 495 (1935).

As you look at the cases here, note how explicit or implicit the reasoning is for overturning precedent and the justification for doing it. For example, in *Erie Railroad Co. v. Tompkins*,[13] the Court is quite explicit in overturning *Swift v. Tyson*.[14] The latter was arguably one of the most important cases in American constitutional law, declaring that federal common law existed. For nearly a century a large body of law was built upon *Swift*, such that when *Erie Railroad* overturns it, it too is one of the most consequential, if least appreciated, cases in American constitutional law. Explaining how this decision affected federal court jurisdiction and application of state law in federal court remains a perplexing issue even to this day. Moreover, to this day, *Erie Railroad* is the case with the longest time period between the original decision (1842) and the overturning of the precedent (1938)—96 years. Given its significance at the time, it is no surprise regarding how explicit the Court was in overturning the precedent.[15]

In many of the cases the Court is clear that it is rejecting precedent, but in some cases it is more subtle. Note also in these cases that the Court does not engage in a theoretical discussion of precedent or offer a theory when it is permissible to reject a past constitutional precedent. Instead, the Court appears to overturn precedent more in terms of error correction (it got the original decision wrong), or there were problems in applying the original precedent in subsequent decisions. Are you persuaded by their arguments in terms of it being legally persuasive versus more reflecting changing Justices and politics? These are questions that should be considered for all the cases in all the chapters.

Finally, especially note *Ashwander v. Tennessee Valley Authority*.[16] Justice Brandeis's "Ashwander Rules" are a classic statement on when the Supreme Court will hear a case and especially on seeking to avoid issuing an opinion based on constitutional reasoning. While these decisional rules are not about precedent per se, they do provide important guidance on how the Court is supposed to address issues to avoid creating unnecessary constitutional precedent.

---

[13]   304 U.S. 64 (1938).
[14]   41 U.S. 1 (1842).
[15]   Nelson, Caleb. 2013. *A Critical Guide to Erie Railroad Co. v. Tompkins*, 54 Wm. & Mary L. Rev. 921.
[16]   297 U.S. 288 (1936).

THE TANEY COURT

The Genesee Chief, 53 U.S. 443 (1851)

Mr. Chief Justice Taney delivered the opinion of the Court.

This is a case of collision on Lake Ontario. The libellants were the owners of the schooner Cuba, and the respondents and present appellants the master and owners of the propeller Genesee Chief. The libellants state that on the 6th of May, 1847, as the Cuba was on her voyage from Sandusky, in the state of Ohio, to Oswego, in the state of New York, the Genesee Chief, which was proceeding on a voyage up the lake, ran foul of her and damaged her so seriously that she shortly afterwards sunk, with her cargo on board; and they also allege that the collision was occasioned by the carelessness and mismanagement of the officers and crew of the propeller, without any fault of the officers or crew of the Cuba. The respondents deny that it was occasioned by the fault of the steamboat, and impute it to the carelessness with which the schooner was managed.

The proceeding is *in rem*, and in substance as well as in form, a proceeding in admiralty. It was instituted under the act of February 26, 1845, (5 Stat. at L., 726), extending the jurisdiction of the district courts to certain cases upon the lakes and navigable waters connecting the same. The District Court decreed in favor of the libellants, and the decision was affirmed in the Circuit Court, from which last-mentioned decree this appeal has been taken.

Before, however, we can look into the merits of the dispute there is question of jurisdiction which meets us at the threshold. When the act of Congress was passed, under which these proceedings were had, serious doubts were entertained of its constitutionality. The language and decision of this court, whenever a question of admiralty jurisdiction had come before it, seemed to imply that under the Constitution of the United States, the jurisdiction was confined to tide-waters. Yet the conviction that this definition of admiralty powers was narrower than the Constitution contemplated, has been growing stronger every day with the growing commerce on the lakes and navigable rivers of the western states. And the difficulties which the language and decisions of this court had thrown in the way, of extending it to these waters, have perhaps led to the inquiry whether the law in question could not be supported under the power granted to Congress to regulate commerce. This proposition has been maintained in a recent work upon the jurisdiction, law, and practice of the courts of the United States in admiralty and maritime causes, which is entitled to much respect, and the same ground has been taken in the argument of the case before us.

The law, however, contains no regulations of commerce; nor any provision in relation to shipping and navigation on the lakes. It merely confers a new jurisdiction on the district courts; and this is its only object and purpose. It is entitled 'An act extending the jurisdiction of the district courts to certain cases upon the lakes and navigable waters connecting the same;' and the enacting clause conforms to the title. It declares that these courts shall have, possess, and exercise the same jurisdiction in matters of contract and tort, arising in or upon or concerning steamboats and other vessels of twenty tons burden and upwards, enrolled and licensed for the coasting trade, and at the time employed in business of commerce and navigation between ports and places in different states and territories, as was at the time of the passage of the law possessed and exercised by the district courts in cases of like steamboats and other vessels employed in navigation and commerce on the high seas, or tide-waters within the admiralty and maritime jurisdiction of the United States.

It is evident, therefore, from the title as well as the body of the law, that Congress, in passing it, did not intend to exercise their power to regulate commerce; nor to derive their authority from that article of the Constitution. And if the constitutionality of this law is supported as a regulation of commerce, we shall impute to the legislature the exercise of a power which it has not claimed under that clause of the Constitution; and which we have no reason to suppose it deemed itself authorized to exercise.

Indeed it would be inconsistent with the plain and ordinary meaning of words, to call a law defining the jurisdiction of certain courts of the United States a regulation of commerce. This law gives jurisdiction to a certain extent over commerce and navigation and authorizes the court to expound the laws that regulate them. But the jurisdiction to administer the existing laws upon these subjects is certainly not a regulation within the meaning of the Constitution. And this act of Congress merely creates a tribunal to carry the laws into execution but does not prescribe them.

Nor can the jurisdiction of the courts of the United States be made to depend on regulations of commerce. They are entirely distinct things, having no necessary connection with one another, and are conferred in the Constitution by separate and distinct grants. The extent of the judicial power is carefully defined and limited, and Congress cannot enlarge it to suit even the wants of commerce, nor for the more convenient execution of its commercial regulations. And the limits fixed by the Constitution to the judicial authority of the courts of the United States, would form an insuperable objection to this law, if its validity depended upon the commercial power.

This power is as extensive upon land as upon water. The Constitution makes no distinction in that respect. And if the admiralty jurisdiction, in matters of contract and tort which the courts of the United States may lawfully exercise on the high seas, can be extended to the lakes under the power to regulate commerce, it can with the same propriety and upon the same construction, be extended to contracts and torts on land when the commerce is between different states. And it may embrace also the vehicles and persons engaged in carrying it on. It would be in the power of Congress to confer admiralty jurisdiction upon its courts, over the cars engaged in transporting passengers or merchandise from one state to another, and over the persons engaged in conducting them, and deny to the parties the trial by jury. Now the judicial power in cases of admiralty and maritime jurisdiction, has never been supposed to extend to contracts made on land and to be executed on land. But if the power of regulating commerce can be made the foundation of jurisdiction in its courts, and a new and extended admiralty jurisdiction beyond its heretofore known and admitted limits, may be created on water under that authority, the same reason would justify the same exercise of power on land.

But if the admiralty jurisdiction is confined to tide-water, the courts of the United States can exercise over the waters in question nothing more than ordinary jurisdiction in cases at common law and equity. And in cases of this description they have no jurisdiction, if the parties are citizens of the same state. This being an express limitation in the grant of judicial power, no act of Congress can enlarge it. And if the validity of the act of 1845 depended upon the power to regulate commerce, it would be unconstitutional, and could confer no authority on the District Courts.

If this law, therefore, is constitutional, it must be supported on the ground that the lakes and navigable waters connecting them are within the scope of admiralty and maritime jurisdiction, as known and understood in the United States when the Constitution was adopted.

The only objection made to this jurisdiction is that there is no tide in the lakes or the waters connecting them; and it is said that the admiralty and maritime jurisdiction, as known and understood in England and this country at the time the Constitution was adopted, was confined to the ebb and flow of the tide.

Now there is certainly nothing in the ebb and flow of the tide that makes the waters peculiarly suitable for admiralty jurisdiction, nor any thing in the absence of a tide that renders it unfit. If it is a public navigable water, on which commerce is carried on between different states or nations, the reason for the jurisdiction is precisely the same. And if a distinction is made on that account, it is merely arbitrary, without any foundation in reason; and, indeed, would seem to be inconsistent with it.

At the time the Constitution of the United States was adopted, and our courts of admiralty went into operation, the definition which had been adopted in England was equally proper here. In the old thirteen states the far greater part of the navigable waters are tide-waters. And in the states which were at that period in any degree commercial, and where courts of admiralty were called on to exercise their jurisdiction, every public river was tide-water to the head of navigation. And, indeed, until the discovery of steamboats, there could be nothing like foreign commerce upon waters with an unchanging current resisting the upward passage. The courts of the United States, therefore, naturally adopted the English mode of defining a public river, and consequently the boundary of admiralty jurisdiction. It measured it by tide-water. And that definition having found its way into our courts, became, after a time, the familiar mode of describing a public river, and was repeated, as cases occurred, without particularly examining whether it was as universally applicable in this country as it was in England. If there were no waters in the United States which are public, as contradistinguished from private, except where there is tide, then unquestionably here as well as in England, tide-water must be the limits of admiralty power. And as the English definition was adopted in our courts, and constantly used in judicial proceedings and forms of pleading, borrowed from England, the public character of the river was in process of time lost sight of, and the jurisdiction of the admiralty treated as if it was limited by the tide. The description of a public navigable river was substituted in the place of the thing intended to be described. And under the natural influence of precedents and established forms, a definition originally correct was adhered to and acted on, after it had ceased, from a change in circumstances, to be the true description of public waters. It was under the influence of these precedents and this usage, that the case of the *Thomas Jefferson*, 10 Wheat., 428, was decided in this court; and the jurisdiction of the courts of admiralty of the United States declared to be limited to the ebb and flow of the tide. *The Steamboat Orleans* v. *Phoebus*, 11 Pet., 175, afterwards followed this case, merely as a point decided.

It is the decision in the case of the *Thomas Jefferson* which mainly embarrasses the court in the present inquiry. We are sensible of the great weight to which it is entitled. But at the same time we are convinced that, if we follow it, we follow an erroneous decision into which the court fell, when the great importance of the question as it now presents itself could not be foreseen; and the subject did not therefore receive that deliberate consideration which at this time would have been given to it by the eminent men who presided here when that case was decided. For the decision was made in 1825, when the commerce on the rivers of the west and on the lakes was in its infancy, and of little importance, and but little regarded compared with that of the present day.

The decree of the Circuit Court must therefore be affirmed with costs.

THE CHASE COURT

Legal Tender Cases, 79 U.S. 457 (1870)

Mr. Justice Strong delivered the opinion of the Court.

The controlling questions in these cases are the following: Are the acts of Congress, known as the legal tender acts, constitutional when applied to contracts made before their passage; and, secondly, are they valid as applicable to debts contracted since their enactment? These questions have been elaborately argued, and they have received from the court that consideration which their great importance demands. It would be difficult to overestimate the consequences which must follow our decision. They will affect the entire business of the country, and take hold of the possible continued existence of the government. If it be held by this court that Congress has no constitutional power, under any circumstances, or in any emergency, to make treasury notes a legal tender for the payment of all debts (a power confessedly possessed by every independent sovereignty other than the United States), the government is without those means of self-preservation which, all must admit, may, in certain contingencies, become indispensable, even if they were not when the acts of Congress now called in question were enacted. It is also clear that if we hold the acts invalid as applicable to debts incurred, or transactions which have taken place since their enactment, our decision must cause, throughout the country, great business derangement, widespread distress, and the rankest injustice...

If now, by our decision, it be established that these debts and obligations can be discharged only by gold coin; if, contrary to the expectation of all parties to these contracts, legal tender notes are rendered unavailable, the government has become an instrument of the grossest injustice; all debtors are loaded with an obligation it was never contemplated they should assume; a large percentage is added to every debt, and such must become the demand for gold to satisfy contracts, that ruinous sacrifices, general distress, and bankruptcy may be expected...

These consequences are too obvious to admit of question. And there is no well-founded distinction to be made between the constitutional validity of an act of Congress declaring treasury notes a legal tender for the payment of debts contracted after its passage and that of an act making them a legal tender for the discharge of all debts, as well those incurred before as those made after its enactment. The consequences of which we have spoken, serious as they are, must be accepted, if there is a clear incompatibility between the Constitution and the legal tender acts. But we are unwilling to precipitate them upon the country unless such an incompatibility plainly appears. A decent respect for a co-ordinate branch of the government demands that the judiciary should presume, until the contrary is clearly shown, that there has been no transgression of power by Congress—all the members of which act under the obligation of an oath of fidelity to the Constitution. Such has always been the rule. And here it is to be observed it is not indispensable to the existence of any power claimed for the Federal government that it can be found specified in the words of the Constitution, or clearly and directly traceable to some one of the specified powers. Its existence may be deduced fairly from more than one of the substantive powers expressly defined, or from them all combined. And it is of importance to observe that Congress has often exercised, without question, powers that are not expressly given nor ancillary to any single enumerated power. Powers thus exercised are what are called by Judge Story in his Commentaries on the Constitution, resulting powers, arising from the aggregate powers of the government...

This is enough to show how, from the earliest period of our existence as a nation, the powers conferred by the Constitution have been construed by Congress and by this court whenever such action by Congress has been called in question.

Happily, the true meaning of the clause authorizing the enactment of all laws necessary and proper for carrying into execution the express powers conferred upon Congress, and all other powers vested in the government of the United States, or in any of its departments or officers, has long since been settled.

It was, however, in *McCulloch* v. *Maryland* that the fullest consideration was given to this clause of the Constitution granting auxiliary powers, and a construction adopted that has ever since been accepted as determining its true meaning. We shall not now go over the ground there trodden. It is familiar to the legal profession, and indeed, to the whole country. Suffice it to say, in that case it was finally settled that in the gift by the Constitution to Congress of authority to enact laws 'necessary and proper' for the execution of all the powers created by it, the necessity spoken of is not to be understood as an absolute one...Even in *Hepburn* v. *Griswold*, both the majority and minority of the court concurred in accepting the doctrines of *McCulloch* v. *Maryland* as sound expositions of the Constitution, though disagreeing in their application.

With these rules of constitutional construction before us, settled at an early period in the history of the government, hitherto universally accepted, and not even now doubted, we have a safe guide to a right decision of the questions before us. Before we can hold the legal tender acts unconstitutional, we must be convinced they were not appropriate means, or means conducive to the execution of any or all of the powers of Congress, or of the government, not appropriate in any degree (for we are not judges of the degree of appropriateness), or we must hold that they were prohibited. ...

We do not, however, rest our assertion of the power of Congress to enact legal tender laws upon this grant. We assert only that the grant can, in no just sense, be regarded as containing an implied prohibition against their enactment, and that, if it raises any implications, they are of complete power over the currency, rather than restraining. We are not aware of anything else which has been advanced in support of the proposition that the legal tender acts were forbidden by either the letter or the spirit of the Constitution... But, without extending our remarks further, it will be seen that we hold the acts of Congress constitutional as applied to contracts made either before or after their passage. In so holding, we overrule so much of what was decided in *Hepburn* v. *Griswold*, 75 U.S. 603 (1870), as ruled the acts unwarranted by the Constitution so far as they apply to contracts made before their enactment. That case was decided by a divided court, and by a court having a less number of judges than the law then in existence provided this court shall have. These cases have been heard before a full court, and they have received our most careful consideration. The questions involved are constitutional questions of the most vital importance to the government and to the public at large. We have been in the habit of treating cases involving a consideration of constitutional power differently from those which concern merely private right. We are not accustomed to hear them in the absence of a full court, if it can be avoided. Even in cases involving only private rights, if convinced we had made a mistake, we would hear another argument and correct our error. And it is no unprecedented thing in courts of last resort, both in this country and in England, to overrule decisions previously made. We agree this should not be done inconsiderately, but in a case of such far-reaching consequences as the present, thoroughly convinced as we are that Congress has not transgressed its powers, we regard it as our duty so to decide and to affirm both these judgments.

THE WAITE COURT

Kilbourn v. Thompson, 103 U.S. 168 (1880)

This is an action for false imprisonment brought by Hallet Kilbourn against John G. Thompson, Michael C. Kerr, John M. Glover, Jeptha D. New, Burwell P. Lewis, and A. Herr Smith. The declaration charges that the defendants with force and arms took the plaintiff from his house, and without any reasonable or probable cause, and against his will, confined him in the common jail of the District of Columbia for the period of forty-five days. The defendant Kerr died before process was served upon him.

Thompson pleaded first the general issue, and secondly a special plea, wherein he set forth that the plaintiff ought not to have or maintain his action, because that long before and at the said time when the force and injuries complained of by him are alleged to have been inflicted, and during all the time in the said declaration mentioned, a congress of the United States was holden at the city of Washington, there duly authorized and required, and was then and there, and during all the time aforesaid, assembled and sitting; that long before and at the time when said force and injuries are alleged to have occurred, and during all the time mentioned, he, the said Thompson, was, and yet is, sergeant-at-arms of the House of Representatives, and by virtue of his office, and by the tenor and effect of the standing rules and orders ordained and established by said House for the determining of the rules of its proceedings, and by the force and effect of the laws and customs of said House and of said Congress, was then and there duly authorized and required, amongst other things, to execute the command of said House, from time to time, together with all such process issued by authority thereof as shall be directed to him by its speaker; that long before and at the time aforementioned one Michael C. Kerr was the speaker of said House, and by virtue of his office, and by the tenor, force, and effect of said standing rules, orders, laws, and customs, was, among other things, duly authorized and required to subscribe with his proper hand, and to seal with the seal of said House, all writs, warrants, and subpoenas issued by its order; that long before and during said time one George M. Adams was the clerk of said House, authorized and required to attest and subscribe with his proper hand all writs, warrants, and subpoenas issued by order of said House; that it was among other things ordained, established, and practised by and under such standing rules, orders, laws, and customs, that all writs, warrants, subpoenas, and other process issued by order of said House shall be under the hand of the speaker and seal of said House, and attested by said clerk; and so being under said hand and seal, and so attested, shall be executed pursuant to the tenor and effect of the same by the sergeant-at-arms; that said Kerr being such speaker, and said Adams such clerk, and the defendant such sergeant-at-arms, and while said Congress was in session, the House of Representatives on the twenty-fourth day of January, 1876.

Mr. Justice Miller, after stating the case, delivered the opinion of the Court.

We are of opinion that the right of the House of Representatives to punish the citizen for a contempt of its authority or a breach of its privileges can derive no support from the precedents and practices of the two Houses of the English Parliament, nor from the adjudged cases in which the English courts have upheld these practices. Nor, taking what has fallen from the English judges, and especially the later cases on which we have just commented, is much aid given to the doctrine, that this power exists as one necessary to enable either House of Congress to exercise successfully their function of legislation.

As we have already said, the Constitution expressly empowers each House to punish its own members for disorderly behavior. We see no reason to doubt that this punishment may in a proper case be imprisonment, and that it may be for refusal to obey some rule on that subject made by the House for the preservation of order.

Whether the power of punishment in either House by fine or imprisonment goes beyond this or not, we are sure that no person can be punished for contumacy as a witness before either House, unless his testimony is required in a matter into which that House has jurisdiction to inquire, and we feel equally sure that neither of these bodies possesses the general power of making inquiry into the private affairs of the citizen.

We are of opinion, for these reasons, that the resolution of the House of Representatives authorizing the investigation was in excess of the power conferred on that body by the Constitution; that the committee, therefore, had no lawful authority to require Kilbourn to testify as a witness beyond what he voluntarily chose to tell; that the orders and resolutions of the House, and the warrant of the speaker, under which Kilbourn was imprisoned, are, in like manner, void for want of jurisdiction in that body, and that his imprisonment was without any lawful authority.

At this point of the inquiry we are met by *Anderson* v. *Dunn* (6 Wheat. 204), which in many respects is analogous to the case now under consideration. Anderson sued Dunn for false imprisonment, and Dunn justified under a warrant of the House of Representatives directed to him as sergeant-at-arms of that body. The warrant recited that Anderson had been found by the House 'guilty of a breach of the privileges of the House, and of a high contempt of the dignity and authority of the same.' The warrant directed the sergeant-at-arms to bring him before the House, when, by its order, he was reprimanded by the speaker. Neither the warrant nor the plea described or gave any clew to the nature of the act which was held by the House to be a contempt. Nor can it be clearly ascertained from the report of the case what it was, though a slight inference may be derived from something in one of the arguments of counsel, that it was an attempt to bribe a member.

But we do not concede that the Houses of Congress possess this general power of punishing for contempt.

The case of *Anderson* v. *Dunn* was decided before the case of *Stockdale* v. *Hansard*, and the more recent cases in the Privy Council to which we have referred. It was decided as a case of the first impression in this court, and undoubtedly under pressure of the strong rulings of the English courts in favor of the privileges of the two Houses of Parliament. Such is not the doctrine, however, of the English courts to-day. In the case of *Stockdale* v. *Hansard* (9 Ad. & E. 1), Mr. Justice Coleridge says: 'The House is not a court of law at all in the sense in which that term can alone be properly applied here. Neither originally nor by appeal can it decide a matter in litigation between two parties; it has no means of doing so; it claims no such power; powers of inquiry and of accusation it has, but it decides nothing judicially, except where it is itself a party, in the case of contempts. ... Considered merely as resolutions or acts, I have yet to learn that this court is to be restrained by the dignity or the power of any body, however exalted, from fearlessly, though respectfully, examining their reasonableness and justice, where the rights of third persons, in litigation before us, depend upon their validity.'

The case of *Kielley* v. *Carson and Others* (4 Moo. P. C. 63), from which we have before quoted so largely, held that the order of the assembly, finding the plaintiff guilty of a contempt, was no defence to the action for imprisonment. And it is to be observed that the case of *Anderson* v. *Dunn* was cited there in argument.

We must, therefore, hold, notwithstanding what is said in the case of *Anderson* v. *Dunn*, that the resolution of the House of Representatives finding Kilbourn guilty of contempt, and the warrant of its speaker for his commitment to prison, are not conclusive in this case, and in fact are no justification, because, as the whole plea shows, the House was without authority in the matter.

THE TAFT COURT

Terral v. Burke Const. Co., 257 U.S. 529 (1922)

Mr. Chief Justice Taft delivered the opinion of the Court.

This is an appeal from the District Court under section 238 of the Judicial Code (Comp. St. § 1215) in a case in which the law of a state is claimed to be in contravention of the Constitution of the United States.

The Burke Construction Company, a corporation organized under the laws of the state of Missouri, filed its bill against Terral, Secretary of State of Arkansas, averring that it has been licensed to do business in the state of Arkansas under an act of the Arkansas Legislature approved May 13, 1907 (Laws 1907, p. 744); that it was organized for the purpose of doing construction work, and carrying on interstate commerce, and was actually so engaged in Arkansas; that the right to do business in the state was a valuable privilege, and the revocation of the license would greatly injure it; that it had brought an original suit in the federal court of Arkansas and had removed a suit brought against it to the same federal court; that the Secretary of State was about to revoke the license because of such suit and such removal, acting under the requirement of section 1 of the act of the Legislature of Arkansas of May 13, 1907, reading as follows:

'If any company shall, without the consent of the other party to any suit or proceeding brought by or against it in any court of this state, remove said suit or proceeding to any federal court, or shall institute any suit or proceeding against any citizen of this state in any federal court, it shall be the duty of the Secretary of State to forthwith revoke all authority to such company and its agents to do business in this state, and to publish such revocation in some newspaper of general circulation published in this state; and if such corporation shall thereafter continue to do business in this state, it shall be subject to the penalty of this act for each day it shall continue to do business in this state after such revocation.'

The penalty fixed is not less than $1,000 and The Construction Company avers that this act is in contravention of section 2, article 3, i. e., the judiciary article of the federal Constitution, and of section 1 of the Fourteenth Amendment.

The defendant filed an answer in which there were many denials. One was that the complainant was engaged in interstate commerce. The answer did not deny, however, that the complainant was a foreign corporation, that it had been duly granted a license to do business in the state of Arkansas, that its right to do business in the state thus licensed was a valuable right, that the complainant had brought suit in the federal District Court and removed another case to that court, that such suit and removal were violations of the license granted by the state of Arkansas, or that the defendant intended to cancel the plaintiff's license. The case was heard on bill and answer, and is to be considered on the averments of the bill which are not denied by the answer.

The sole question presented on the record is whether a state law is unconstitutional which revokes a license to a foreign corporation to do business within the state because, while doing only a domestic business in the state, it resorts to the federal court sitting in the state.

The cases in this court in which the conflict between the power of a state to exclude a foreign corporation from doing business within its borders, and the federal constitutional right of such foreign corporation to resort to the federal courts has been considered, cannot be reconciled. They began with Home Insurance Co. v. Morse, 20 Wall. 445, 22 L. Ed. 365, which was followed by Doyle v. Continental Ins. Co., 94 U. S. 535, 24 L. Ed. 148; Barron v. Burnside, 121 U. S. 186, 7 Sup. Ct. 931, 30 L. Ed. 915; Southern Pacific Co. v. Denton, 146 U. S. 202, 13 Sup. Ct. 44, 36 L. Ed. 942; Martin v. Baltimore, 151 U. S. 673, 684, 14 Sup. Ct. 533, 38 L. Ed. 311; Barrow Steamship Co. v. Kane, 170 U. S. 100, 111, 18 Sup. Ct. 526, 42 L. Ed. 964; Security Mutual Life Ins. Co. v. Prewitt, 202 U. S. 246, 26 Sup. Ct. 619, 50 L. Ed. 1013, 6 Ann. Cas. 317; Herndon v. Chicago, Rock Island & Pac. Ry. Co., 218 U. S. 135, 30 Sup. Ct. 633, 54 L. Ed. 970; Harrison v. St. Louis & San Francisco R. R. Co., 232 U. S. 318, 34 Sup. Ct. 333, 58 L. Ed. 621, L. R. A. 1915F, 1187; and Wisconsin v. Philadelphia & Reading Coal Co., 241 U. S. 329, 36 Sup. Ct. 563, 60 L. Ed. 1027.

The principle established by the more recent decisions of this court is that a state may not, in imposing conditions upon the privilege of a foreign corporation's doing business in the state, exact from it a waiver of the exercise of its constitutional right to resort to the federal courts, or thereafter withdraw the privilege of doing business because of its exercise of such right, whether waived in advance or not. The principle does not depend for its application on the character of the business the corporation does, whether state or interstate, although that has been suggested

as a distinction in some cases. It rests on the ground that the federal Constitution confers upon citizens of one state the right to resort to federal courts in another, that state action, whether legislative or executive, necessarily calculated to curtail the free exercise of the right thus secured is void because the sovereign power of a state in excluding foreign corporations, as in the exercise of all others of its sovereign powers, is subject to the limitations of the supreme fundamental law. It follows that the cases of Doyle v. Continental Insurance Co., 94 U. S. 535, 24 L. Ed. 148, and Security Mutual Life Ins. Co. v. Prewitt, 202 U. S. 246, 26 Sup. Ct. 619, 50 L. Ed. 1013, must be considered as overruled and that the views of the minority judges in those cases have become the law of this court. The appellant in proposing to comply with the statute in question and revoke the license was about to violate the constitutional right of the appellee. In enjoining him the District Court was right, and its decree is
Affirmed.

THE HUGHES COURT

Ashwander v. Tennessee Valley Authority, 297 U.S. 288 (1936)

Mr. Justice Brandeis (concurring).

The Court has frequently called attention to the 'great gravity and delicacy' of its function in passing upon the validity of an act of Congress; and has restricted exercise of this function by rigid insistence that the jurisdiction of federal courts is limited to actual cases and controversies; and that they have no power to give advisory opinions. On this ground it has in recent years ordered the dismissal of several suits challenging the constitutionality of important acts of Congress. In Texas v. Interstate Commerce Commission, 258 U.S. 158, 162, 42 S.Ct. 261, 66 L.Ed. 531, the validity of titles 3 and 4 of the Transportation Act of 1920 (41 Stat. 456). In New Jersey v. Sargent, 269 U.S. 328, 46 S.Ct. 122, 70 L.Ed. 289, the validity of parts of the Federal Water Power Act (41 Stat. 1063). In Arizona v. California, 283 U.S. 423, 51 S.Ct. 522, 75 L.Ed. 1154, the validity of the Boulder Canyon Project Act (43 U.S.C.A. s 617 et seq.). Compare United States v. West Virginia, 295 U.S. 463, 55 S.Ct. 789, 79 L.Ed. 1546, involving the Federal Water Power Act and Liberty Warehouse Co. v. Grannis, 273 U.S. 70, 47 S.Ct. 282, 71 L.Ed. 541, where this Court affirmed the dismissal of a suit to test the validity of a Kentucky statute concerning the sale of tobacco; also, Massachusetts State Grange v. Benton, 272 U.S. 525, 47 S.Ct. 189, 71 L.Ed. 387.
The Court developed, for its own governance in the cases confessedly within its jurisdiction, a series of rules under which it has avoided passing upon a large part of all the constitutional questions pressed upon it for decision. They are:
1. The Court will not pass upon the constitutionality of legislation in a friendly, nonadversary, proceeding, declining because to decide such questions 'is legitimate only in the last resort, and as a necessity in the determination of real, earnest, and vital controversy between individuals. It never was the thought that, by means of a friendly suit, a party beaten in the legislature could transfer to the courts an inquiry as to the constitutionality of the legislative act.' Chicago & Grand Trunk Ry. Co. v. Wellman, 143 U.S. 339, 345, 12 S.Ct. 400, 402, 36

L.Ed. 176. Compare Lord v. Veazie, 8 How. 251, 12 L.Ed. 1067; Atherton Mills v. Johnston, 259 U.S. 13, 15, 42 S.Ct. 422, 66 L.Ed. 814.

2. The Court will not 'anticipate a question of constitutional law in advance of the necessity of deciding it.' Liverpool, N.Y. & Phila. Steamship Co. v. Emigration Commissioners, 113 U.S. 33, 39, 5 S.Ct. 352, 355, 28 L.Ed. 899; Abrams v. Van Schaick, 293 U.S. 188, 55 S.Ct. 135, 79 L.Ed. 278; Wilshire Oil Co. v. United States, 295 U.S. 100, 55 S.Ct. 673, 79 L.Ed. 1329. 'It is not the habit of the court to decide questions of a constitutional nature unless absolutely necessary to a decision of the case.' Burton v. United States, 196 U.S. 283, 295, 25 S.Ct. 243, 245, 49 L.Ed. 482.

3. The Court will not 'formulate a rule of constitutional law broader than is required by the precise facts to which it is to be applied.' Liverpool, N.Y. & Phila. Steamship Co. v. Emigration Commissioners, supra. Compare Hammond v. Schappi Bus Line, Inc., 275 U.S. 164, 169–172, 48 S.Ct. 66, 72 L.Ed. 218.

4. The Court will not pass upon a constitutional question although properly presented by the record, if there is also present some other ground upon which the case may be disposed of. This rule has found most varied application. Thus, if a case can be decided on either of two grounds, one involving a constitutional question, the other a question of statutory construction or general law, the Court will decide only the latter. Siler v. Louisville & Nashville R. Co., 213 U.S. 175, 191, 29 S.Ct. 451, 53 L.Ed. 753; Light v. United States, 220 U.S. 523, 538, 31 S.Ct. 485, 55 L.Ed. 570. Appeals from the highest court of a state challenging its decision of a question under the Federal Constitution are frequently dismissed because the judgment can be sustained on an independent state ground. Berea College v. Kentucky, 211 U.S. 45, 53, 29 S.Ct. 33, 53 L.Ed. 81.

5. The Court will not pass upon the validity of a statute upon complaint of one who fails to show that he is injured by its operation. Tyler v. Judges, etc., 179 U.S. 405, 21 S.Ct. 206, 45 L.Ed. 252; Hendrick v. Maryland, 235 U.S. 610, 621, 35 S.Ct. 140, 59 L.Ed. 385. Among the many applications of this rule, none is more striking than the denial of the right of challenge to one who lacks a personal or property right. Thus, the challenge by a public official interested only in the performance of his official duty will not be entertained. Columbus & Greenville Ry. Co. v. Miller, 283 U.S. 96, 99, 100, 51 S.Ct. 392, 75 L.Ed. 861. In Fairchild v. Hughes, 258 U.S. 126, 42 S.Ct. 274, 66 L.Ed. 499, the Court affirmed the dismissal of a suit brought by a citizen who sought to have the Nineteenth Amendment declared unconstitutional. In Massachusetts v. Mellon, 262 U.S. 447, 43 S.Ct. 597, 67 L.Ed. 1078, the challenge of the federal Maternity Act was not entertained although made by the commonwealth on behalf of all its citizens.

6. The Court will not pass upon the constitutionality of a statute at the instance of one who has availed himself of its benefits. Great Falls Mfg. Co. v. Attorney General, 124 U.S. 581, 8 S.Ct. 631, 31 L.Ed. 527; Wall v. Parrot Silver & Copper Co., 244 U.S. 407, 411, 412, 37 S.Ct. 609, 61 L.Ed. 1229; St. Louis Malleable Casting Co. v. Prendergast Construction Co., 260 U.S. 469, 43 S.Ct. 178, 67 L.Ed. 351.

7. 'When the validity of an act of the Congress is drawn in question, and even if a serious doubt of constitutionality is raised, it is a cardinal principle that this Court will first ascertain whether a construction of the statute is fairly possible by which the question may be avoided.' Crowell v. Benson, 285 U.S. 22, 62, 52 S.Ct. 285, 296, 76 L.Ed. 598.

West Coast Hotel Co. v. Parrish, 300 U.S. 379 (1937)

Mr. Chief Justice Hughes delivered the opinion of the Court.

This case presents the question of the constitutional validity of the minimum wage law of the state of Washington.

The appellant relies upon the decision of this Court in Adkins v. Children's Hospital, 261 U.S. 525, which held invalid the District of Columbia Minimum Wage Act (40 Stat. 960) which was attacked under the due process clause of the Fifth Amendment. On the argument at bar, counsel for the appellees attempted to distinguish the Adkins Case upon the ground that the appellee was employed in a hotel and that the business of an innkeeper was affected with a public interest. That effort at distinction is obviously futile, as it appears that in one of the cases ruled by the Adkins opinion the employee was a woman employed as an elevator operator in a hotel.

The Supreme Court of Washington has upheld the minimum wage statute of that state. It has decided that the statute is a reasonable exercise of the police power of the state. In reaching that conclusion, the state court has invoked principles long established by this Court in the application of the Fourteenth Amendment. The state court has refused to regard the decision in the Adkins Case as determinative and has pointed to our decisions both before and since that case as justifying its position. We are of the opinion that this ruling of the state court demands on our part a re-examination of the Adkins Case. The importance of the question, in which many states having similar laws are concerned, the close division by which the decision in the Adkins Case was reached, and the economic conditions which have supervened, and in the light of which the reasonableness of the exercise of the protective power of the state must be considered, make it not only appropriate, but we think imperative, that in deciding the present case the subject should receive fresh consideration.

The principle which must control our decision is not in doubt. The constitutional provision invoked is the due process clause of the Fourteenth Amendment governing the states, as the due process clause invoked in the Adkins Case governed Congress. In each case the violation alleged by those attacking minimum wage regulation for women is deprivation of freedom of contract. What is this freedom? The Constitution does not speak of freedom of contract. It speaks of liberty and prohibits the deprivation of liberty without due process of law. In prohibiting that deprivation, the Constitution does not recognize an absolute and uncontrollable liberty. Liberty in each of its phases has its history and connotation. But the liberty safeguarded is liberty in a social organization which requires the protection of law against the evils which menace the health, safety, morals, and welfare of the people. Liberty under the Constitution is thus necessarily subject to the restraints of due process, and regulation which is reasonable in relation to its subject and is adopted in the interests of the community is due process. This essential limitation of liberty in general governs freedom of contract in particular. More than twenty-five years ago we set forth the applicable principle in these words, after referring to the cases where the liberty guaranteed by the Fourteenth Amendment had been broadly described.

This power under the Constitution to restrict freedom of contract has had many illustrations.

The point that has been strongly stressed that adult employees should be deemed competent to make their own contracts was decisively met nearly forty years ago in

Holden v. Hardy, supra, where we pointed out the inequality in the footing of the parties...

And we added that the fact 'that both parties are of full age, and competent to contract, does not necessarily deprive the state of the power to interfere, where the parties do not stand upon an equality, or where the public health demands that one party to the contract shall be protected against himself.' 'The state still retains an interest in his welfare, however reckless he may be. The whole is no greater than the sum of all the parts, and when the individual health, safety, and welfare are sacrificed or neglected, the state must suffer.'

It is manifest that this established principle is peculiarly applicable in relation to the employment of women in whose protection the state has a special interest. That phase of the subject received elaborate consideration in Muller v. Oregon (1908) 208 U.S. 412, where the constitutional authority of the state to limit the working hours of women was sustained. We emphasized the consideration that 'woman's physical structure and the performance of maternal functions place her at a disadvantage in the struggle for subsistence' and that her physical well being 'becomes an object of public interest and care in order to preserve the strength and vigor of the race.' We emphasized the need of protecting women against oppression despite her possession of contractual rights. We said that 'though limitations upon personal and contractual rights may be removed by legislation, there is that in her disposition and habits of life which will operate against a full assertion of those rights. She will still be where some legislation to protect her seems necessary to secure a real equality of right.' Hence she was 'properly placed in a class by herself, and legislation designed for her protection may be sustained, even when like legislation is not necessary for men, and could not be sustained.' We concluded that the limitations which the statute there in question 'places upon her contractual powers, upon her right to agree with her employer, as to the time she shall labor' were 'not imposed solely for her benefit, but also largely for the benefit of all.' We referred to recognized classifications on the basis of sex with regard to hours of work and in other matters, and we observed that the particular points at which that difference shall be enforced by legislation were largely in the power of the state. In later rulings this Court sustained the regulation of hours of work of women employees in Riley v. Massachusetts, 232 U.S. 671, 34 S.Ct. 469, 58 L.Ed. 788 (factories), Miller v. Wilson, 236 U.S. 373, 35 S.Ct. 342, 59 L.Ed. 628, L.R.A.1915F, 829 (hotels), and Bosley v. McLaughlin, 236 U.S. 385, 35 S.Ct. 345, 59 L.Ed. 632 (hospitals).

This array of precedents and the principles they applied were thought by the dissenting Justices in the Adkins Case to demand that the minimum wage statute be sustained. The validity of the distinction made by the Court between a minimum wage and a maximum of hours in limiting liberty of contract was especially challenged. That challenge persists and is without any satisfactory answer.

We think that the views thus expressed are sound and that the decision in the Adkins Case was a departure from the true application of the principles governing the regulation by the state of the relation of employer and employed. Those principles have been reenforced by our subsequent decisions. Thus in Radice v. New York, 264 U.S. 292, 44 S.Ct. 325, 68 L.Ed. 690, we sustained the New York statute which restricted the employment of women in restaurants at night. In O'Gorman & Young v. Hartford Fire Insurance Company, 282 U.S. 251, 51 S.Ct. 130, 75 L.Ed. 324, 72 A.L.R. 1163, which upheld an act regulating the commissions of insurance agents, we pointed to the presumption of the constitutionality of a statute dealing with a subject within the scope of the police power and to the absence of any factual foundation of record for deciding that the limits of power had been transcended. In Nebbia v. New York, 291 U.S. 502, 54 S.Ct. 505, 78 L.Ed. 940, 89 A.L.R. 1469, dealing with the New York statute providing for minimum prices for milk, the general subject of the regulation of the use of private property and of the making of private contracts received an exhaustive examination, and we again declared that if such laws 'have a reasonable relation to a proper legislative purpose, and are neither arbitrary nor discriminatory, the requirements of due process are satisfied'; that 'with the wisdom of the policy adopted, with the adequacy or practicability of the law enacted to forward it, the courts are both incompetent and unauthorized to deal'; that 'times without number we have said that the Legislature is primarily the judge of the necessity of such an enactment, that every possible presumption is in favor of its validity, and that though the court may hold views inconsistent with the wisdom of the law, it may not be annulled unless palpably in excess of legislative power.'

With full recognition of the earnestness and vigor which characterize the prevailing opinion in the Adkins Case, we find it impossible to reconcile that ruling with these well-considered declarations. What can be closer to the public interest than the health of women and their protection from unscrupulous and overreaching employers? And if the protection of women is a legitimate end of the exercise of state power, how can it be said that the requirement of the payment of a minimum wage fairly fixed in order to meet the very necessities of existence is not an admissible means to that end? The Legislature of the state was clearly entitled to consider the situation of women in employment, the fact that they are in the class receiving the least pay, that their bargaining power is relatively weak, and that they are the ready victims of those who would take advantage of their necessitous circumstances...The Legislature had the right to consider that its minimum wage requirements would be an important aid in carrying out its policy of protection.

There is an additional and compelling consideration which recent economic experience has brought into a strong light. The exploitation of a class of workers who are in an unequal position with respect to bargaining power and are thus relatively defenseless against the denial of a living wage is not only detrimental to their health and well being, but casts a direct burden for their support upon the community. What these workers lose in wages the taxpayers are called upon to pay. The bare cost of living must be met. We may take judicial notice of the unparalleled demands for relief which arose during the recent period of depression and still continue to an alarming extent despite the degree of economic recovery which has been achieved. It is unnecessary to cite official statistics to establish what is of common knowledge through the length and breadth of the land.

Our conclusion is that the case of Adkins v. Children's Hospital, supra, should be, and it is, overruled. The judgment of the Supreme Court of the state of Washington is affirmed.

Affirmed.

Erie Railroad v. Tompkins, 304 U.S. 64 (1938)

Mr. Justice Brandeis delivered the opinion of the Court.

The question for decision is whether the oft-challenged doctrine of *Swift v. Tyson*, shall now be disapproved.

Tompkins, a citizen of Pennsylvania, was injured on a dark night by a passing freight train of the Erie Railroad Company while walking along its right of way at Hughestown in that state. He claimed that the accident occurred through negligence in the operation, or maintenance, of the train; that he was rightfully on the premises as licensee because on a commonly used beaten footpath which ran for a short distance alongside the tracks; and that he was struck by something which looked like a door projecting from one of the moving cars. To enforce that claim he brought an action in the federal court for Southern New York, which had jurisdiction because the company is a corporation of that state. It denied liability; and the case was tried by a jury.

The Erie insisted that its duty to Tompkins was no greater than that owed to a trespasser. It contended, among other things, that its duty to Tompkins, and hence its liability, should be determined in accordance with the Pennsylvania law; that under the law of Pennsylvania, as declared by its highest court, persons who use pathways along the railroad right of way—that is, a longitudinal pathway as distinguished from a crossing—are to be deemed trespassers; and that the railroad is not liable for injuries to undiscovered trespassers resulting from its negligence, unless it be wanton or willful. Tompkins denied that any such rule had been established by the decisions of the Pennsylvania courts; and contended that, since there was no statute of the state on the subject, the railroad's duty and liability is to be determined in federal courts as a matter of general law.

The trial judge refused to rule that the applicable law precluded recovery. The jury brought in a verdict of $30,000; and the judgment entered thereon was affirmed by the Circuit Court of Appeals.

The Erie had contended that application of the Pennsylvania rule was required, among other things, by section 34 of the Federal Judiciary Act of September 24, 1789 which provides: 'The laws of the several States, except where the Constitution, treaties, or statutes of the United States otherwise require or provide, shall be regarded as rules of decision in trials at common law, in the courts of the United States, in cases where they apply.'

Because of the importance of the question whether the federal court was free to disregard the alleged rule of the Pennsylvania common law, we granted certiorari.

First. Swift v. Tyson, 16 Pet. 1, 18, 10 L.Ed. 865, held that federal courts exercising jurisdiction on the ground of diversity of citizenship need not, in matters of general jurisprudence, apply the unwritten law of the state as declared by its highest court; that they are free to exercise an independent judgment as to what the common law of the state is—or should be; and that, as there stated by Mr. Justice Story, 'the true interpretation of the 34th section limited its application to state laws, strictly local, that is to say, to the positive statutes of the state, and the construction thereof adopted by the local tribunals, and to rights and titles to things having a permanent locality, such as the rights and titles to real estate, and other matters immovable and intra-territorial in their nature and character. It never has been supposed by us, that the section did apply, or was designed to apply, to questions of a more general nature, not at all dependent upon local statutes or local usages of a fixed and permanent operation, as, for example, to the construction of ordinary contracts or other written instruments, and especially to questions of general commercial law, where the state tribunals are called upon to perform the like functions as ourselves, that is, to ascertain, upon general reasoning and legal analogies, what is the true exposition of the contract or instrument, or what is the just rule furnished by the principles of commercial law to govern the case.'

The Court in applying the rule of section 34 to equity cases, in Mason v. United States, 260 U.S. 545, 559, 43 S.Ct. 200, 204, 67 L.Ed. 396, said: 'The statute, however, is merely declarative of the rule which would exist in the absence of the statute.' The federal courts assumed, in the broad field of 'general law,' the power to declare rules of decision which Congress was confessedly without power to enact as statutes. Doubt was repeatedly expressed as to the correctness of the construction given section 34, and as to the soundness of the rule which it introduced. But it was the more recent research of a competent scholar, who examined the original document, which established that the construction given to it by the Court was erroneous; and that the purpose of the section was merely to make certain that, in all matters except those in which some federal law is controlling, the federal courts exercising jurisdiction in diversity of citizenship cases would apply as their rules of decision the law of the state, unwritten as well as written.

Criticism of the doctrine became widespread after the decision of Black & White Taxicab & Transfer Co. v. Brown & Yellow Taxicab & Transfer Co. There, Brown &Yellow, a Kentucky corporation owned by Kentuckians, and the Louisville & Nashville Railroad, also a Kentucky corporation, wished that the former should have the exclusive privilege of soliciting passenger and baggage transportation at the Bowling Green, Ky., Railroad station; and that the Black & White, a competing Kentucky corporation, should be prevented from interfering with that privilege. Knowing that such a contract would be void under the common law of Kentucky, it was arranged that the Brown & Yellow reincorporate under the law of Tennessee, and that the contract with the railroad should be executed there. The suit was then brought by the Tennessee corporation in the federal court for Western Kentucky to enjoin competition by the Black & White; an injunction issued by the District Court was sustained by the Court of Appeals; and this Court, citing many decisions in which the doctrine of Swift & Tyson had been applied, affirmed the decree.

Second. Experience in applying the doctrine of Swift v. Tyson, had revealed its defects, political and social; and the benefits expected to flow from the rule did not accrue. Persistence of state courts in their own opinions on questions of common law prevented uniformity; and the impossibility of discovering a satisfactory line of demarcation between the province of general law and that of local law developed a new well of uncertainties.

On the other hand, the mischievous results of the doctrine had become apparent. Diversity of citizenship jurisdiction was conferred in order to prevent apprehended discrimination in state courts against those not citizens of the state. Swift v. Tyson introduced grave discrimination by noncitizens against citizens. It made rights enjoyed under the unwritten 'general law' vary according to whether enforcement was sought in the state or in the federal court; and the privilege of selecting the court in which the right should be determined was conferred upon the noncitizen. Thus, the doctrine rendered impossible equal protection of the law. In attempting to promote uniformity of law throughout the United States, the doctrine had prevented uniformity in the administration of the law of the state.

The discrimination resulting became in practice far-reaching. This resulted in part from the broad province accorded to the so-called 'general law' as to which federal courts exercised an independent judgment. In addition to questions of purely commercial law, 'general law' was held to include the obligations under contracts entered into and to be performed within the state, the extent to which a carrier operating within a state may stipulate for exemption from liability for his own negligence or that of his employee; the liability for torts committed within the state upon persons resident or property located there, even where the question of liability depended upon the scope of a property right conferred by the state; and the right to exemplary or punitive damages. Furthermore, state decisions construing local deeds, mineral conveyances, and even devises of real estate, were disregarded.

The injustice and confusion incident to the doctrine of Swift v. Tyson have been repeatedly urged as reasons for abolishing or limiting diversity of citizenship jurisdiction. Other legislative relief has been proposed. If only a question of statutory construction were involved, we should not be prepared to abandon a doctrine so widely applied throughout nearly a century. But the unconstitutionality of the course pursued has now been made clear, and compels us to do so.

Third. Except in matters governed by the Federal Constitution or by acts of Congress, the law to be applied in any case is the law of the state. And whether the law of the state shall be declared by its Legislature in a statute or by its highest court in a decision is not a matter of federal concern. There is no federal general common law. Congress has no power to declare substantive rules of common law applicable in a state whether they be local in their nature or 'general,' be they commercial law or a part of the law of torts. And no clause in the Constitution purports to confer such a power upon the federal courts.

The fallacy underlying the rule declared in Swift v. Tyson is made clear by Mr. Justice Holmes. The doctrine rests upon the assumption that there is 'a transcendental body of law outside of any particular State but obligatory within it unless and until changed by statute,' that federal courts have the power to use their judgment as to what the rules of common law are; and that in the federal courts 'the parties are entitled to an independent judgment on matters of general law'.

Reversed.

Mr. Justice Cardozo took no part in the consideration or decision of this case.

Mr. Justice Butler (dissenting).

No constitutional question was suggested or argued below or here. And as a general rule, this Court will not consider any question not raised below and presented by the petition. Here it does not decide either of the questions presented, but, changing the rule of decision in force since the foundation of the government, remands the case to be adjudged according to a standard never before deemed permissible.

The opinion just announced states that: 'The question for decision is whether the oft-challenged doctrine of Swift v. Tyson shall now be disapproved.'

The doctrine of that case has been followed by this Court in an unbroken line of decisions. So far as appears, it was not questioned until more than 50 years later, and then by a single judge.

And since that decision, the division of opinion in this Court has been of the same character as it was before. In 1910, Mr. Justice Holmes, speaking for himself and two other Justices, dissented from the holding that a court of the United States was bound to exercise its own independent judgment in the construction of a conveyance made before the state courts had rendered an authoritative decision as to its meaning and effect.

This Court has often emphasized its reluctance to consider constitutional questions and that legislation will not be held invalid as repugnant to the fundamental law if the case may be decided upon any other ground. In view of grave consequences liable to result from erroneous exertion of its power to set aside legislation, the Court should move cautiously, seek assistance of counsel, act only after ample deliberation, show that the question is before the Court, that its decision cannot be avoided by construction of the statute assailed or otherwise, indicate precisely the principle or provision of the Constitutional held to have been transgressed, and fully disclose the reasons and authorities found to warrant the conclusion of invalidity. These safeguards against the improvident use of the great power to invalidate legislation are so well-grounded and familiar that statement of reasons or citation of authority to support them is no longer necessary.

I am of opinion that the constitutional validity of the rule need not be considered, because under the law, as found by the courts of Pennsylvania and generally throughout the country, it is plain that the evidence required a finding that plaintiff was guilty of negligence that contributed to cause his injuries, and that the judgment below should be reversed upon that ground.

STONE AND VINSON COURTS

The Supreme Court under Chief Justices Harlan Fiske Stone (1941–1945) and Frederick Vinson (1946–1953) were both consolidational and transitional. By that, the Courts consolidated the constitutional jurisprudence that upheld or ratified the New Deal reforms under Franklin D. Roosevelt (FDR), but also paved the way for the emergence of the more sweeping changes that would eventually occur under Earl Warren and his Court (1953–1969). In the process, they were perceived as having overturned many precedents.[17]

The roots of the Stone and Vinson Courts reside in the 1936 re-election of FDR. During his first term as president, and especially in his first 100 days in office, Roosevelt and Congress passed a significant amount of legislation aimed at repairing and restructuring the economy. However, the Supreme

---

[17]   Jackson, Robert. 1944. *Decisional Law and Stare Decisis*, 30 A. B. A. J. 334.

Court struck down much of that legislation as unconstitutional, violating either the Commerce Clause or the Delegation Doctrine. No doubt angered or frustrated by the Court's action, on March 9, 1937, soon after his second term started, FDR gave a speech proposing enlargement of the number of Justices on the Supreme Court. He wanted to add one new Justice for each one currently more than age 70.[18]

Ostensibly the extra Justices were proposed to address the workload for the aging jurists, but the reality was that he was targeting his Court opponents. This Court Packing Plan, as discussed earlier, did not pass Congress but nonetheless the Justices got his point. On June 2, 1937, Willis Van Devanter retired and Roosevelt replaced him with Hugh Black. This began what the media called the famous "switch in time that saved nine," where the composition of the Court changed. Between 1937 and 1946, when Vinson became Chief Justice, the entire composition of the Supreme Court changed. Roosevelt was effectively able to pack the Court without enlarging it; he merely needed to outlast the Justices who retired or died.

With a change in Court personnel came a new approach to the law. In cases such as *U.S. v. Darby*,[19] the Court continued the direction of the later Hughes Court and begin to uphold the second wave of New Deal legislation, finding that there were no longer Commerce Clause or Delegation Doctrine problems. In effect, the Roosevelt Court helped usher in what could be called the *Carolene Products* era of jurisprudence. This reference to *United States v. Carolene Products Company*,[20] and especially its footnote number four, foretold a Court more supportive of economic regulation and protection of individual rights than before. Legal scholars such as John Hart Ely would argue that the full force of the logic or implications of footnote four would eventually be the inspiration for the Warren Court.[21]

Part of the New Deal or *Carolene Products* legal revolution came with revisiting constitutional precedents. As noted, these precedents addressed mostly economic or business regulation issues. But increasingly the Court began to confront issues of race and individual rights. The adoption of the Fourteenth Amendment and the Due Process Clause in 1870 eventually became the vehicles for the Court beginning the process of gradually incorporating various provisions of the Bill of Rights to the states. The question of which rights, if at all, to incorporate became an issue for the Stone and

---

[18] Leuchtenburg, William E. 1996. *The Supreme Court Reborn: The Constitutional Revolution in the Age of Roosevelt.* New York: Oxford University Press.
[19] 312 U.S. 100 (1941).
[20] 304 U.S. 144 (1938).
[21] Ely, John Hart. 1980. *Democracy and Distrust: A Theory of Judicial Review.* Cambridge, MA: Harvard University Press.

Vinson Courts. Additionally, partially because of legal action by the NAACP to challenge and reverse *Plessy v. Ferguson*,[22] the Court confronted racial discrimination in America. Look at *Smith v. Allwright* as a case where the Stone Court struggled with race, and *Angel v. Bullington*,[23] where the Vinson Court addressed the implications of the *Erie Railroad* decision. Both cases were in reaction to decisions by earlier courts, especially the Hughes Court.

Finally, with the onset of World War II, loyalty to the United States became an issue as states and the federal government adopted laws to encourage patriotism, such as mandatory Pledges of Allegiance in school. Here the Stone Court concludes in *West Virginia v. Barnette*[24] that the Hughes Court decision in *Minersville School District v. Gobitis*[25] simply got it wrong.

Overall, the Stone and Vinson Courts facilitated a transition in constitutional law. Between them they overturned 14 of their own constitutional precedents. This was more than the Hughes Court at 12, and these decisions set the context for the Warren Court. In looking at their decisions rejecting constitutional precedent, note how the emphasis seems to be on both how the previous Court got the decision wrong, and it needed to be corrected, or how confusion in the law created by the original decision necessitated the overruling of the precedent.

THE STONE COURT

U.S. v. Darby, 312 U.S. 100 (1941)

Mr. Justice Stone delivered the opinion of the Court.

> The two principal questions raised by the record in this case are, first, whether Congress has constitutional power to prohibit the shipment in interstate commerce of lumber manufactured by employees whose wages are less than a prescribed minimum or whose weekly hours of labor at that wage are greater than a prescribed maximum, and, second, whether it has power to prohibit the employment of workmen in the production of goods 'for interstate commerce' at other than prescribed wages and hours. A subsidiary question is whether in connection with such prohibitions Congress can require the employer subject to them to keep records showing the hours worked each day and week by each of his employees including those engaged 'in the production and manufacture of goods to wit, lumber, for "interstate commerce."'
>
> The power of Congress over interstate commerce 'is complete in itself, may be exercised to its utmost extent, and acknowledges no limitations, other than are

---

[22]   163 U.S. 537 (1896).
[23]   330 U.S. 183 (1947).
[24]   319 U.S. 624 (1943).
[25]   310 U.S. 586 (1940).

prescribed by the constitution.' Gibbons v. Ogden, supra, 9 Wheat. 196, 6 L.Ed. 23. That power can neither be enlarged nor diminished by the exercise or non-exercise of state power. Kentucky Whip & Collar Co. v. Illinois Central R. Co., supra. Congress, following its own conception of public policy concerning the restrictions which may appropriately be imposed on interstate commerce, is free to exclude from the commerce articles whose use in the states for which they are destined it may conceive to be injurious to the public health, morals or welfare, even though the state has not sought to regulate their use. Such regulation is not a forbidden invasion of state power merely because either its motive or its consequence is to restrict the use of articles of commerce within the states of destination and is not prohibited unless by other Constitutional provisions. It is no objection to the assertion of the power to regulate interstate commerce that its exercise is attended by the same incidents which attend the exercise of the police power of the states. The motive and purpose of the present regulation are plainly to make effective the Congressional conception of public policy that interstate commerce should not be made the instrument of competition in the distribution of goods produced under substandard labor conditions, which competition is injurious to the commerce and to the states from and to which the commerce flows. The motive and purpose of a regulation of interstate commerce are matters for the legislative judgment upon the exercise of which the Constitution places no restriction and over which the courts are given no control. McCray v. United States, 195 U.S. 27; Sonzinsky v. United States, 300 U.S. 506, 513, 57 S.Ct. 554, 555, 81 L.Ed. 772, and cases cited. 'The judicial cannot prescribe to the legislative departments of the government limitations upon the exercise of its acknowledged power.' Whatever their motive and purpose, regulations of commerce which do not infringe some constitutional prohibition are within the plenary power conferred on Congress by the Commerce Clause. Subject only to that limitation, presently to be considered, we conclude that the prohibition of the shipment interstate of goods produced under the forbidden substandard labor conditions is within the constitutional authority of Congress.

In the more than a century which has elapsed since the decision of Gibbons v. Ogden, these principles of constitutional interpretation have been so long and repeatedly recognized by this Court as applicable to the Commerce Clause, that there would be little occasion for repeating them now were it not for the decision of this Court twenty-two years ago in Hammer v. Dagenhart. In that case it was held by a bare majority of the Court over the powerful and now classic dissent of Mr. Justice Holmes setting forth the fundamental issues involved, that Congress was without power to exclude the products of child labor from interstate commerce. The reasoning and conclusion of the Court's opinion there cannot be reconciled with the conclusion which we have reached, that the power of Congress under the Commerce Clause is plenary to exclude any article from interstate commerce subject only to the specific prohibitions of the Constitution.

Hammer v. Dagenhart has not been followed. The distinction on which the decision was rested that Congressional power to prohibit interstate commerce is limited to articles which in themselves have some harmful or deleterious property—a distinction which was novel when made and unsupported by any provision of the Constitution—has long since been abandoned. The thesis of the opinion that the motive of the prohibition or its effect to control in some measure the use or production within the states of the article thus excluded from the commerce can operate to deprive the regulation of its constitutional authority has long since ceased to have force. And finally we have declared 'The authority of the Federal Government over

interstate commerce does not differ in extent or character from that retained by the states over intrastate commerce.'
The conclusion is inescapable that Hammer v. Dagenhart, was a departure from the principles which have prevailed in the interpretation of the commerce clause both before and since the decision and that such vitality, as a precedent, as it then had has long since been exhausted. It should be and now is overruled.

West Virginia State Board of Education v. Barnette, 319 U.S. 624 (1943)

Mr. Justice Jackson delivered the opinion of the Court.

Following the decision by this Court on June 3, 1940, in Minersville School District v. Gobitis, 310 U.S. 586, the West Virginia legislature amended its statutes to require all schools therein to conduct courses of instruction in history, civics, and in the Constitutions of the United States and of the State 'for the purpose of teaching, fostering and perpetuating the ideals, principles and spirit of Americanism, and increasing the knowledge of the organization and machinery of the government.' Appellant Board of Education was directed, with advice of the State Superintendent of Schools, to 'prescribe the courses of study covering these subjects' for public schools. The Act made it the duty of private, parochial and denominational schools to prescribe courses of study 'similar to those required for the public schools.'
The Board of Education on January 9, 1942, adopted a resolution containing recitals taken largely from the Court's Gobitis opinion and ordering that the salute to the flag become 'a regular part of the program of activities in the public schools,' that all teachers and pupils 'shall be required to participate in the salute honoring the Nation represented by the Flag; provided, however, that refusal to salute the Flag be regarded as an Act of insubordination, and shall be dealt with accordingly.'
The resolution originally required the 'commonly accepted salute to the Flag' which it defined. Objections to the salute as 'being too much like Hitler's' were raised by the Parent and Teachers Association, the Boy and Girl Scouts, the Red Cross, and the Federation of Women's Clubs. Some modification appears to have been made in deference to these objections, but no concession was made to Jehovah's Witnesses. What is now required is the 'stiff-arm' salute, the saluter to keep the right hand raised with palm turned up while the following is repeated: 'I pledge allegiance to the Flag of the United States of America and to the Republic for which it stands; one Nation, indivisible, with liberty and justice for all.'
Failure to conform is 'insubordination' dealt with by expulsion. Readmission is denied by statute until compliance. Meanwhile the expelled child is 'unlawfully absent' and may be proceeded against as a delinquent. His parents or guardians are liable to prosecution, and if convicted are subject to fine not exceeding $50 and jail term not exceeding thirty days.
The Gobitis decision, however, assumed, as did the argument in that case and in this, that power exists in the State to impose the flag salute discipline upon school children in general. The Court only examined and rejected a claim based on religious beliefs of immunity from an unquestioned general rule. The question which underlies the flag salute controversy is whether such a ceremony so touching matters of opinion and political attitude may be imposed upon the individual by official authority under powers committed to any political organization under our Constitution. We examine rather than assume existence of this power and, against

this broader definition of issues in this case, re-examine specific grounds assigned for the Gobitis decision.

It was said that the flag-salute controversy confronted the Court with 'the problem which Lincoln cast in memorable dilemma: "Must a government of necessity be too strong for the liberties of its people, or too weak to maintain its own existence?"' and that the answer must be in favor of strength.

Government of limited power need not be anemic government. Assurance that rights are secure tends to diminish fear and jealousy of strong government, and by making us feel safe to live under it makes for its better support. Without promise of a limiting Bill of Rights it is doubtful if our Constitution could have mustered enough strength to enable its ratification. To enforce those rights today is not to choose weak government over strong government. It is only to adhere as a means of strength to individual freedom of mind in preference to officially disciplined uniformity for which history indicates a disappointing and disastrous end.

The subject now before us exemplifies this principle. Free public education, if faithful to the ideal of secular instruction and political neutrality, will not be partisan or enemy of any class, creed, party, or faction. If it is to impose any ideological discipline, however, each party or denomination must seek to control, or failing that, to weaken the influence of the educational system. Observance of the limitations of the Constitution will not weaken government in the field appropriate for its exercise.

It was also considered in the Gobitis case that functions of educational officers in states, counties and school districts were such that to interfere with their authority 'would in effect make us the school board for the country.'

The Fourteenth Amendment, as now applied to the States, protects the citizen against the State itself and all of its creatures—Boards of Education not excepted. These have, of course, important, delicate, and highly discretionary functions, but none that they may not perform within the limits of the Bill of Rights. That they are educating the young for citizenship is reason for scrupulous protection of Constitutional freedoms of the individual, if we are not to strangle the free mind at its source and teach youth to discount important principles of our government as mere platitudes.

Such Boards are numerous and their territorial jurisdiction often small. But small and local authority may feel less sense of responsibility to the Constitution, and agencies of publicity may be less vigilant in calling it to account. The action of Congress in making flag observance voluntary and respecting the conscience of the objector in a matter so vital as raising the Army contrasts sharply with these local regulations in matters relatively trivial to the welfare of the nation. There are village tyrants as well as village Hampdens, but none who acts under color of law is beyond reach of the Constitution.

The Gobitis opinion reasoned that this is a field 'where courts possess no marked and certainly no controlling competence,' that it is committed to the legislatures as well as the courts to guard cherished liberties and that it is constitutionally appropriate to 'fight out the wise use of legislative authority in the forum of public opinion and before legislative assemblies rather than to transfer such a contest to the judicial arena,' since all the 'effective means of inducing political changes are left free.'

The very purpose of a Bill of Rights was to withdraw certain subjects from the vicissitudes of political controversy, to place them beyond the reach of majorities and officials and to establish them as legal principles to be applied by the courts. One's right to life, liberty, and property, to free speech, a free press, freedom of worship and assembly, and other fundamental rights may not be submitted to vote; they depend on the outcome of no elections.

In weighing arguments of the parties it is important to distinguish between the due process clause of the Fourteenth Amendment as an instrument for transmitting the principles of the First Amendment and those cases in which it is applied for its own sake. The test of legislation which collides with the Fourteenth Amendment, because it also collides with the principles of the First, is much more definite than the test when only the Fourteenth is involved. Much of the vagueness of the due process clause disappears when the specific prohibitions of the First become its standard. The right of a State to regulate, for example, a public utility may well include, so far as the due process test is concerned, power to impose all of the restrictions which a legislature may have a 'rational basis' for adopting. But freedoms of speech and of press, of assembly, and of worship may not be infringed on such slender grounds. They are susceptible of restriction only to prevent grave and immediate danger to interests which the state may lawfully protect. It is important to note that while it is the Fourteenth Amendment which bears directly upon the State it is the more specific limiting principles of the First Amendment that finally govern this case.

Nor does our duty to apply the Bill of Rights to assertions of official authority depend upon our possession of marked competence in the field where the invasion of rights occurs. True, the task of translating the majestic generalities of the Bill of Rights, conceived as part of the pattern of liberal government in the eighteenth century, into concrete restraints on officials dealing with the problems of the twentieth century, is one to disturb self-confidence. These principles grew in soil which also produced a philosophy that the individual was the center of society, that his liberty was attainable through mere absence of governmental restraints, and that government should be entrusted with few controls and only the mildest supervision over men's affairs. We must transplant these rights to a soil in which the laissez-faire concept or principle of non-interference has withered at least as to economic affairs, and social advancements are increasingly sought through closer integration of society and through expanded and strengthened governmental controls. These changed conditions often deprive precedents of reliability and cast us more than we would choose upon our own judgment. But we act in these matters not by authority of our competence but by force of our commissions. We cannot, because of modest estimates of our competence in such specialties as public education, withhold the judgment that history authenticates as the function of this Court when liberty is infringed.

Lastly, and this is the very heart of the Gobitis opinion, it reasons that 'National unity is the basis of national security,' that the authorities have 'the right to select appropriate means for its attainment,' and hence reaches the conclusion that such compulsory measures toward 'national unity' are constitutional. Upon the verity of this assumption depends our answer in this case.

National unity as an end which officials may foster by persuasion and example is not in question. The problem is whether under our Constitution compulsion as here employed is a permissible means for its achievement.

Struggles to coerce uniformity of sentiment in support of some end thought essential to their time and country have been waged by many good as well as by evil men. Nationalism is a relatively recent phenomenon but at other times and places the ends have been racial or territorial security, support of a dynasty or regime, and particular plans for saving souls. As first and moderate methods to attain unity have failed, those bent on its accomplishment must resort to an ever-increasing severity.

As governmental pressure toward unity becomes greater, so strife becomes more bitter as to whose unity it shall be. Probably no deeper division of our people could proceed from any provocation than from finding it necessary to choose what doctrine and whose program public educational officials shall compel youth to unite in embracing. Ultimate futility of such attempts to compel coherence is the lesson of every such effort from the Roman drive to stamp out Christianity as a disturber of its pagan unity, the Inquisition, as a means to religious and dynastic unity, the Siberian exiles as a means to Russian unity, down to the fast failing efforts of our present totalitarian enemies. Those who begin coercive elimination of dissent soon find themselves exterminating dissenters. Compulsory unification of opinion achieves only the unanimity of the graveyard.

The case is made difficult not because the principles of its decision are obscure but because the flag involved is our own. Nevertheless, we apply the limitations of the Constitution with no fear that freedom to be intellectually and spiritually diverse or even contrary will disintegrate the social organization. To believe that patriotism will not flourish if patriotic ceremonies are voluntary and spontaneous instead of a compulsory routine is to make an unflattering estimate of the appeal of our institutions to free minds. We can have intellectual individualism and the rich cultural diversities that we owe to exceptional minds only at the price of occasional eccentricity and abnormal attitudes.

If there is any fixed star in our constitutional constellation, it is that no official, high or petty, can prescribe what shall be orthodox in politics, nationalism, religion, or other matters of opinion or force citizens to confess by word or act their faith therein. If there are any circumstances which permit an exception, they do not now occur to us.

The decision of this Court in Minersville School District v. Gobitis and the holdings of those few per curiam decisions which preceded and foreshadowed it are overruled, and the judgment enjoining enforcement of the West Virginia Regulation is affirmed.

Affirmed.

Mr. Justice Frankfurter, dissenting.

The admonition that judicial self-restraint alone limits arbitrary exercise of our authority is relevant every time we are asked to nullify legislation. The Constitution does not give us greater veto power when dealing with one phase of 'liberty' than with another, or when dealing with grade school regulations than with college regulations that offend conscience, as was the case in Hamilton v. Regents, 293 U.S. 245. In neither situation is our function comparable to that of a legislature or are we free to act as though we were a superlegislature. Judicial self-restraint is equally necessary whenever an exercise of political or legislative power is challenged. There is no warrant in the constitutional basis of this Court's authority for attributing different roles to it depending upon the nature of the challenge to the legislation. Our power does not vary according to the particular provision of the Bill of Rights which is invoked. The right not to have property taken without just compensation has, so far as the scope of judicial power is concerned, the same constitutional dignity as the right to be protected against unreasonable searches and seizures, and the latter has no less claim than freedom of the press or freedom of speech or religious freedom. In no instance is this Court the primary protector of the particular liberty that is invoked. This Court has recognized, what hardly could be denied, that all the provisions of the first ten Amendments are 'specific' prohibitions, United States v. Carolene Products Co., 304 U.S. 144, 152, 58 S.Ct. 778, 783, 82 L.Ed. 1234, note 4. But each specific Amendment, in so far as embraced within the Fourteenth Amendment, must be equally respected, and the function of this Court does not differ in passing on the constitutionality of legislation challenged under different Amendments.

When Mr. Justice Holmes, speaking for this Court, wrote that 'it must be remembered that legislatures are ultimate guardians of the liberties and welfare of the people in quite as great a degree as the courts', Missouri, Kansas & Texas R. Co. v. May, 194 U.S. 267, 270, 24 S.Ct. 638, 639, 48 L.Ed. 971, he went to the very essence of our constitutional system and the democratic conception of our society. He did not mean that for only some phases of civil government this Court was not to supplant legislatures and sit in judgment upon the right or wrong of a challenged measure. He was stating the comprehensive judicial duty and role of this Court in our constitutional scheme whenever legislation is sought to be nullified on any ground, namely, that responsibility for legislation lies with legislatures, answerable as they are directly to the people, and this Court's only and very narrow function is to determine whether within the broad grant of authority vested in legislatures they have exercised a judgment for which reasonable justification can be offered.

Under our constitutional system the legislature is charged solely with civil concerns of society. If the avowed or intrinsic legislative purpose is either to promote or to discourage some religious community or creed, it is clearly within the constitutional restrictions imposed on legislatures and cannot stand. But it by no means follows that legislative power is wanting whenever a general non-discriminatory civil regulation in fact touches conscientious scruples or religious beliefs of an individual or a group. Regard for such scruples or beliefs undoubtedly presents one of the most reasonable claims for the exertion of legislative accommodation. It is, of course, beyond our power to rewrite the state's requirement, by providing exemptions for those who do not wish to participate in the flag salute or by making some other accommodations to meet their scruples. That wisdom might suggest the making of such accommodations and that school administration would not find it too difficult to make them and yet maintain the ceremony for those not refusing to conform, is outside our province to suggest. Tact, respect, and generosity toward variant views will always commend themselves to those charged with the duties of legislation so as to achieve a maximum of good will and to require a minimum of unwilling submission to a general law. But the real question is, who is to make such accommodations, the courts or the legislature?

If the function of this Court is to be essentially no different from that of a legislature, if the considerations governing constitutional construction are to be substantially those that underlie legislation, then indeed judges should not have life tenure and they should be made directly responsible to the electorate. There have been many but unsuccessful proposals in the last sixty years to amend the Constitution to that end.

Smith v. Allwright, 321 U.S. 649 (1944)

Mr. Justice Reed delivered the opinion of the Court.

This writ of certiorari brings here for review a claim for damages in the sum of $5,000 on the part of petitioner, a Negro citizen of the 48th precinct of Harris County, Texas, for the refusal of respondents, election and associate election judges respectively of that precinct, to give petitioner a ballot or to permit him to cast a ballot in the primary election of July 27, 1940, for the nomination of Democratic candidates for the United States Senate and House of Representatives, and Governor and other state officers. The refusal is alleged to have been solely because of the race and color of the proposed voter.

The actions of respondents are said to violate Sections 31 and 759 43 of Title 8 of the United States Code, 8 U.S.C.A. ss 31 and 43, in that petitioner was deprived of rights secured by Sections 2 and 4 of Article I and the Fourteenth, Fifteenth and Seventeenth Amendments to the United States Constitution. The suit was filed in the District Court of the United States for the Southern District of Texas, which had jurisdiction under Judicial Code Section 24, subsection 14, 28 U.S.C.A. s 41 (14).

The District Court denied the relief sought and the Circuit Court of Appeals quite properly affirmed its action on the authority of Grovey v. Townsend, 295 U.S. 45. We granted the petition for certiorari to resolve a claimed inconsistency between the decision in the Grovey case and that of United States v. Classic, 313 U.S. 299.

The State of Texas by its Constitution and statutes provides that every person, if certain other requirements are met which are not here in issue, qualified by residence in the district or county 'shall be deemed a qualified elector.' Constitution of Texas, Article VI, Section 2 Vernon's Ann.St.; Vernon's Civil Statutes (1939 ed.), Article 2955. Primary elections for United States Senators, Congressmen and state officers are provided for by Chapters Twelve and Thirteen of the statutes. Under these chapters, the Democratic Party was required to hold the primary which was the occasion of the alleged wrong to petitioner. A summary of the state statutes regulating primaries appears in the footnote. These nominations are to be made by the qualified voters of the party.

The Democratic Party of Texas is held by the Supreme Court of that state to be a 'voluntary association,' Bell v. Hill, 123 Tex. 531, 534, 74 S.W.2d 113, protected by Section 27 of the Bill of Rights, Art. 1, Constitution of Texas, from interference by the state except that:

'In the interest of fair methods and a fair expression by their members of their preferences in the selection of their nominees, the State may regulate such elections by proper laws.'

The Democratic party on May 24, 1932, in a State Convention adopted the following resolution, which has not since been 'amended, abrogated, annulled or avoided':
'Be it resolved that all white citizens of the State of Texas who are qualified to vote under the Constitution and laws of the State shall be eligible to membership in the Democratic party and, as such, entitled to participate in its deliberations.' It was by virtue of this resolution that the respondents refused to permit the petitioner to vote.

Texas is free to conduct her elections and limit her electorate as she may deem wise, save only as her action may be affected by the prohibitions of the United States Constitution or in conflict with powers delegated to and exercised by the National Government. The Fourteenth Amendment forbids a state from making or enforcing any law which abridges the privileges or immunities of citizens of the United States and the Fifteenth Amendment specifically interdicts any denial or abridgement by a state of the right of citizens to vote on account of color. Respondents appeared in the District Court and the Circuit Court of Appeals and defended on the ground that the Democratic party of Texas is a voluntary organization with members banded together for the purpose of selecting individuals of the group representing the common political beliefs as candidates in the general election. As such a voluntary organization, it was claimed, the Democratic party is free to select its own membership and limit to whites participation in the party primary. Such action, the answer asserted, does not violate the Fourteenth, Fifteenth or Seventeenth Amendment as officers of government cannot be chosen at primaries and the Amendments are applicable only to general elections where governmental officers are actually elected. Primaries, it is said, are political party affairs, handled by party not governmental officers. No appearance for respondents is made in this Court. Arguments presented here by the Attorney General of Texas and the Chairman of the State Democratic Executive Committee of Texas, as amici curiae, urged substantially the same grounds as those advanced by the respondents.

The right of a Negro to vote in the Texas primary has been considered heretofore by this Court. The first case was Nixon v. Herndon, 273 U.S. 536, 47 S.Ct. 446, 71 L.Ed. 759. At that time, 1924, the Texas statute, Art. 3093a, Acts 1923, 2d Called Sess., c. 32, afterwards numbered Art. 3107, Rev.Stat.1925, declared 'in no event shall a Negro be eligible to participate in a Democratic party primary election * * * in the State of Texas.' Nixon was refused the right to vote in a Democratic primary and brought a suit for damages against the election officers under R.S. s 1979 and 2004, the present sections 43 and 31 of Title 8, U.S.C., 8 U.S.C.A. ss 43 and 31, respectively. It was urged to this Court that the denial of the franchise to Nixon violated his Constitutional rights under the Fourteenth and Fifteenth Amendments. Without consideration of the Fifteenth, this Court held that the action of Texas in denying the ballot to Negroes by statute was in violation of the equal protection clause of the Fourteenth Amendment and reversed the dismissal of the suit.

The legislature of Texas reenacted the article but gave the State Executive Committee of a party the power to prescribe the qualifications of its members for voting or other participation. This article remains in the statutes. The State Executive Committee of the Democratic party adopted a resolution that white Democrats and none other might participate in the primaries of that party. Nixon was refused again the privilege of voting in a primary and again brought suit for damages by virtue of Section 31, Title 8 U.S.C., 18 U.S.C.A. s 31. This Court again reversed the dismissal of the suit for the reason that the Committee action was deemed to be State action and invalid as discriminatory under the Fourteenth Amendment. The test was said to be whether the Committee operated as representative of the State in the discharge of the State's authority. Nixon v. Condon, 286 U.S. 73, 52 S.Ct. 484, 76 L.Ed. 984, 88 A.L.R. 458. The question of the inherent power of a political party in Texas 'without restraint by any law to determine its own membership' was left open. Id., 286 U.S. 83, 84, 85, 52 S.Ct. 485.

In Grovey v. Townsend, this Court had before it another suit for damages for the refusal in a primary of a county clerk, a Texas officer with only public functions to perform, to furnish petitioner, a Negro, an absentee ballot. The refusal was solely on the ground of race. This case differed from Nixon v. Condon, supra, in that a state convention of the Democratic party had passed the resolution of May 24, 1932, hereinbefore quoted. It was decided that the determination by the state convention

of the membership of the Democratic party made a significant change from a determination by the Executive Committee. The former was party action, voluntary in
character. The latter, as had been held in the Condon case, was action by authority
of the State. The managers of the primary election were therefore declared not to be
state officials in such sense that their action was state action. A state convention of
a party was said not to be an organ of the state. This Court went on to announce that
to deny a vote in a primary was a mere refusal of party membership with which 'the
state need have no concern,' while for a state to deny a vote in a general election
on the ground of race or color violated the Constitution. Consequently, there was
found no ground for holding that the county clerk's refusal of a ballot because of
racial ineligibility for party membership denied the petitioner any right under the
Fourteenth or Fifteenth Amendments.

Since Grovey v. Townsend and prior to the present suit, no case from Texas involving primary elections has been before this Court. We did decide, however, United
States v. Classic, 313 U.S. 299, 61 S.Ct. 1031, 85 L.Ed. 1368. We there held that
Section 4 of Article I of the Constitution authorized Congress to regulate primary as
well as general elections, 'where the primary is by law made an integral part of the
election machinery.' Consequently, in the Classic case, we upheld the applicability
to frauds in a Louisiana primary of ss 19 and 20 of the Criminal Code, 18 U.S.C.A.
ss 51, 52 Thereby corrupt acts of election officers were subjected to Congressional
sanctions because that body had power to protect rights of Federal suffrage secured
by the Constitution in primary as in general elections. This decision depended, too,
on the determination that under the Louisiana statutes the primary was a part of the
procedure for choice of Federal officials. By this decision the doubt as to whether
or not such primaries were a part of 'elections' subject to Federal control, which
had remained unanswered since Newberry v. United States was erased. The Nixon
cases were decided under the equal protection clause of the Fourteenth Amendment
without a determination of the status of the primary as a part of the electoral process.
The exclusion of Negroes from the primaries by action of the State was held invalid
under that Amendment. The fusing by the Classic case of the primary and general
elections into a single instrumentality for choice of officers has a definite bearing
on the permissibility under the Constitution of excluding Negroes from primaries.
This is not to say that the Classic case cuts directly into the rationale of Grovey v.
Townsend. This latter case was not mentioned in the opinion. Classic bears upon
Grovey v. Townsend not because exclusion of Negroes from primaries is any more
or less state action by reason of the unitary character of the electoral process but
because the recognition of the place of the primary in the electoral scheme makes
clear that state delegation to a party of the power to fix the qualifications of primary
elections is delegation of a state function that may make the party's action the action
of the state. When Grovey v. Townsend was written, the Court looked upon the
denial of a vote in a primary as a mere refusal by a party of party membership. As
the Louisiana statutes for holding primaries are similar to those of Texas, our ruling
in Classic as to the unitary character of the electoral process calls for a reexamina-
tion as to whether or not the exclusion of Negroes from a Texas party primary was
state action.

The statutes of Texas relating to primaries and the resolution of the Democratic
party of Texas extending the privileges of membership to white citizens only are
the same in substance and effect today as they were when Grovey v. Townsend was
decided by a unanimous Court. The question as to whether the exclusionary action
of the party was the action of the State persists as the determinative factor. In again

entering upon consideration of the inference to be drawn as to state action from a substantially similar factual situation, it should be noted that Grovey v. Townsend upheld exclusion of Negroes from primaries through the denial of party membership by a party convention. A few years before this Court refused approval of exclusion by the State Executive Committee of the party. A different result was reached on the theory that the Committee action was state authorized and the Convention action was unfettered by statutory control. Such a variation in the result from so slight a change in form influences us to consider anew the legal validity of the distinction which has resulted in barring Negroes from participating in the nominations of candidates of the Democratic party in Texas. Other precedents of this Court forbid the abridgement of the right to vote.

It may now be taken as a postulate that the right to vote in such a primary for the nomination of candidates without discrimination by the State, like the right to vote in a general election, is a right secured by the Constitution. United States v. Classic, 313 U.S. at page 314, 61 S.Ct. at page 1037, 85 L.Ed. 1368; Myers v. Anderson, 238 U.S. 368, 35 S.Ct. 932, 59 L.Ed. 1349; Ex parte Yarbrough, 110 U.S. 651, 663 et seq., 4 S.Ct. 152, 158, 28 L.Ed. 274. By the terms of the Fifteenth Amendment that right may not be abridged by any state on account of race. Under our Constitution the great privilege of the ballot may not be denied a man by the State because of his color.

Primary elections are conducted by the party under state statutory authority. The county executive committee selects precinct election officials and the county, district or state executive committees, respectively, canvass the returns. These party committees or the state convention certify the party's candidates to the appropriate officers for inclusion on the official ballot for the general election. No name which has not been so certified may appear upon the ballot for the general election as a candidate of a political party. No other name may be printed on the ballot which has not been placed in nomination by qualified voters who must take an oath that they did not participate in a primary for the selection of a candidate for the office for which the nomination is made.

The privilege of membership in a party may be, as this Court said in Grovey v. Townsend, no concern of a state. But when, as here, that privilege is also the essential qualification for voting in a primary to select nominees for a general election, the state makes the action of the party the action of the state. In reaching this conclusion we are not unmindful of the desirability of continuity of decision in constitutional questions. However, when convinced of former error, this Court has never felt constrained to follow precedent. In constitutional questions, where correction depends upon amendment and not upon legislative action this Court throughout its history has freely exercised its power to reexamine the basis of its constitutional decisions. This has long been accepted practice, and this practice has continued to this day. This is particularly true when the decision believed erroneous is the application of a constitutional principle rather than an interpretation of the Constitution to extract the principle itself. Here we are applying, contrary to the recent decision in Grovey v. Townsend, the well established principle of the Fifteenth Amendment, forbidding the abridgement by a state of a citizen's right to vote. Grovey v. Townsend is overruled.

THE VINSON COURT

Angel v. Bullington, 330 U.S. 183 (1947)

Justice Frankfurter delivered the opinion of the Court.

In 1940, Bullington, a citizen of Virginia, sold land in Virginia to Angel, a citizen of North Carolina. Only part of the purchase price was paid. For the balance, Angel executed a series of notes secured by a deed of trust on the land. Upon default on one of the notes, Bullington, acting upon an acceleration clause in the deed, caused all other notes to become due and called upon the trustees to sell the land. The sale was duly made in Virginia and the proceeds of the sale applied to the payment of the notes. This controversy concerns attempts to collect the deficiency.

Bullington began suit for the deficiency in the Superior Court of Macon County, North Carolina. Angel countered with a demurrer, the substance of which was that a statute of North Carolina (c. 36, Public Laws 1933, Mitchie's Code s 2593(f)) precluded recovery of such a deficiency judgment.

The Superior Court overruled the demurrer, and an appeal to the Supreme Court of North Carolina followed. Bullington supported his Superior Court judgment on the ground that the United States Constitution precluded North Carolina from shutting the doors of its courts to him. The North Carolina Supreme Court, holding that the North Carolina Act of 1933 barred Bullington's suit against Angel, reversed the Superior Court and dismissed the action. 220 N.C. 18, 16 S.E.2d 411, 136 A.L.R. 1054. Bullington did not seek to review this judgment here. Instead, he sued Angel for the deficiency in the United States District Court for the Western District of North Carolina. Angel pleaded in bar the judgment in the North Carolina action. The District Court gave judgment for Bullington and the Circuit Court of Appeals for the Fourth Circuit affirmed. We granted certiorari because the failure to dismiss this action, on the ground that the judgment in the North Carolina court precluded the right thereafter to recover on the same cause of action in the federal court, presented an important question in the administration of justice.

We start with the fact that the prevailing rule as to res judicata is settled law in North Carolina. An adjudication bars future litigation between the same parties not only as to all issues actually raised and decided but also as to those which could have been raised. ... If the North Carolina action had been dismissed because it was brought in one North Carolina court rather than in another, of course no federal issue would have been involved. Had that been the case, a suit for the same cause of action could have been initiated in a North Carolina federal district court, just as another suit could have been brought in the proper North Carolina State court. But that is not the present situation. A quite different situation is before us. Being somewhat unusual, it calls for a critical consideration of the scope and purpose of the doctrine of res judicata.

The judgment of the Supreme Court of North Carolina would clearly bar this suit had it been brought anew in a state court. For purposes of diversity jurisdiction a federal court is 'in effect, only another court of the State.' That the adjudication of federal questions by the North Carolina Supreme Court may have been erroneous is immaterial for purposes of res judicata. A higher court was available for an authoritative adjudication of the federal questions involved. And so the question is whether federal rights were necessarily involved and adjudicated in the litigation in the State courts.

Here, claims based on the United States Constitution were plainly and reasonably made in the North Carolina suit. The North Carolina Supreme Court met these claims. It met them by saying that the North Carolina statute did not deal with substantive matters but merely with matters regulating local procedure. But whether the claims are based on a federal right or are merely of local concern is itself a federal question on which this Court, and not the Supreme Court of North Carolina, has the last say.

The merits of this controversy were adjudicated by the North Carolina Supreme Court since that court, or this Court on appeal, might have decided that the North Carolina statute did not bar Bullington's first action. The North Carolina statute might have been found unconstitutional. Federal issues were thus involved in the adjudication by the North Carolina Supreme Court. Bullington knew that there were federal issues in the State suit because he raised them...

The essence of diversity jurisdiction is that a federal court enforces State law and State policy. If North Carolina has authoritatively announced that deficiency judgments cannot be secured within its borders, it contradicts the presuppositions of diversity jurisdiction for a federal court in that State to give such a deficiency judgment. North Carolina would hardly allow defeat of a State-wide policy through occasional suits in a federal court. What is more important, diversity jurisdiction must follow State law and policy. A federal court in North Carolina, when invoked on grounds of diversity of citizenship, cannot give that which North Carolina has withheld. Availability of diversity jurisdiction which was put into the Constitution so as to prevent discrimination against outsiders is not to effect discrimination against the great body of local citizens.

Cases like David Lupton's Sons v. Automobile Club of America, 225 U.S. 489, are obsolete insofar as they are based on a view of diversity jurisdiction which came to an end with Erie Railroad Co. v. Tompkins, 304 U.S. 64, 58. That decision drastically limited the power of federal district courts to entertain suits in diversity cases that could not be brought in the respective State courts or were barred by defenses controlling in the State courts.

Judgment reversed.

2.   The Warren Court

INTRODUCTION

If the Stone and Vinson Courts represented the consolidation of the New Deal constitutional reforms, the Court under Chief Justice Earl Warren (1953–1969) was the full blossoming and articulation of the trends that had been building under these Chief Justices. Under Earl Warren the Court reversed 32 constitutional precedents, compared with 36 reversals in the entire history of the Supreme Court until Warren became Chief Justice. Up to 2020, the Warren Court has reversed more constitutional precedents than any other Court, and while the percentage of reversal is still quite small, it is greater than any other Court so far.

Across a variety of areas, the Court's past precedents clashed with a new world that the Warren Court faced. The three most notable areas of law that the Warren Court changed came in terms of race, criminal due process, and voting rights. Arguably among the most famous Supreme Court cases in history is *Brown v. Board of Education*,[1] which reversed the "separate but equal" doctrine of *Plessy v. Ferguson*.[2] In issuing the *Brown* opinion the Court helped pave the wave for the civil rights movement of the 1960s and beyond, and it was also the basis of many other court cases that challenged segregation and discrimination in America.

Baker v. Carr[3] reversed *Colgrove v. Green*.[4] The latter had declared that matters of malapportionment were political questions beyond the scope of judicial review. *Baker* declared that the courts could address issues regarding redistricting and not ask plaintiffs perhaps futilely to go speak to the very legislatures who malapportioned to cure the problem they created to solve the problem. *Baker* pushed the federal courts center into trying to open the channels of the political process (to paraphrase part of *Caroline Products* footnote number four) that had been closed to discrete and insular minorities. Nearly 60 years after *Baker*, the courts remain a major player in the redistricting process.

---

[1]   347 U.S. 483 (1954).
[2]   163 U.S. 537 (1896).
[3]   369 U.S. 186 (1962).
[4]   328 U.S. 549 (1946).

Gideon v. Wainwright[5] reversed *Betts v. Brady*,[6] ruling that even in non-capital murder cases, individuals had a Sixth Amendment right to counsel. *Gideon* along with a host of other criminal justice cases redid the legal landscape when it came to the rights of those accused of crimes. In many cases the Court also reversed constitutional precedents and incorporated Bill of Rights protections to the states.

One accusation of the Warren Court is that it acted not on legal principle but politics or upon other considerations.[7] Consider the *Brown* decision. What was the basis for the Court reversing *Plessy*? Was it that the latter was wrongly decided? The Court seems to suggest that. It also seems to suggest that decisions after *Plessy* had problems in it, and no doubt the NAACP, which adopted a legal strategy to overturn it, exploited and created those problems.[8] But look at footnote 11 and the introduction of psychological evidence on the impact of segregation on black children. How does this evidence factor in?

In *Baker*, how much did the Court consider practical alternative when it came to claims regarding voting rights and redistricting? If the Court did not intervene, what would happen? What were the institutional alternatives to remedy a perceived wrong? In *Gideon*, did it argue that *Betts v. Brady* was simply wrong or unworkable or that there were practical considerations in applying it? Ask the same question about *Mapp v. Ohio*[9] and the reasons for its reversal of *Wolf v. Colorado*.[10] The Warren Court seems to consider practical application of past precedents and how workable they are as major factors when considering to overturn them. Is there anything wrong with that from the perspective of a theory of precedent?

Brown v. Board of Education of Topeka, 347 U.S. 483 (1954)

Mr. Chief Justice Warren delivered the opinion of the Court.

> These cases come to us from the States of Kansas, South Carolina, Virginia, and Delaware. They are premised on different facts and different local conditions, but

---

[5]   372 U.S. 335 (1963).
[6]   316 U.S. 455 (1942).
[7]   Bickel, Alexander. 1962. *The Least Dangerous Branch*. Indianapolis: Bobbs-Merrill.
[8]   Kluger, Richard. 2004. *Simple Justice: The History of Brown v. Board of Education and Black America's Struggle for Equality*. New York: Vintage.
[9]   367 U.S. 643 (1961).
[10] 338 U.S. 25 (1949).

a common legal question justifies their consideration together in this consolidated opinion.

In each of the cases, minors of the Negro race, through their legal representatives, seek the aid of the courts in obtaining admission to the public schools of their community on a nonsegregated basis. In each instance, they have been denied admission to schools attended by white children under laws requiring or permitting segregation according to race. This segregation was alleged to deprive the plaintiffs of the equal protection of the laws under the Fourteenth Amendment. In each of the cases other than the Delaware case, a three-judge federal district court denied relief to the plaintiffs on the so-called 'separate but equal' doctrine announced by this Court in Plessy v. Ferguson, 163 U.S. 537, 16 S.Ct. 1138, 41 L.Ed. 256. Under that doctrine, equality of treatment is accorded when the races are provided substantially equal facilities, even though these facilities be separate. In the Delaware case, the Supreme Court of Delaware adhered to that doctrine, but ordered that the plaintiffs be admitted to the white schools because of their superiority to the Negro schools.

The plaintiffs contend that segregated public schools are not 'equal' and cannot be made 'equal,' and that hence they are deprived of the equal protection of the laws. Because of the obvious importance of the question presented, the Court took jurisdiction.

The doctrine of 'separate but equal' did not make its appearance in this court until 1896 in the case of Plessy v. Ferguson, involving not education but transportation. American courts have since labored with the doctrine for over half a century. In this Court, there have been six cases involving the 'separate but equal' doctrine in the field of public education. In Cumming v. Board of Education of Richmond County, 175 U.S. 528, 20 S.Ct. 197, 44 L.Ed. 262, and Gong Lum v. Rice, 275 U.S. 78, 48 S.Ct. 91, 72 L.Ed. 172, the validity of the doctrine itself was not challenged. In more recent cases, all on the graduate school level, inequality was found in that specific benefits enjoyed by white students were denied to Negro students of the same educational qualifications. State of Missouri ex rel. Gaines v. Canada, 305 U.S. 337, 59 S.Ct. 232, 83 L.Ed. 208; Sipuel v. Board of Regents of University of Oklahoma, 332 U.S. 631, 68 S.Ct. 299, 92 L.Ed. 247; Sweatt v. Painter, 339 U.S. 629, 70 s.Ct. 848, 94 L.Ed. 1114; McLaurin v. Oklahoma State Regents, 339 U.S. 637, 70 S.Ct. 851, 94 L.Ed. 1149. In none of these cases was it necessary to re-examine the doctrine to grant relief to the Negro plaintiff. And in Sweatt v. Painter, supra, the Court expressly reserved decision on the question whether Plessy v. Ferguson should be held inapplicable to public education.

In the instant cases, that question is directly presented. Here, unlike Sweatt v. Painter, there are findings below that the Negro and white schools involved have been equalized, or are being equalized, with respect to buildings, curricula, qualifications and salaries of teachers, and other 'tangible' factors. Our decision, therefore, cannot turn on merely a comparison of these tangible factors in the Negro and white schools involved in each of the cases. We must look instead to the effect of segregation itself on public education.

In approaching this problem, we cannot turn the clock back to 1868 when the Amendment was adopted, or even to 1896 when Plessy v. Ferguson was written. We must consider public education in the light of its full development and its present place in American life throughout the Nation. Only in this way can it be determined if segregation in public schools deprives these plaintiffs of the equal protection of the laws.

Today, education is perhaps the most important function of state and local governments. Compulsory school attendance laws and the great expenditures for education both demonstrate our recognition of the importance of education to our democratic society. It is required in the performance of our most basic public responsibilities, even service in the armed forces. It is the very foundation of good citizenship. Today it is a principal instrument in awakening the child to cultural values, in preparing him for later professional training, and in helping him to adjust normally to his environment. In these days, it is doubtful that any child may reasonably be expected to succeed in life if he is denied the opportunity of an education. Such an opportunity, where the state has undertaken to provide it, is a right which must be made available to all on equal terms.

We come then to the question presented: Does segregation of children in public schools solely on the basis of race, even though the physical facilities and other 'tangible' factors may be equal, deprive the children of the minority group of equal educational opportunities? We believe that it does.

In Sweatt v. Painter, in finding that a segregated law school for Negroes could not provide them equal educational opportunities, this Court relied in large part on 'those qualities which are incapable of objective measurement but which make for greatness in a law school.' In McLaurin v. Oklahoma State Regents, supra (339 U.S. 637, 70 S.Ct. 853), the Court, in requiring that a Negro admitted to a white graduate school be treated like all other students, again resorted to intangible considerations: '* * * his ability to study, to engage in discussions and exchange views with other students, and, in general, to learn his profession.' Such considerations apply with added force to children in grade and high schools. To separate them from others of similar age and qualifications solely because of their race generates a feeling of inferiority as to their status in the community that may affect their hearts and minds in a way unlikely ever to be undone. The effect of this separation on their educational opportunities was well stated by a finding in the Kansas case by a court which nevertheless felt compelled to rule against the Negro plaintiffs:

> 'Segregation of white and colored children in public schools has a detrimental effect upon the colored children. The impact is greater when it has the sanction of the law; for the policy of separating the races is usually interpreted as denoting the inferiority of the negro group. A sense of inferiority affects the motivation of a child to learn. Segregation with the sanction of law, therefore, has a tendency to (retard) the educational and mental development of Negro children and to deprive them of some of the benefits they would receive in a racial(ly) integrated school system.'

Whatever may have been the extent of psychological knowledge at the time of Plessy v. Ferguson, this finding is amply supported by modern authority.[11] Any language in Plessy v. Ferguson contrary to this finding is rejected.

We conclude that in the field of public education the doctrine of 'separate but equal' has no place. Separate educational facilities are inherently unequal. Therefore, we hold that the plaintiffs and others similarly situated for whom the actions have been brought are, by reason of the segregation complained of, deprived of the equal protection of the laws guaranteed by the Fourteenth Amendment. This disposition makes unnecessary any discussion whether such segregation also violates the Due Process Clause of the Fourteenth Amendment.

It is so ordered.

11. K. B. Clark, Effect of Prejudice and Discrimination on Personality Development (Midcentury White House Conference on Children and Youth, 1950); Witmer and Kotinsky, Personality in the Making (1952), c. VI; Deutscher and Chein, The Psychological Effects of Enforced Segregation: A Survey of Social Science Opinion, 26 J.Psychol. 259 (1948); Chein, What are the Psychological Effects of Segregation Under Conditions of Equal Facilities?, 3 Int. J. Opinion and Attitude Res. 229 (1949); Brameld, Educational Costs, in Discrimination and National Welfare (MacIver, ed., 1949), 44–48; Frazier, The Negro in the United States (1949), 674–681. And see generally Myrdal, An American Dilemma (1944).

Barenblatt v. United States, 360 U.S. 109 (1959)

Mr. Justice Harlan delivered the opinion of the Court.

The case is before us for the second time. We again granted certiorari, to consider petitioner's statutory and constitutional challenges to his conviction, and particularly his claim that the judgment below cannot stand under our decision in the Watkins case.

Pursuant to a subpoena, and accompanied by counsel, petitioner on June 28, 1954, appeared as a witness before this congressional Subcommittee. After answering a few preliminary questions and testifying that he had been a graduate student and teaching fellow at the University of Michigan from 1947 to 1950 and an instructor in psychology at Vassar College from 1950 to shortly before his appearance before the Subcommittee, petitioner objected generally to the right of the Subcommittee to inquire into his 'political' and 'religious' beliefs or any 'other personal and private affairs' or 'associational activities,' upon grounds set forth in a previously prepared memorandum which he was allowed to file with the Subcommittee. Thereafter petitioner specifically declined to answer each of the following five questions:

'Are you now a member of the Communist Party? (Count One.)

'Have you ever been a member of the Communist Party? (Count Two.)

'Now, you have stated that you knew Francis Crowley. Did you know Francis Crowley as a member of the Communist Party? (Count Three.)

'Were you ever a member of the Haldane Club of the Communist Party while at the University of Michigan? (Count Four.)

'Were you a member while a student of the University of Michigan Council of Arts, Sciences, and Professions?' (Count Five.)

In each instance the grounds for refusal were those set forth in the prepared statement. Petitioner expressly disclaimed reliance upon 'the Fifth Amendment.'

Following receipt of the Subcommittee's report of these occurrences the House duly certified the matter to the District of Columbia United States Attorney for contempt proceedings. An indictment in five Counts, each embracing one of petitioner's several refusals to answer, ensued. With the consent of both sides the case was tried to the court without a jury, and upon conviction under all Counts a general sentence of six months' imprisonment and a fine of $250 was imposed.

Since this sentence was less than the maximum punishment authorized by the statute for conviction under any one Count, the judgment below must be upheld if the conviction upon any of the Counts is sustainable. As we conceive the ultimate issue in this case to be whether petitioner could properly be convicted of contempt for refusing to answer questions relating to his participation in or knowledge of alleged Communist Party activities at educational institutions in this country, we find it unnecessary to consider the validity of his conviction under the Third and Fifth Counts, the only ones involving questions which on their face do not directly relate to such participation or knowledge.

Petitioner's various contentions resolve themselves into three propositions: First, the compelling of testimony by the Subcommittee was neither legislatively authorized nor constitutionally permissible because of the vagueness of Rule XI of the House of Representatives, Eighty-third Congress, the charter of authority of the parent Committee. Second, petitioner was not adequately apprised of the pertinency of the Subcommittee's questions to the subject matter of the inquiry. Third, the questions petitioner refused to answer infringed rights protected by the First Amendment.

Subcommittee's Authority to Compel Testimony.

At the outset it should be noted that Rule XI authorized this Subcommittee to compel testimony within the framework of the investigative authority conferred on the Un-American Activities Committee. Petitioner contends that Watkins v. United States, supra, nevertheless held the grant of this power in all circumstances ineffective because of the vagueness of Rule XI in delineating the Committee jurisdiction to which its exercise was to be appurtenant. This view of Watkins was accepted by two of the dissenting judges below.

The Watkins case cannot properly be read as standing for such a proposition. A principal contention in Watkins was that the refusals to answer were justified because the requirement of 2 U.S.C. s 192, 2 U.S.C.A. s 192 that the questions asked be 'pertinent to the question under inquiry' had not been satisfied.

In short, while Watkins was critical of Rule XI, it did not involve the broad and inflexible holding petitioner now attributes to it.

Petitioner also contends, independently of Watkins, that the vagueness of Rule XI deprived the Subcommittee of the right to compel testimony in this investigation into Communist activity. We cannot agree with this contention which in its furthest reach would mean that the House Un-American Activities Committee under its existing authority has no right to compel testimony in any circumstances. Granting the vagueness of the Rule, we may not read it in isolation from its long history in the House of Representatives.

The essence of that history can be briefly stated. The Un-American Activities Committee, originally known as the Dies Committee, was first established by the House in 1938. The Committee was principally a consequence of concern over the activities of the German-American Bund, whose members were suspected of allegiance to Hitler Germany, and of the Communist Party, supposed by many to be under the domination of the Soviet Union. From the beginning, without interruption to the present time, and with the undoubted knowledge and approval of the House, the Committee has devoted a major part of its energies to the investigation of Communist activities. More particularly, in 1947 the Committee announced a wide-range program in this field, pursuant to which during the years 1948 to 1952 it conducted diverse inquiries into such alleged Communist activities as espionage; efforts to learn atom bomb secrets; infiltration into labor, farmer, veteran, professional, youth, and motion picture groups; and in addition held a number of hearings upon various legislative proposals to curb Communist activities.

In light of this long and illuminating history it can hardly be seriously argued that the investigation of Communist activities generally, and the attendant use of compulsory process, was beyond the purview of the Committee's intended authority under Rule XI.

Pertinency Claim.

Undeniably a conviction for contempt under 2 U.S.C. s 192, 2 U.S.C.A. s 192 cannot stand unless the questions asked are pertinent to the subject matter of the investigation. Watkins v. United States, supra, 354 U.S. at pages 214–215, 77 S.Ct. at pages 1193–1194. But the factors which led us to rest decision on this ground in Watkins were very different from those involved here.

In Watkins the petitioner had made specific objection to the Subcommittee's questions on the ground of pertinency; the question under inquiry had not been disclosed in any illuminating manner; and the questions asked the petitioner were not only amorphous on their face, but in some instances clearly foreign to the alleged subject matter of the investigation—'Communism in labor.' In contrast, petitioner in the case before us raised no objections on the ground of pertinency at the time any of the questions were put to him. It is true that the memorandum which petitioner brought with him to the Subcommittee hearing contained the statement, 'to ask me whether I am or have been a member of the Communist Party may have dire consequences. I might wish to * * * challenge the pertinency of the question to the investigation,' and at another point quoted from this Court's opinion in Jones v. Securities & Exchange Comm., 298 U.S. 1, 56 S.Ct. 654, 80 L.Ed. 1015, language relating to a witness' right to be informed of the pertinency of questions asked him by an administrative agency. These statements cannot, however, be accepted as the equivalent of a pertinency objection. At best they constituted but a contemplated objection to questions still unasked, and buried as they were in the context of petitioner's general challenge to the power of the Subcommittee they can hardly be considered adequate, within the meaning of what was said in Watkins, supra, 354 U.S. at pages 214–215, 77 S.Ct. at pages 1193–1194, to trigger what would have been the Subcommittee's reciprocal obligation had it been faced with a pertinency objection. Petitioner's contentions on this aspect of the case cannot be sustained.

Constitutional Contentions.

The precise constitutional issue confronting us is whether the Subcommittee's inquiry into petitioner's past or present membership in the Communist Party transgressed the provisions of the First Amendment, which of course reach and limit congressional investigations.

The Court's past cases establish sure guides to decision. Undeniably, the First Amendment in some circumstances protects an individual from being compelled to disclose his associational relationships. However, the protections of the First Amendment, unlike a proper claim of the privilege against self-incrimination under the Fifth Amendment, do not afford a witness the right to resist inquiry in all circumstances. Where First Amendment rights are asserted to bar governmental interrogation resolution of the issue always involves a balancing by the courts of the competing private and public interests at stake in the particular circumstances shown. These principles were recognized in the Watkins case, where, in speaking of the First Amendment in relation to congressional inquiries, we said 'It is manifest that despite the adverse effects which follow upon compelled disclosure of private matters, not all such inquiries are barred. * * * The critical element is the existence of, and the weight to be ascribed to, the interest of the Congress in demanding disclosures from an unwilling witness.'

The first question is whether this investigation was related to a valid legislative purpose, for Congress may not constitutionally require an individual to disclose his political relationships or other private affairs except in relation to such a purpose.

That Congress has wide power to legislate in the field of Communist activity in this Country, and to conduct appropriate investigations in aid thereof, is hardly debatable. The existence of such power has never been questioned by this Court, and it is sufficient to say, without particularization, that Congress has enacted or considered in this field a wide range of legislative measures, not a few of which have stemmed from recommendations of the very Committee whose actions have been drawn in question here.

On these premises, this Court in its constitutional adjudications has consistently refused to view the Communist Party as an ordinary political party, and has upheld federal legislation aimed at the Communist problem which in a different context would certainly have raised constitutional issues of the gravest character. On the same premises this Court has upheld under the Fourteenth Amendment state legislation requiring those occupying or seeking public office to disclaim knowing membership in any organization advocating overthrow of the Government by force and violence, which legislation none can avoid seeing was aimed at membership in the Communist Party. Similarly, in other areas, this Court has recognized the close nexus between the Communist Party and violent overthrow of government. To suggest that because the Communist Party may also sponsor peaceable political reforms the constitutional issues before us should now be judged as if that Party were just an ordinary political party from the standpoint of national security, is to ask this Court to blind itself to world affairs which have determined the whole course of our national policy since the close of World War II, affairs to which Judge Learned Hand gave vivid expression in his opinion in United States v. Dennis, 2 Cir., 183 F.2d 201, 213, and to the vast burdens which these conditions have entailed for the entire Nation.

Nor can we accept the further contention that this investigation should not be deemed to have been in furtherance of a legislative purpose because the true objective of the Committee and of the Congress was purely 'exposure.' So long as Congress acts in pursuance of its constitutional power, the Judiciary lacks authority to intervene on the basis of the motives which spurred the exercise of that power

Finally, the record is barren of other factors which in themselves might sometimes lead to the conclusion that the individual interests at stake were not subordinate to those of the state. There is no indication in this record that the Subcommittee was attempting to pillory witnesses. Nor did petitioner's appearance as a witness follow from indiscriminate dragnet procedures, lacking in probable cause for belief that he possessed information which might be helpful to the Subcommittee. And the relevancy of the questions put to him by the Subcommittee is not open to doubt. We conclude that the balance between the individual and the governmental interests here at stake must be struck in favor of the latter, and that therefore the provisions of the First Amendment have not been offended.

We hold that petitioner's conviction for contempt of Congress discloses no infirmity, and that the judgment of the Court of Appeals must be affirmed. Affirmed.

Mapp v. Ohio, 367 U.S. 643 (1961)

Mr. Justice Clark delivered the opinion of the Court.

Appellant stands convicted of knowingly having had in her possession and under her control certain lewd and lascivious books, pictures, and photographs in violation of s 2905.34 of Ohio's Revised Code.[1] As officially stated in the syllabus to its opinion, the Supreme Court of Ohio found that her conviction was valid though 'based primarily upon the introduction in evidence of lewd and lascivious books and pictures unlawfully seized during an unlawful search of defendant's home * * *.'

On May 23, 1957, three Cleveland police officers arrived at appellant's residence in that city pursuant to information that 'a person (was) hiding out in the home, who was wanted for questioning in connection with a recent bombing, and that there was a large amount of policy paraphernalia being hidden in the home.' Miss Mapp and her daughter by a former marriage lived on the top floor of the two-family dwelling. Upon their arrival at that house, the officers knocked on the door and demanded entrance but appellant, after telephoning her attorney, refused to admit them without a search warrant. They advised their headquarters of the situation and undertook a surveillance of the house.

The officers again sought entrance some three hours later when four or more additional officers arrived on the scene. When Miss Mapp did not come to the door immediately, at least one of the several doors to the house was forcibly opened[2] and the policemen gained admittance. Meanwhile Miss Mapp's attorney arrived, but the officers, having secured their own entry, and continuing in their defiance of the law, would permit him neither to see Miss Mapp nor to enter the house. It appears that Miss Mapp was halfway down the stairs from the upper floor to the front door when the officers, in this highhanded manner, broke into the hall. She demanded to see the search warrant. A paper, claimed to be a warrant, was held up by one of the officers. She grabbed the 'warrant' and placed it in her bosom. A struggle ensued in which the officers recovered the piece of paper and as a result of which they handcuffed appellant because she had been 'belligerent' in resisting their official rescue of the 'warrant' from her person. Running roughshod over appellant, a policeman 'grabbed' her, 'twisted (her) hand,' and she 'yelled (and) pleaded with him' because 'it was hurting.' Appellant, in handcuffs, was then forcibly taken upstairs to her bedroom where the officers searched a dresser, a chest of drawers, a closet and some suitcases. They also looked into a photo album and through personal papers belonging to the appellant. The search spread to the rest of the second floor including the child's bedroom, the living room, the kitchen and a dinette. The basement of the building and a trunk found therein were also searched. The obscene materials for possession of which she was ultimately convicted were discovered in the course of that widespread search.

At the trial no search warrant was produced by the prosecution, nor was the failure to produce one explained or accounted for. At best, 'There is, in the record, considerable doubt as to whether there ever was any warrant for the search of defendant's home.'

The State says that even if the search were made without authority, or otherwise unreasonably, it is not prevented from using the unconstitutionally seized evidence at trial, citing Wolf v. People of State of Colorado, 1949, 338 U.S. 25, at page 33, 69 S.Ct. 1359. at page 1364, 93 L.Ed. 1782, in which this Court did indeed hold 'that in a prosecution in a State court for a State crime the Fourteenth Amendment does not forbid the admission of evidence obtained by an unreasonable search and seizure.' On this appeal, of which we have noted probable jurisdiction, it is urged once again that we review that holding.

I.

Seventy-five years ago, in Boyd v. United States, 1886, 116 U.S. 616, 630, 6 S.Ct. 524, 532, 29 L.Ed. 746, considering the Fourth and Fifth Amendments as running 'almost into each other'[5] on the facts before it, this Court held that the doctrines of those Amendments 'apply to all invasions on the part of the government and its employees of the sanctity of a man's home and the privacies of life. It is not the breaking of his doors, and the rummaging of his drawers, that constitutes the essence of the offence; but it is the invasion of his indefeasible right of personal security, personal liberty and private property * * *. Breaking into a house and opening boxes and drawers are circumstances of aggravation; but any forcible and compulsory extortion of a man's own testimony or of his private papers to be used as evidence to convict him of crime or to forfeit his goods, is within the condemnation * * * (of those Amendments).' The Court noted that 'constitutional provisions for the security of person and property should be liberally construed. * * * It is the duty of courts to be watchful for the constitutional rights of the citizen, and against any stealthy encroachments thereon.'

Less than 30 years after Boyd, this Court, in Weeks v. United States, 1914, 232 U.S. 383, at pages 391–392, 34 S.Ct. 341, at page 344, 58 L.Ed. 652, stated that

'the 4th Amendment * * * put the courts of the United States and Federal officials, in the exercise of their power and authority, under limitations and restraints (and) * * * forever secure(d) the people, their persons, houses, papers, and effects, against all unreasonable searches and seizures under the guise of law * * * and the duty of giving to it force and effect is obligatory upon all entrusted under our Federal system with the enforcement of the laws.'

Specifically dealing with the use of the evidence unconstitutionally seized, the Court concluded: 'If letters and private documents can thus be seized and held and used in evidence against a citizen accused of an offense, the protection of the Fourth Amendment declaring his right to be secure against such searches and seizures is of no value, and, so far as those thus placed are concerned, might as well be stricken from the Constitution. The efforts of the courts and their officials to bring the guilty to punishment, praiseworthy as they are, are not to be aided by the sacrifice of those

great principles established by years of endeavor and suffering which have resulted in their embodiment in the fundamental law of the land.'
Finally, the Court in that case clearly stated that use of the seized evidence involved 'a denial of the constitutional rights of the accused.' Thus, in the year 1914, in the Weeks case, this Court 'for the first time' held that 'in a federal prosecution the Fourth Amendment barred the use of evidence secured through an illegal search and seizure.' This Court has ever since required of federal law officers a strict adherence to that command which this Court has held to be a clear, specific, and constitutionally required—even if judicially implied—deterrent safeguard without insistence upon which the Fourth Amendment would have been reduced to 'a form of words.' Holmes J., Silverthorne Lumber Co. v. United States, 1920, 251 U.S. 385, 392, 40 S.Ct. 182, 183, 64 L.Ed. 319. It meant, quite simply, that 'conviction by means of unlawful seizures and enforced confessions * * * should find no sanction in the judgments of the courts * * *,' Weeks v. United States, supra, 232 U.S. at page 392, 34 S.Ct. at page 344, and that such evidence 'shall not be used at all.' There are in the cases of this Court some passing references to the Weeks rule as being one of evidence. But the plain and unequivocal language of Weeks—and its later paraphrase in Wolf—to the effect that the Weeks rule is of constitutional origin, remains entirely undisturbed. In Byars v. United States, 1927, 273 U.S. 28, at pages 29–30, 47 S.Ct. 248, at pages 248–249, 71 L.Ed. 520, a unanimous Court declared that 'the doctrine (cannot) * * * be tolerated under our constitutional system, that evidences of crime discovered by a federal officer in making a search without lawful warrant may be used against the victim of the unlawful search where a timely challenge has been interposed.' (Emphasis added.) The Court, in Olmstead v. United States, 1928, 277 U.S. 438, at page 462, 48 S.Ct. 564, 567, 72 L.Ed. 944, in unmistakable language restated the Weeks rule:
'The striking outcome of the Weeks case and those which followed it was the sweeping declaration that the Fourth Amendment, although not referring to or limiting the use of evidence in court, really forbade its introduction if obtained by government officers through a violation of the amendment.'
In McNabb v. United States, 1943, 318 U.S. 332, at pages 339–340, 63 S.Ct. 608, at page 612, 87 L.Ed. 819, we note this statement: '(A) conviction in the federal courts, the foundation of which is evidence obtained in disregard of liberties deemed fundamental by the Constitution, cannot stand. Boyd v. United States * * * Weeks v. United States * * *. And this Court has, on Constitutional grounds, set aside convictions, both in the federal and state courts, which were based upon confessions "secured by protracted and repeated questioning of ignorant and untutored persons, in whose minds the power of officers was greatly magnified" * * * or "who have been unlawfully held incommunicado without advice of friends or counsel" * * *.'

II.

In 1949, 35 years after Weeks was announced, this Court, in Wolf v. People of State of Colorado, supra, again for the first time,[6] discussed the effect of the Fourth

Amendment upon the States through the operation of the Due Process Clause of the Fourteenth Amendment. It said:

'(W)e have no hesitation in saying that were a State affirmatively to sanction such police incursion into privacy it would run counter to the guaranty of the Fourteenth Amendment.'

Nevertheless, after declaring that the 'security of one's privacy against arbitrary intrusion by the police' is 'implicit in "the concept of ordered liberty" and as such enforceable against the States through the Due Process Clause,' cf. Palko v. State of Connecticut, 1937, 302 U.S. 319, 58 S.Ct. 149, 82 L.Ed. 288, and announcing that it 'stoutly adhere(d)' to the Weeks decision, the Court decided that the Weeks exclusionary rule would not then be imposed upon the States as 'an essential ingredient of the right.' 338 U.S. at pages 27–29, 69 S.Ct. at page 1362. The Court's reasons for not considering essential to the right to privacy, as a curb imposed upon the States by the Due Process Clause, that which decades before had been posited as part and parcel of the Fourth Amendment's limitations upon federal encroachment of individual privacy, were bottomed on factual considerations.

While they are not basically relevant to a decision that the exclusionary rule is an essential ingredient of the Fourth Amendment as the right it embodies is vouchsafed against the States by the Due Process Clause, we will consider the current validity of the factual grounds upon which Wolf was based.

The Court in Wolf first stated that '(t)he contrariety of views of the States' on the adoption of the exclusionary rule of Weeks was 'particularly impressive' and, in this connection that it could not 'brush aside the experience of States which deem the incidence of such conduct by the police too slight to call for a deterrent remedy * * * by overriding the (States') relevant rules of evidence.' While in 1949, prior to the Wolf case, almost two-thirds of the States were opposed to the use of the exclusionary rule, now, despite the Wolf case, more than half of those since passing upon it, by their own legislative or judicial decision, have wholly or partly adopted or adhered to the Weeks rule. Significantly, among those now following the rule is California, which, according to its highest court, was 'compelled to reach that conclusion because other remedies have completely failed to secure compliance with the constitutional provisions * * *.' People v. Cahan, 1955, 44 Cal.2d 434, 445, 282 P.2d 905, 911, 50 A.L.R.2d 513. In connection with this California case, we note that the second basis elaborated in Wolf in support of its failure to enforce the exclusionary doctrine against the States was that 'other means of protection' have been afforded 'the right to privacy.'[7] 338 U.S. at page 30, 69 S.Ct. at page 1362. The experience of California that such other remedies have been worthless and futile is buttressed by the experience of other States. The obvious futility of relegating the Fourth Amendment of the protection of other remedies has, moreover, been recognized by this Court since Wolf. See Irvine v. People of State of California, 1954, 347 U.S. 128, 137, 74 S.Ct. 381, 385, 98 L.Ed. 561.

Likewise, time has set its face against what Wolf called the 'weighty testimony' of People v. Defore, 1926, 242 N.Y. 13, 150 N.E. 585. There Justice (then Judge) Cardozo, rejecting adoption of the Weeks exclusionary rule in New York, had said that '(t)he Federal rule as it stands is either too strict or too lax.' However, the force of that reasoning has been largely vitiated by later decisions of this Court. These include the recent discarding of the 'silver platter' doctrine which allowed federal judicial use of evidence seized in violation of the Constitution by state agents, Elkins v. United States, supra; the relaxation of the formerly strict requirements as to standing to challenge the use of evidence thus seized, so that now the procedure of exclusion, 'ultimately referable to constitutional safeguards,' is available to anyone even 'legitimately on (the) premises' unlawfully searched, Jones v. United States, 1960, 362 U.S. 257, 266–267, 80 S.Ct. 725, 734, 4 L.Ed.2d 697; and finally, the formulation of a method to prevent state use of evidence unconstitutionally seized by federal agents, Rea v. United States, 1956, 350 U.S. 214, 76 S.Ct. 292, 100 L.Ed. 233. Because there can be no fixed formula, we are admittedly met with 'recurring questions of the reasonableness of searches,' but less is not to be expected when dealing with a Constitution, and, at any rate, '(r)easonableness is in the first instance for the (trial court) to determine.'

It, therefore, plainly appears that the factual considerations supporting the failure of the Wolf Court to include the Weeks exclusionary rule when it recognized the enforceability of the right to privacy against the States in 1949, while not basically relevant to the constitutional consideration, could not, in any analysis, now be deemed controlling.

III.

Some five years after Wolf, in answer to a plea made here Term after Term that we overturn its doctrine on applicability of the Weeks exclusionary rule, this Court indicated that such should not be done until the States had 'adequate opportunity to adopt or reject the (Weeks) rule.' There again it was said: 'Never until June of 1949 did this Court hold the basic search-and-seizure prohibition in any way applicable to the states under the Fourteenth Amendment.'

And only last Term, after again carefully re-examining the Wolf doctrine in Elkins v. United States, supra, the Court pointed out that 'the controlling principles' as to search and seizure and the problem of admissibility 'seemed clear' (364 U.S. at page 212, 1441 of 80 S.Ct.) until the announcement in Wolf 'that the Due Process Clause of the Fourteenth Amendment does not itself require state courts to adopt the exclusionary rule' of the Weeks case. At page 213 of 364 U.S., at page 1442 of 80 S.Ct. At the same time, the Court pointed out, 'the underlying constitutional doctrine which Wolf established * * * that the Federal Constitution * * * prohibits unreasonable searches and seizures by state officers' had undermined the 'foundation upon which the admissibility of stateseized evidence in a federal trial originally rested * * *.' Ibid. The Court concluded that it was therefore obliged to hold, although it chose the narrower ground on which to do so, that all evidence obtained by an unconstitutional search and seizure was inadmissible in a federal court regardless of its source. Today we once again examine Wolf's constitutional documentation of the right to privacy free from unreasonable state intrusion, and, after its dozen years on our books, are led by it to close the only courtroom door remaining open to evidence secured by official lawlessness in flagrant abuse of that basic right, reserved to all persons as a specific guarantee against that very same unlawful conduct. We hold that all evidence obtained by searches and seizures in violation of the Constitution is, by that same authority, inadmissible in a state court.

IV.

Since the Fourth Amendment's right of privacy has been declared enforceable against the States through the Due Process Clause of the Fourteenth, it is enforceable against them by the same sanction of exclusion as is used against the Federal

Government. Were it otherwise, then just as without the Weeks rule the assurance against unreasonable federal searches and seizures would be 'a form of words', valueless and undeserving of mention in a perpetual charter of inestimable human liberties, so too, without that rule the freedom from state invasions of privacy would be so ephemeral and so neatly severed from its conceptual nexus with the freedom from all brutish means of coercing evidence as not to merit this Court's high regard as a freedom 'implicit in "the concept of ordered liberty."' At the time that the Court held in Wolf that the Amendment was applicable to the States through the Due Process Clause, the cases of this Court, as we have seen, had steadfastly held that as to federal officers the Fourth Amendment included the exclusion of the evidence seized in violation of its provisions. Even Wolf 'stoutly adhered' to that proposition. The right to privacy, when conceded operatively enforceable against the States, was not susceptible of destruction by avulsion of the sanction upon which its protection and enjoyment had always been deemed dependent under the Boyd, Weeks and Silverthorne cases. Therefore, in extending the substantive protections of due process to all constitutionally unreasonable searches—state or federal—it was logically and constitutionally necessary that the exclusion doctrine—an essential part of the right to privacy—be also insisted upon as an essential ingredient of the right newly recognized by the Wolf case. In short, the admission of the new constitutional right by Wolf could not consistently tolerate denial of its most important constitutional privilege, namely, the exclusion of the evidence which an accused had been forced to give by reason of the unlawful seizure. To hold otherwise is to grant the right but in reality to withhold its privilege and enjoyment. Only last year the Court itself recognized that the purpose of the exclusionary rule 'is to deter—to compel respect for the constitutional guaranty in the only effectively available way—by removing the incentive to disregard it.'

Indeed, we are aware of no restraint, similar to that rejected today, conditioning the enforcement of any other basic constitutional right. The right to privacy, no less important than any other right carefully and particularly reserved to the people, would stand in marked contrast to all other rights declared as 'basic to a free society.' This Court has not hesitated to enforce as strictly against the States as it does against the Federal Government the rights of free speech and of a free press, the rights to notice and to a fair, public trial, including, as it does, the right not to be convicted by use of a coerced confession, however logically relevant it be, and without regard to its reliability. And nothing could be more certain than that when a coerced confession is involved, 'the relevant rules of evidence' are overridden without regard to 'the incidence of such conduct by the police,' slight or frequent. Why should not the same rule apply to what is tantamount to coerced testimony by way of unconstitutional seizure of goods, papers, effect, documents, etc.? We find that, as to the Federal Government, the Fourth and Fifth Amendments and, as to the States, the freedom from unconscionable invasions of privacy and the freedom from convictions based upon coerced confessions do enjoy an 'intimate relation'[8] in their perpetuation of 'principles of humanity and civil liberty (secured) * * * only after years of struggle.' Bram v. United States, 1897, 168 U.S. 532, 543–544, 18 S.Ct. 183, 187, 42 L.Ed. 568. They express 'supplementing phases of the same constitutional purpose—to maintain inviolate large areas of personal privacy.' Feldman v. United States, 1944, 322 U.S. 487, 489–490, 64 S.Ct. 1082, 1083, 88 L.Ed. 1408. The philosophy of each Amendment and of each freedom is complementary to, although not dependent upon, that of the other in its sphere of influence—the very least that together they assure in either sphere is that no man is to be convicted on unconstitutional evidence. Cf. Rochin v. People of State of California, 1952, 342 U.S. 165, 173, 72 S.Ct. 205, 210, 96 L.Ed. 183.

V.

Moreover, our holding that the exclusionary rule is an essential part of both the Fourth and Fourteenth Amendments is not only the logical dictate of prior cases, but it also makes very good sense. There is no war between the Constitution and common sense. Presently, a federal prosecutor may make no use of evidence illegally seized, but a State's attorney across the street may, although he supposedly is operating under the enforceable prohibitions of the same Amendment. Thus the State, by admitting evidence unlawfully seized, serves to encourage disobedience to the Federal Constitution which it is bound to uphold.

Baker v. Carr, 369 U.S. 186 (1962)

Mr. Justice Brennan delivered the opinion of the Court.

This civil action was brought under 42 U.S.C. ss 1983 and 1988, 42 U.S.C.A. ss 1983, 1988 to redress the alleged deprivation of federal constitutional rights. The complaint, alleging that by means of a 1901 statute of Tennessee apportioning the members of the General Assembly among the State's 95 counties, 'these plaintiffs and others similarly situated, are denied the equal protection of the laws accorded them by the Fourteenth Amendment to the Constitution of the United States by virtue of the debasement of their votes,' was dismissed by a three-judge court convened under 28 U.S.C. s 2281, 28 U.S.C.A. s 2281 in the Middle District of Tennessee. The court held that it lacked jurisdiction of the subject matter and also that no claim was stated upon which relief could be granted. 179 F.Supp. 824. We noted probable jurisdiction of the appeal. 364 U.S. 898, 81 S.Ct. 230, 5 L.Ed.2d 193. We hold that the dismissal was error, and remand the cause to the District Court for trial and further proceedings consistent with this opinion.

The General Assembly of Tennessee consists of the Senate with 33 members and the House of Representatives with 99 members. The Tennessee Constitution provides in Art. II as follows: 'Sec. 3. Legislative authority—Term of office.—The Legislative authority of this State shall be vested in a General Assembly, which shall consist of a Senate and House of Representatives, both dependent on the people; who shall hold their offices for two years from the day of the general election.

Thus, Tennessee's standard for allocating legislative representation among her counties is the total number of qualified voters resident in the respective counties, subject only to minor qualifications. Decennial reapportionment in compliance with the constitutional scheme was effected by the General Assembly each decade from 1871 to 1901. The 1871 apportionment was preceded by an 1870 statute requiring an enumeration. The 1881 apportionment involved three statutes, the first authorizing an enumeration, the second enlarging the Senate from 25 to 33 members and the House from 75 to 99 members, and the third apportioning the membership of both Houses. In 1891 there were both an enumeration and an apportionment. In 1901 the General Assembly abandoned separate enumeration in favor of reliance upon the Federal Census and passed the Apportionment Act here in controversy. In the more than 60 years since that action, all proposals in both Houses of the General Assembly for reapportionment have failed to pass.

Between 1901 and 1961, Tennessee has experienced substantial growth and redistribution of her population. In 1901 the population was 2,020,616, of whom 487,380 were eligible to vote. The 1960 Federal Census reports the State's population at 3,567,089, of whom 2,092,891 are eligible to vote. The relative standings of the counties in terms of qualified voters have changed significantly. It is primarily the continued application of the 1901 Apportionment Act to this shifted and enlarged voting population which gives rise to the present controversy.

Indeed, the complaint alleges that the 1901 statute, even as of the time of its passage, 'made no apportionment of Representatives and Senators in accordance with the constitutional formula * * *, but instead arbitrarily and capriciously apportioned representatives in the Senate and House without reference * * * to any logical or reasonable formula whatever.' It is further alleged that 'because of the population changes since 1900, and the failure of the Legislature to reapportion itself since 1901,' the 1901 statute became 'unconstitutional and obsolete.' Appellants also argue that, because of the composition of the legislature effected by the 1901 Apportionment Act, redress in the form of a state constitutional amendment to change the entire mechanism for reapportioning, or any other change short of that, is difficult or impossible. The complaint concludes that 'these plaintiffs and others similarly situated, are denied the equal protection of the laws accorded them by the Fourteenth Amendment to the Constitution of the United States by virtue of the debasement of their votes.' They seek a declaration that the 1901 statute is unconstitutional and an injunction restraining the appellees from acting to conduct any further elections under it.

I.
The District Court's Opinion and Order of Dismissal.

Because we deal with this case on appeal from an order of dismissal granted on appellees' motions, precise identification of the issues presently confronting us demands clear exposition of the grounds upon which the District Court rested in dismissing the case. The dismissal order recited that the court sustained the appellees' grounds '(1) that the Court lacks jurisdiction of the subject matter, and (2) that the complaint fails to state a claim upon which relief can be granted * * *.'

In the setting of a case such as this, the recited grounds embrace two possible reasons for dismissal:

First: That the facts and injury alleged, the legal bases invoked as creating the rights and duties relied upon, and the relief sought, fail to come within that language of Article III of the Constitution and of the jurisdictional statutes which define those matters concerning which United States District Courts are empowered to act;

Second: That, although the matter is cognizable and facts are alleged which establish infringement of appellants' rights as a result of state legislative action departing from a federal constitutional standard, the court will not proceed because the matter is considered unsuited to judicial inquiry or adjustment.

We treat the first ground of dismissal as 'lack of jurisdiction of the subject matter.' The second we consider to result in a failure to state a justiciable cause of action.

The District Court's dismissal order recited that it was issued in conformity with the court's per curiam opinion. The opinion reveals that the court rested its dismissal upon lack of subject-matter jurisdiction and lack of a justiciable cause of action without attempting to distinguish between these grounds.

II.
Jurisdiction of the Subject Matter.

The District Court was uncertain whether our cases withholding federal judicial relief rested upon a lack of federal jurisdiction or upon the inappropriateness of the subject matter for judicial consideration—what we have designated 'nonjusticiability.' The distinction between the two grounds is significant. In the instance of nonjusticiability, consideration of the cause is not wholly and immediately foreclosed; rather, the Court's inquiry necessarily proceeds to the point of deciding whether the duty asserted can be judicially identified and its breach judicially determined, and whether protection for the right asserted can be judicially molded. In the instance of lack of jurisdiction the cause either does not 'arise under' the Federal Constitution, laws or treaties (or fall within one of the other enumerated categories of Art. III, s 2), or is not a 'case or controversy' within the meaning of that section; or the cause is not one described by any jurisdictional statute. Our conclusion, that this cause presents no nonjusticiable 'political question' settles the only possible doubt that it is a case or controversy. Under the present heading of 'Jurisdiction of the Subject Matter' we hold only that the matter set forth in the complaint does arise under the Constitution and is within 28 U.S.C. s 1343, 28 U.S.C.A. s 1343.

Article III, s 2, of the Federal Constitution provides that 'The judicial Power shall extend to all Cases, in Law and Equity, arising under this Constitution, the Laws of the United States, and Treaties made, or which shall be made, under their Authority * * *.' It is clear that the cause of action is one which 'arises under' the Federal Constitution. The complaint alleges that the 1901 statute effects an apportionment that deprives the appellants of the equal protection of the laws in violation of the Fourteenth Amendment. Dismissal of the complaint upon the ground of lack of jurisdiction of the subject matter would, therefore, be justified only if that claim were 'so attenuated and unsubstantial as to be absolutely devoid of merit.'

Since the complaint plainly sets forth a case arising under the Constitution, the subject matter is within the federal judicial power defined in Art. III, s 2, and so within the power of Congress to assign to the jurisdiction of the District Courts. Congress has exercised that power in 28 U.S.C. s 1343(3), 28 U.S.C.A. s 1343(3): 'The district courts shall have original jurisdiction of any civil action authorized by law to be commenced by any person * * * (t)o redress the deprivation, under color of any State law, statute, ordinance, regulation, custom or usage, of any right, privilege or immunity secured by the Constitution of the United States.'

An unbroken line of our precedents sustains the federal courts' jurisdiction of the subject matter of federal constitutional claims of this nature. The first cases involved the redistricting of States for the purpose of electing Representatives to the Federal Congress. When the Ohio Supreme Court sustained Ohio legislation against an attack for repugnancy to Art. I, s 4, of the Federal Constitution, we affirmed on the merits and expressly refused to dismiss for want of jurisdiction: 'In view * * * of the subject-matter of the controversy and the Federal characteristics which inhere in it * * *.' Ohio ex rel. Davis v. Hildebrant, 241 U.S. 565, 570, 36 S.Ct. 708, 710, 60 L.Ed. 1172. When the Minnesota Supreme Court affirmed the dismissal of a suit to enjoin the Secretary of State of Minnesota from acting under Minnesota redistricting legislation, we reviewed the constitutional merits of the legislation and reversed the State Supreme Court. Smiley v. Holm, 285 U.S. 355, 52 S.Ct. 397, 76 L.Ed. 795. And see companion cases from the New York Court of Appeals and the Missouri Supreme Court, Koenig v. Flynn, 285 U.S. 375, 52 S.Ct. 403, 76 L.Ed. 805; Carroll v. Becker, 285 U.S. 380, 52 S.Ct. 402, 76 L.Ed. 807. When a three-judge District Court exercising jurisdiction under the predecessor of 28 U.S.C. s 1343(3), 28 U.S.C.A. s 1343(3), permanently enjoined officers of the State of Mississippi from conducting an election of Representatives under a Mississippi redistricting act, we reviewed the federal questions on the merits and reversed the District Court. A similar decree of a District Court, exercising jurisdiction under the same statute, concerning a Kentucky redistricting act, was reviewed and the decree reversed.

The appellees refer to Colegrove v. Green, as authority that the District Court lacked jurisdiction of the subject matter. Appellees misconceive the holding of that case. The holding was precisely contrary to their reading of it. Seven members of the Court participated in the decision. Unlike many other cases in this field which have assumed without discussion that there was jurisdiction, all three opinions filed in Colegrove discussed the question. Two of the opinions expressing the views of four of the Justices, a majority, flatly held that there was jurisdiction of that subject matter. Mr. Justice Black joined by Mr. Justice Douglas and Mr. Justice Murphy stated: 'It is my judgment that the District Court had jurisdiction * * *,' citing the predecessor of 28 U.S.C. s 1343(3), 28 U.S.C.A. s 1343(3), and Bell v. Hood. Mr. Justice Rutledge, writing separately, expressed agreement with this conclusion. Indeed, it is even questionable that the opinion of Mr. Justice Frankfurter, joined by Justices Reed and Burton, doubted jurisdiction of the subject matter.

Several subsequent cases similar to Colegrove have been decided by the Court in summary per curiam statements. None was dismissed for want of jurisdiction of the subject matter.

Two cases decided with opinions after Colegrove likewise plainly imply that the subject matter of this suit is within District Court jurisdiction. In MacDougall v. Green, the District Court dismissed for want of jurisdiction, which had been invoked under 28 U.S.C. s 1343(3), 28 U.S.C.A. s 1343(3), a suit to enjoin enforcement of the requirement that nominees for state-wide elections be supported by a petition signed by a minimum number of persons from at least 50 of the State's 102 counties. This Court's disagreement with that action is clear since the Court affirmed the judgment after a review of the merits and concluded that the particular claim there was without merit. In South v. Peters, we affirmed the dismissal of an attack on the Georgia 'county unit' system but founded our action on a ground that plainly would not have been reached if the lower court lacked jurisdiction of the subject matter, which allegedly existed under 28 U.S.C. s 1343(3), 28 U.S.C.A. s 1343(3). The express words of our holding were that 'Federal courts consistently refuse to exercise their equity powers in cases posing political issues arising from a state's geographical distribution of electoral strength among its political subdivisions.'

We hold that the District Court has jurisdiction of the subject matter of the federal constitutional claim asserted in the complaint.

IV.

Justiciability.

In holding that the subject matter of this suit was not justiciable, the District Court relied on Colegrove v. Green, supra, and subsequent per curiam cases. The court stated: 'From a review of these decisions there can be no doubt that the federal rule * * * is that the federal courts * * * will not intervene in cases of this type to compel legislative reapportionment.' We understand the District Court to have read the cited cases as compelling the conclusion that since the appellants sought to have a legislative apportionment held unconstitutional, their suit presented a 'political question' and was therefore nonjusticiable. We hold that this challenge to an apportionment presents no nonjusticiable 'political question.' The cited cases do not hold the contrary.

Of course the mere fact that the suit seeks protection of a political right does not mean it presents a political question. Such an objection 'is little more than a play upon words.' Rather, it is argued that apportionment cases, whatever the actual wording of the complaint, can involve no federal constitutional right except one resting on the guaranty of a republican form of government, and that complaints based on that clause have been held to present political questions which are nonjusticiable. We hold that the claim pleaded here neither rests upon nor implicates the Guaranty Clause and that its justiciability is therefore not foreclosed by our decisions of cases involving that clause. The District Court misinterpreted Colegrove v. Green and other decisions of this Court on which it relied. Appellants' claim that they are being denied equal protection is justiciable, and if 'discrimination is sufficiently shown, the right to relief under the equal protection clause is not diminished by the fact that the discrimination relates to political rights.' To show why we reject the argument based on the Guaranty Clause, we must examine the authorities under it. But because there appears to be some uncertainty as to why those cases did present political questions, and specifically as to whether this apportionment case is like those cases, we deem it necessary first to consider the contours of the 'political question' doctrine.

Our discussion, even at the price of extending this opinion, requires review of a number of political question cases, in order to expose the attributes of the doctrine—attributes which, in various settings, diverge, combine, appear, and disappear in seeming disorderliness. Since that review is undertaken solely to demonstrate that neither singly nor collectively do these cases support a conclusion that this apportionment case is nonjusticiable, we of course do not explore their implications in other contexts. That review reveals that in the Guaranty Clause cases and in the other 'political question' cases, it is the relationship between the judiciary and the coordinate branches of the Federal Government, and not the federal judiciary's relationship to the States, which gives rise to the 'political question.' We have said that 'In determining whether a question falls within (the political question) category, the appropriateness under our system of government of attributing finality to the action of the political departments and also the lack of satisfactory criteria for a judicial determination are dominant considerations.' The nonjusticiability of a political question is primarily a function of the separation of powers. Much confusion results from the capacity of the 'political question' label to obscure the need for case-by-case inquiry. Deciding whether a matter has in any measure been committed by the Constitution to another branch of government, or whether the action of that branch exceeds whatever authority has been committed, is itself a delicate exercise in constitutional interpretation, and is a responsibility of this Court as ultimate interpreter of the Constitution. To demonstrate this requires no less than to analyze representative cases and to infer from them the analytical threads that make up the political question doctrine. We shall then show that none of those threads catches this case.

We have already noted that the District Court's holding that the subject matter of this complaint was nonjusticiable relied upon Colegrove v. Green, and later cases. Some of those concerned the choice of members of a state legislature, as in this case; others, like Colegrove itself and earlier precedents, concerned the choice of Representatives in the Federal Congress.

Article I, ss 2, 4, and 5, and Amendment XIV, s 2, relate only to congressional elections and obviously do not govern apportionment of state legislatures. However, our decisions in favor of justiciability even in light of those provisions plainly afford no support for the District Court's conclusion that the subject matter of this controversy presents a political question. Indeed, the refusal to award relief in Colegrove resulted only from the controlling view of a want of equity. Nor is anything contrary to be found in those per curiams that came after Colegrove.

We conclude that the complaint's allegations of a denial of equal protection present a justiciable constitutional cause of action upon which appellants are entitled to a trial and a decision. The right asserted is within the reach of judicial protection under the Fourteenth Amendment.

The judgment of the District Court is reversed and the cause is remanded for further proceedings consistent with this opinion.

Reversed and remanded.

Dissenting opinion of Mr. Justice Harlan, whom Mr. Justice Frankfurter joins.

The dissenting opinion of Mr. Justice Frankfurter, in which I join, demonstrates the abrupt departure the majority makes from judicial history by putting the federal courts into this area of state concerns—an area which, in this instance, the Tennessee state courts themselves have refused to enter.

Once one cuts through the thicket of discussion devoted to 'jurisdiction,' 'standing,' 'justiciability,' and 'political question,' there emerges a straightforward issue which, in my view, is determinative of this case. Does the complaint disclose a violation of a federal constitutional right, in other words, a claim over which a United States District Court would have jurisdiction under 28 U.S.C. s 1343(3), 28 U.S.C.A. s 1343(3) and 42 U.S.C. s 1983, 42 U.S.C.A. s 1983? The majority opinion does not actually discuss this basic question, but, as one concurring Justice observes, seems to decide it 'sub silentio.' However, in my opinion, appellants' allegations, accepting all of them as true, do not, parsed down or as a whole, show an infringement by Tennessee of any rights assured by the Fourteenth Amendment. Accordingly, I believe the complaint should have been dismissed for 'failure to state a claim upon which relief can be granted.'

It is at once essential to recognize this case for what it is. The issue here relates not to a method of state electoral apportionment by which seats in the federal House of Representatives are allocated, but solely to the right of a State to fix the basis of representation in its own legislature. Until it is first decided to what extent that right is limited by the Federal Constitution, and whether what Tennessee has done or failed to do in this instance runs afoul of any such limitation, we need not reach the issues of 'justiciability' or 'political question' or any of the other considerations which in such cases as Colegrove v. Green, 328 U.S. 549, 66 S.Ct. 1198, 90 L.Ed. 1432, led the Court to decline to adjudicate a challenge to a state apportionment affecting seats in the federal House of Representatives, in the absence of a controlling Act of Congress.

In short, there is nothing in the Federal Constitution to prevent a State, acting not irrationally, from choosing any electoral legislative structure it thinks best suited to the interests, temper, and customs of its people. I would have thought this proposition settled by MacDougall v. Green, in which the Court observed that to 'assume that political power is a function exclusively of numbers is to disregard the practicalities of government,' and reaffirmed by South v. Peters. A State's choice to distribute electoral strength among geographical units, rather than according to a census of population, is certainly no less a rational decision of policy than would be its choice to levy a tax on property rather than a tax on income. Both are legislative judgments entitled to equal respect from this Court.

Gideon v. Wainwright, 372 U.S. 335 (1963)

Mr. Justice Black delivered the opinion of the Court.

Petitioner was charged in a Florida state court with having broken and entered a poolroom with intent to commit a misdemeanor. This offense is a felony under Florida law. Appearing in court without funds and without a lawyer, petitioner asked the court to appoint counsel for him, whereupon the following colloquy took place:

'The COURT: Mr. Gideon, I am sorry, but I cannot appoint Counsel to represent you in this case. Under the laws of the State of Florida, the only time the Court can appoint Counsel to represent a Defendant is when that person is charged with a capital offense. I am sorry, but I will have to deny your request to appoint Counsel to defend you in this case.

'The DEFENDANT: The United States Supreme Court says I am entitled to be represented by Counsel.'

Put to trial before a jury, Gideon conducted his defense about as well as could be expected from a layman. He made an opening statement to the jury, cross-examined the State's witnesses, presented witnesses in his own defense, declined to testify himself, and made a short argument 'emphasizing his innocence to the charge contained in the Information filed in this case.' The jury returned a verdict of guilty, and petitioner was sentenced to serve five years in the state prison. Later, petitioner filed in the Florida Supreme Court this habeas corpus petition attacking his conviction and sentence on the ground that the trial court's refusal to appoint counsel for him denied him rights 'guaranteed by the Constitution and the Bill of Rights by the United States Government.' Treating the petition for habeas corpus as properly before it, the State Supreme Court, 'upon consideration thereof' but without an opinion, denied all relief. Since 1942, when Betts v. Brady, 316 U.S. 455, 62 S.Ct. 1252, 86 L.Ed. 1595, was decided by a divided Court, the problem of a defendant's federal constitutional right to counsel in a state court has been a continuing source of controversy and litigation in both state and federal courts. To give this problem another review here, we granted certiorari. 370 U.S. 908, 82 S.Ct. 1259, 8 L.Ed.2d 403. Since Gideon was proceeding in forma pauperis, we appointed counsel to represent him and requested both sides to discuss in their briefs and oral arguments the following: 'Should this Court's holding in Betts v. Brady, be reconsidered?'

I.

The facts upon which Betts claimed that he had been unconstitutionally denied the right to have counsel appointed to assist him are strikingly like the facts upon which Gideon here bases his federal constitutional claim. Betts was indicted for robbery in a Maryland state court. On arraignment, he told the trial judge of his lack of funds to hire a lawyer and asked the court to appoint one for him. Betts was advised that it was not the practice in that county to appoint counsel for indigent defendants except in murder and rape cases. He then pleaded not guilty, had witnesses summoned, cross-examined the State's witnesses, examined his own, and chose not to testify himself. He was found guilty by the judge, sitting without a jury, and sentenced to eight years in prison. Like Gideon, Betts sought release by habeas corpus, alleging that he had been denied the right to assistance of counsel in violation of the Fourteenth Amendment. Betts was denied any relief, and on review this Court affirmed. It was held that a refusal to appoint counsel for an indigent defendant charged with a felony did not necessarily violate the Due Process Clause of the Fourteenth Amendment, which for reasons given the Court deemed to be the only applicable federal constitutional provision.

Treating due process as 'a concept less rigid and more fluid than those envisaged in other specific and particular provisions of the Bill of Rights,' the Court held that refusal to appoint counsel under the particular facts and circumstances in the Betts case was not so 'offensive to the common and fundamental ideas of fairness' as to amount to a denial of due process. Since the facts and circumstances of the two cases are so nearly indistinguishable, we think the Betts v. Brady holding if left standing would require us to reject Gideon's claim that the Constitution guarantees him the assistance of counsel. Upon full reconsideration we conclude that Betts v. Brady should be overruled.

II.

The Sixth Amendment provides, 'In all criminal prosecutions, the accused shall enjoy the right * * * to have the Assistance of Counsel for his defence.' We have construed this to mean that in federal courts counsel must be provided for defendants unable to employ counsel unless the right is competently and intelligently waived. Betts argued that this right is extended to indigent defendants in state courts by the Fourteenth Amendment. In response the Court stated that, while the Sixth Amendment laid down 'no rule for the conduct of the states, the question recurs whether the constraint laid by the amendment upon the national courts expresses a rule so fundamental and essential to a fair trial, and so, to due process of law, that it is made obligatory upon the states by the Fourteenth Amendment.' In order to decide whether the Sixth Amendment's guarantee of counsel is of this fundamental nature, the Court in Betts set out and considered '(r)elevant data on the subject * * * afforded by constitutional and statutory provisions subsisting in the colonies and the states prior to the inclusion of the Bill of Rights in the national Constitution, and in the constitutional, legislative, and judicial history of the states to the present date.' On the basis of this historical data the Court concluded that 'appointment of counsel is not a fundamental right, essential to a fair trial.' It was for this reason the Betts Court refused to accept the contention that the Sixth Amendment's guarantee of counsel for indigent federal defendants was extended to or, in the words of that Court, 'made obligatory upon the states by the Fourteenth Amendment.' Plainly, had the Court concluded that appointment of counsel for an indigent criminal defendant was 'a fundamental right, essential to a fair trial,' it would have held that the Fourteenth Amendment requires appointment of counsel in a state court, just as the Sixth Amendment requires in a federal court.

We think the Court in Betts had ample precedent for acknowledging that those guarantees of the Bill of Rights which are fundamental safeguards of liberty immune from federal abridgment are equally protected against state invasion by the Due Process Clause of the Fourteenth Amendment. This same principle was recognized, explained, and applied in Powell v. Alabama, 287 U.S. 45, 53 S.Ct. 55, 77 L.Ed. 158 (1932), a case upholding the right of counsel, where the Court held that despite sweeping language to the contrary in Hurtado v. California, 110 U.S. 516, 4 S.Ct. 292, 28 L.Ed. 232 (1884), the Fourteenth Amendment 'embraced' those 'fundamental principles of liberty and justice which lie at the base of all our civil and political institutions,' even though they had been 'specifically dealt with in another part of the Federal Constitution.' In many cases other than Powell and Betts, this Court has looked to the fundamental nature of original Bill of Rights guarantees to decide whether the Fourteenth Amendment makes them obligatory on the States. Explicitly recognized to be of this 'fundamental nature' and therefore made immune from state invasion by the Fourteenth, or some part of it, are the First Amendment's freedoms of speech, press, religion, assembly, association, and petition for redress of grievances. For the same reason, though not always in precisely the same terminology, the Court has made obligatory on the States the Fifth Amendment's command that private property shall not be taken for public use without just compensation, the Fourth Amendment's prohibition of unreasonable searches and seizures, and the Eighth's ban on cruel and unusual punishment. On the other hand, this Court in Palko v. Connecticut, 302 U.S. 319, 58 S.Ct. 149, 82 L.Ed. 288 (1937), refused to hold that the Fourteenth Amendment made the double jeopardy provision of the Fifth Amendment obligatory on the States.

In so refusing, however, the Court, speaking through Mr. Justice Cardozo, was careful to emphasize that 'immunities that are valid as against the federal government by force of the specific pledges of particular amendments have been found to be implicit in the concept of ordered liberty, and thus, through the Fourteenth Amendment, become valid as against the states' and that guarantees 'in their origin * * * effective against the federal government alone' had by prior cases 'been taken over from the earlier articles of the Federal Bill of Rights and brought within the Fourteenth Amendment by a process of absorption.' We accept Betts v. Brady's assumption, based as it was on our prior cases, that a provision of the Bill of Rights which is 'fundamental and essential to a fair trial' is made obligatory upon the States by the Fourteenth Amendment. We think the Court in Betts was wrong, however, in concluding that the Sixth Amendment's guarantee of counsel is not one of these fundamental rights. Ten years before Betts v. Brady, this Court, after full consideration of all the historical data examined in Betts, had unequivocally declared that 'the right to the aid of counsel is of this fundamental character.' Powell v. Alabama, 287 U.S. 45, 68, 53 S.Ct. 55, 63, 77 L.Ed. 158 (1932). While the Court at the close of its Powell opinion did by its language, as this Court frequently does, limit its holding to the particular facts and circumstances of that case, its conclusions about the fundamental nature of the right to counsel are unmistakable. Several years later, in 1936, the Court reemphasized what it had said about the fundamental nature of the right to counsel in this language: 'We concluded that certain fundamental rights, safeguarded by the first eight amendments against federal action, were also safeguarded against state action by the due process of law clause of the Fourteenth Amendment, and among them the fundamental right of the accused to the aid of counsel in a criminal prosecution.' Grosjean v. American Press Co., 297 U.S. 233, 243–244, 56 S.Ct. 444, 446, 80 L.Ed. 660 (1936). And again in 1938 this Court said: '(The assistance of counsel) is one of the safeguards of the Sixth Amendment deemed necessary to insure fundamental human rights of life and liberty. * * * The Sixth Amendment stands as a constant admonition that if the constitutional safeguards it provides be lost, justice will not "still be done."' Johnson v. Zerbst, 304 U.S. 458, 462, 58 S.Ct. 1019, 1022, 82 L.Ed. 1461 (1938).

In light of these and many other prior decisions of this Court, it is not surprising that the Betts Court, when faced with the contention that 'one charged with crime, who is unable to obtain counsel, must be furnished counsel by the state,' conceded that '(e)xpressions in the opinions of this court lend color to the argument * * *' The fact is that in deciding as it did—that 'appointment of counsel is not a fundamental right, essential to a fair trial'—the Court in Betts v. Brady made an abrupt break with its own well-considered precedents. In returning to these old precedents, sounder we believe than the new, we but restore constitutional principles established to achieve a fair system of justice. Not only these precedents but also reason and reflection require us to recognize that in our adversary system of criminal justice, any person haled into court, who is too poor to hire a lawyer, cannot be assured a fair trial unless counsel is provided for him. This seems to us to be an obvious truth. Governments, both state and federal, quite properly spend vast sums of money to establish machinery to try defendants accused of crime. Lawyers to prosecute are everywhere deemed essential to protect the public's interest in an orderly society.

Similarly, there are few defendants charged with crime, few indeed, who fail to hire the best lawyers they can get to prepare and present their defenses. That government hires lawyers to prosecute and defendants who have the money hire lawyers to defend are the strongest indications of the wide-spread belief that lawyers in criminal courts are necessities, not luxuries. The right of one charged with crime to counsel may not be deemed fundamental and essential to fair trials in some countries, but it is in ours. From the very beginning, our state and national constitutions and laws have laid great emphasis on procedural and substantive safeguards designed to assure fair trials before impartial tribunals in which every defendant stands equal before the law. This noble ideal cannot be realized if the poor man charged with crime has to face his accusers without a lawyer to assist him. A defendant's need for a lawyer is nowhere better stated than in the moving words of Mr. Justice Sutherland in Powell v. Alabama: The Court in Betts v. Brady departed from the sound wisdom upon which the Court's holding in Powell v. Alabama rested. Florida, supported by two other States, has asked that Betts v. Brady be left intact. Twenty-two States, as friends of the Court, argue that Betts was 'an anachronism when handed down' and that it should now be overruled. We agree.

The judgment is reversed and the cause is remanded to the Supreme Court of Florida for further action not inconsistent with this opinion.

Brandenburg v. Ohio, 395 U.S. 444 (1969)

PER CURIAM.

The appellant, a leader of a Ku Klux Klan group, was convicted under the Ohio Criminal Syndicalism statute for 'advocat(ing) * * * the duty, necessity, or propriety of crime, sabotage, violence, or unlawful methods of terrorism as a means of accomplishing industrial or political reform' and for 'voluntarily assembl(ing) with any society, group, or assemblage of persons formed to teach or advocate the doctrines of criminal syndicalism.' He was fined $1,000 and sentenced to one to 10 years' imprisonment. The appellant challenged the constitutionality of the criminal syndicalism statute under the First and Fourteenth Amendments to the United States Constitution, but the intermediate appellate court of Ohio affirmed his conviction without opinion. The Supreme Court of Ohio dismissed his appeal, sua sponte, 'for the reason that no substantial constitutional question exists herein.' It did not file an opinion or explain its conclusions. Appeal was taken to this Court, and we noted probable jurisdiction.

The record shows that a man, identified at trial as the appellant, telephoned an announcer-reporter on the staff of a Cincinnati television station and invited him to come to a Ku Klux Klan 'rally' to be held at a farm in Hamilton County. With the cooperation of the organizers, the reporter and a cameraman attended the meeting and filmed the events. Portions of the films were later broadcast on the local station and on a national network.

The prosecution's case rested on the films and on testimony identifying the appellant as the person who communicated with the reporter and who spoke at the rally. The State also introduced into evidence several articles appearing in the film, including a pistol, a rifle, a shotgun, ammunition, a Bible, and a red hood worn by the speaker in the films.

One film showed 12 hooded figures, some of whom carried firearms. They were gathered around a large wooden cross, which they burned. No one was present other than the participants and the newsmen who made the film. Most of the words uttered during the scene were incomprehensible when the film was projected, but scattered phrases could be understood that were derogatory of Negroes and, in one instance, of Jews. Another scene on the same film showed the appellant, in Klan regalia, making a speech. The speech, in full, was as follows:

'This is an organizers' meeting. We have had quite a few members here today which are—we have hundreds, hundreds of members throughout the State of Ohio. I can quote from a newspaper clipping from the Columbus, Ohio Dispatch, five weeks ago Sunday morning. The Klan has more members in the State of Ohio than does any other organization. We're not a revengent organization, but if our President, our Congress, our Supreme Court, continues to suppress the white, Caucasian race, it's possible that there might have to be some revengeance taken.

'We are marching on Congress July the Fourth, four hundred thousand strong. From there we are dividing into two groups, one group to march on St. Augustine, Florida, the other group to march into Mississippi. Thank you.'

The second film showed six hooded figures one of whom, later identified as the appellant, repeated a speech very similar to that recorded on the first film. The reference to the possibility of 'revengeance' was omitted, and one sentence was added:

'Personally, I believe the nigger should be returned to Africa, the Jew returned to Israel.' Though some of the figures in the films carried weapons, the speaker did not. The Ohio Criminal Syndicalism Statute was enacted in 1919. From 1917 to 1920, identical or quite similar laws were adopted by 20 States and two territories. In 1927, this Court sustained the constitutionality of California's Criminal Syndicalism Act, the text of which is quite similar to that of the laws of Ohio. Whitney v. California, 274 U.S. 357, 47 S.Ct. 641, 71 L.Ed. 1095 (1927). The Court upheld the statute on the ground that, without more, 'advocating' violent means to effect political and economic change involves such danger to the security of the State that the State may outlaw it. But Whitney has been thoroughly discredited by later decisions. See Dennis v. United States, 341 U.S. 494, at 507, 71 S.Ct. 857, at 866, 95 L.Ed. 1137 (1951). These later decisions have fashioned the principle that the constitutional guarantees of free speech and free press do not permit a State to forbid or proscribe advocacy of the use of force or of law violation except where such advocacy is directed to inciting or producing imminent lawless action and is likely to incite or produce such action. As we said in Noto v. United States, 367 U.S. 290, 297–298 (1961), 'the mere abstract teaching * * * of the moral propriety or even moral necessity for a resort to force and violence, is not the same as preparing a group for violent action and steeling it to such action.' See also Herndon v. Lowry, 301 U.S. 242, 259–261, (1937); Bond v. Floyd, 385 U.S. 116, 134, (1966). A statute which fails to draw this distinction impermissibly intrudes upon the freedoms guaranteed by the First and Fourteenth Amendments. It sweeps within its condemnation speech which our Constitution has immunized from governmental control.

Measured by this test, Ohio's Criminal Syndicalism Act cannot be sustained. The Act punishes persons who 'advocate or teach the duty, necessity, or propriety' of violence 'as a means of accomplishing industrial or political reform'; or who publish or circulate or display any book or paper containing such advocacy; or who 'justify' the commission of violent acts 'with intent to exemplify, spread or advocate the propriety of the doctrines of criminal syndicalism'; or who 'voluntarily assemble' with a group formed 'to teach or advocate the doctrines of criminal syndicalism.' Neither the indictment nor the trial judge's instructions to the jury in any way refined the statute's bald definition of the crime in terms of mere advocacy not distinguished from incitement to imminent lawless action.

Accordingly, we are here confronted with a statute which, by its own words and as applied, purports to punish mere advocacy and to forbid, on pain of criminal punishment, assembly with others merely to advocate the described type of action. Such a statute falls within the condemnation of the First and Fourteenth Amendments. The contrary teaching of Whitney v. California, supra, cannot be supported, and that decision is therefore overruled.

Mr. Justice Black, concurring.

I agree with the views expressed by Mr. Justice DOUGLAS in his concurring opinion in this case that the 'clear and present danger' doctrine should have no place in the interpretation of the First Amendment. I join the Court's opinion, which, as I understand it, simply cites Dennis v. United States, but does not indicate any agreement on the Court's part with the 'clear and present danger' doctrine on which Dennis purported to rely.

3.   The Burger Court

INTRODUCTION

Vincent Blasi once described the Supreme Court under Chief Justice Warren Burger (1969–1986) as the "counter-revolution that wasn't."[1] Richard Nixon ran for president in 1968 as a law-and-order candidate, challenging the Supreme Court as soft on crime. He promised Justices who would be tougher on criminals, who would support the police, and who would read the Constitution in a way to that would limit Justices' ability to make policy. He wanted "strict constructionists." He wanted Justices who would not follow in the steps of the Warren Court and instead perhaps reverse many of their precedents.

Almost immediately President Nixon had his opportunity. In 1968 Earl Warren announced his intention to retire, giving President Lyndon Johnson an opportunity to replace him. He selected liberal Abe Fortas to be Chief Justice, but the nomination failed, leaving it to Nixon to fill the replacement. In 1969 Nixon nominated District of Columbia Court of Appeals Judge Warren Burger to be Chief Justice. He was assumed to be more conservative that Fortas and Warren, and it was presumed by Nixon that Burger would be the start of the former's remaking of the Supreme Court.

Yet Burger was only one vote. For several years, and in fact, through the entirety of the Burger Court, many of the Warren Court's most liberal members, such as William Brennan and Thurgood Marshall, remained on the bench. This produced a Court that was not entirely in Nixon's image, much like the Stone and Vinson Courts were for Franklin Roosevelt. Thus, the Burger Court, at least initially, did not go about dismantling Warren-era precedents in the way some anticipated. The continuity of Justices in part explains that, but so does the strength of legal precedent.

As noted in the Introduction, it is not necessarily easy for the Court simply to dismiss or overturn precedents it does not like. Once decided, even if it is constitutional precedent (which supposedly has less judicial deference than statutory precedent), it is still precedent and the Court needs to explain why it

---

[1]   Blasi, Vincent. 1986. *The Burger Court: The Counter-Revolution That Wasn't.* New Haven, CT: Yale University Press.

is rejecting it. To do that, the Court also needs a case to reverse a precedent. Thousands of cases come to the Supreme Court every year on petitions of certiorari, asking it to take their case. It takes four Justices to grant cert or a petition for review. Thus, just getting the right case before the Court that four Justices want to hear is difficult, but then after oral arguments one needs five votes to reverse precedent. These practical considerations weigh against reversing precedent, let alone considering all the other legal and policy factors discussed in the Introduction that weigh in favor of retaining precedents. These are issues not unique to the Burger Court.

But during the Burger Court there was a lot going on in America. The Civil Rights Movement was fully blossoming, and the need to confront the reality of race and racial discrimination was imperative. Programs such as affirmative action or setting aside programs or grants for people of color became mechanisms for addressing discrimination. During the 1970s and 1980s, second-generation feminism sought changes in the law to help women, and attorneys and then judges such as Ruth Bader Ginsburg were instrumental in challenging gender stereotypes in the law. The 1969 demonstrations in New York City at the Stonewall Inn by the gay community to protest police brutality against their members placed civil rights for the LGBTQ on the political agenda. But the 1970s and 1980s also saw new challenges in criminal justice, such as with the death penalty or public access to trials, or a rethinking of national and state power. All of these issues were matters for the Burger Court to address.

Several notable decisions by the Burger Court stand out (for this book). The first is *Roe v. Wade*,[2] declaring the women have a constitutional right to terminate their pregnancies under certain circumstances. That decision has polarized America, leading also to efforts by many to overturn it. When we get to the Rehnquist Court we will visit *Planned Parenthood v. Casey*,[3] a decision that both reaffirms and reinterprets the *Roe* precedent. There are many other decisions beyond the scope of this book that have sought to narrow or reverse it, but as of 2020, *Roe* remains precedent.

Another important decision for this book is *Bowers v. Hardwick*,[4] where the Court declared that same-sex couples did not have a constitutional right to engage in consensual sex acts. That decision is important because it was later reversed in *Lawrence v. Texas*[5] under the Rehnquist Court. That reversal of constitutional precedent will be discussed in the next chapter.

---

[2]   410 U.S. 113 (1973).
[3]   505 U.S. 833 (1992).
[4]   478 U.S. 186 (1986).
[5]   539 U.S. 558 (2003).

As with the Supreme Court after FDR's 1936 re-election, the Burger Court did gradually see holdovers from the Warren Court leave, to be replaced first by appointees by Richard Nixon and then Ronald Reagan. The Court became more conservative over time, eventually reversing not simply some of the Warren or earlier precedents, but some of those it had established earlier under Burger compared to later. Examples of this include cases on federalism, where the Court, initially in *National League of Cities v. Usery*,[6] placed limits on the national government's ability to regulate the working conditions of state government, only to reverse less than a decade in *Garcia v. San Antonio Metropolitan Transit Authority*.[7] In *Spinelli v. United States*,[8] the Court issued a two-step process for use of an informant's information to secure a search warrant, only to see it overruled in *Illinois v. Gates*.[9] The Court also rejected its precedent in *Gannett Co. v. DePasquale*,[10] which had given judges broad authority to close trial, and held in *Richmond Newspapers, Inc. v. Virginia*[11] that the First Amendment gave the media a right to attend trials. In *Gregg v. Georgia*,[12] it reversed its decision in *Furman v. Georgia*,[13] regarding procedural defects in the use of the death penalty.

Overall, the Burger Court reversed 32 constitutional precedents, the exact same number as the Warren Court. But because it issued that many reversals with nearly 700 more decisions, its rate of precedent rejection was lower than the Warren Court. When examining these opinions, consider the reasons for constitutional precedent reversal. Error correction seems to dominate, as well as considerations of the confusion or unworkability of the original precedent. This is the case, for example, with *Miller v. California*,[14] where the Court saw prior cases on determining obscenity simply as having failed. Unworkability applied as well as in the three decisions of its own that it reversed. *In Craig v. Boren*,[15] how much of the decision here is simply a change in societal thinking and conceptions regarding women's roles? Was *Reed v. Reed*[16] wrongly decided at the time, or have we (society or the Court) come to view it as wrong now? There is an old expression that says that the Supreme Court follows election returns. Does this adage explain the Burger Court approach to precedent?

---

6   426 U.S. 833 (1976).
7   469 U.S. 528 (1985).
8   393 U.S. 410 (1969).
9   462 U.S. 213 (1983).
10   443 U.S. 368 (1979).
11   448 U.S. 555 (1980).
12   428 U.S. 153 (1976).
13   408 U.S. 238 (1972).
14   413 U.S. 15 (1973).
15   429 U.S. 190 (1976).
16   404 U.S. 71 (1971).

Miller v. California, 413 U.S. 15 (1973)

Mr. Chief Justice Burger delivered the opinion of the Court.

This is one of a group of 'obscenity-pornography' cases being reviewed by the Court in a re-examination of standards enunciated in earlier cases involving what Mr. Justice Harlan called 'the intractable obscenity problem.'
Appellant conducted a mass mailing campaign to advertise the sale of illustrated books, euphemistically called 'adult' material. After a jury trial, he was convicted of violating California Penal Code s 311.2(a), a misdemeanor, by knowingly distributing obscene matter, and the Appellate Department, Superior Court of California, County of Orange, summarily affirmed the judgment without opinion. Appellant's conviction was specifically based on his conduct in causing five unsolicited advertising brochures to be sent through the mail in an envelope addressed to a restaurant in Newport Beach, California. The envelope was opened by the manager of the restaurant and his mother. They had not requested the brochures; they complained to the police.
The brochures advertise four books entitled 'Intercourse,' 'Man-Woman,' 'Sex Orgies Illustrated,' and 'An Illustrated History of Pornography,' and a film entitled 'Marital Intercourse.' While the brochures contain some descriptive printed material, primarily they consist of pictures and drawings very explicitly depicting men and women in groups of two or more engaging in a variety of sexual activities, with genitals often prominently displayed.

I

This case involves the application of a State's criminal obscenity statute to a situation in which sexually explicit materials have been thrust by aggressive sales action upon unwilling recipients who had in no way indicated any desire to receive such materials. This Court has recognized that the States have a legitimate interest in prohibiting dissemination or exhibition of obscene material when the mode of dissemination carries with it a significant danger of offending the sensibilities of unwilling recipients or of exposure to juveniles. It is in this context that we are called on to define the standards which must be used to identify obscene material that a State may regulate without infringing on the First Amendment as applicable to the States through the Fourteenth Amendment.
The dissent of Mr. Justice BRENNAN reviews the background of the obscenity problem, but since the Court now undertakes to formulate standards more concrete than those in the past, it is useful for us to focus on two of the landmark cases in the somewhat tortured history of the Court's obscenity decisions. In Roth v. United States, 354 U.S. 476 (1957), the Court sustained a conviction under a federal statute punishing the mailing of 'obscene, lewd, lascivious or filthy...' materials. The key to that holding was the Court's rejection of the claim that obscene materials were protected by the First Amendment. Five Justices joined in the opinion stating:
'All ideas having even the slightest redeeming social importance—unorthodox ideas, controversial ideas, even ideas hateful to the prevailing climate of opinion—have the full protection of the (First Amendment) guaranties, unless excludable because they encroach upon the limited area of more important interests. But implicit in the history of the First Amendment is the rejection of

obscenity as utterly without redeeming social importance. ... This is the same judgment expressed by this Court in Chaplinsky v. New Hampshire, 315 U.S. 568, 571–572.
'We hold that obscenity is not within the area of constitutionally protected speech or press.' 354 U.S., at 484–485, 77 S.Ct., 1309 (footnotes omitted).
Nine years later, in Memoirs v. Massachusetts, 383 U.S. 413 (1966), the Court veered sharply away from the Roth concept and, with only three Justices in the plurality opinion, articulated a new test of obscenity. The plurality held that under the Roth definition

'as elaborated in subsequent cases, three elements must coalesce: it must be established that (a) the dominant theme of the material taken as a whole appeals to a prurient interest in sex; (b) the material is patently offensive because if affronts contemporary community standards relating to the description or representation of sexual matters; and (c) the material is utterly without redeeming social value.'

The sharpness of the break with Roth, represented by the third element of the Memoirs test and emphasized by Mr. Justice White's dissent, was further underscored when the Memoirs plurality went on to state:

'The Supreme Judicial Court erred in holding that a book need not be "unqualifiedly worthless before it can be deemed obscene." A book cannot be proscribed unless it is found to be utterly without redeeming social value.'

While Roth presumed 'obscenity' to be 'utterly without redeeming social importance,' Memoirs required that to prove obscenity it must be affirmatively established that the material is 'utterly without redeeming social value.' Thus, even as they repeated the words of Roth, the Memoirs plurality produced a drastically altered test that called on the prosecution to prove a negative, i.e., that the material was 'utterly without redeeming social value'—a burden virtually impossible to discharge under our criminal standards of proof. Such considerations caused Mr. Justice Harlan to wonder if the 'utterly without redeeming social value' test had any meaning at all. See Memoirs v. Massachusetts, id., at 459, 86 S.Ct., at 998 (Harlan, J., dissenting). Apart from the initial formulation in the Roth case, no majority of the Court has at any given time been able to agree on a standard to determine what constitutes obscene, pornographic material subject to regulation under the States' police power. We have seen 'a variety of views among the members of the Court unmatched in any other course of constitutional adjudication.' This is not remarkable, for in the area of freedom of speech and press the courts must always remain sensitive to any infringement on genuinely serious literary, artistic, political, or scientific expression. This is an area in which there are few eternal verities.
The case we now review was tried on the theory that the California Penal Code s 311 approximately incorporates the three-stage Memoirs test, supra. But now the Memoirs test has been abandoned as unworkable by its author, and no Member of the Court today supports the Memoirs formulation.

II

This much has been categorically settled by the Court, that obscene material is unprotected by the First Amendment. The First and Fourteenth Amendments have never been treated as absolutes. We acknowledge, however, the inherent dangers of undertaking to regulate any form of expression. State statutes designed to regulate obscene materials must be carefully limited. As a result, we now confine the permissible scope of such regulation to works which depict or describe sexual conduct. That conduct must be specifically defined by the applicable state law, as written or authoritatively construed. A state offense must also be limited to works which, taken as a whole, appeal to the prurient interest in sex, which portray sexual conduct in a patently offensive way, and which, taken as a whole, do not have serious literary, artistic, political, or scientific value. The basic guidelines for the trier of fact must be: (a) whether 'the average person, applying contemporary community standards' would find that the work, taken as a whole, appeals to the prurient interest, Kois v. Wisconsin, supra, 408 U.S., at 230, 92 S.Ct., at 2246, quoting Roth v. United States, supra, 354 U.S., at 489, 77 S.Ct., at 1311; (b) whether the work depicts or describes, in a patently offensive way, sexual conduct specifically defined by the applicable state law; and (c) whether the work, taken as a whole, lacks serious literary, artistic, political, or scientific value. We do not adopt as a constitutional standard the 'utterly without redeeming social value' test of Memoirs v. Massachusetts, 383 U.S., at 419, 86 S.Ct., at 977; that concept has never commanded the adherence of more than three Justices at one time. If a state law that regulates obscene material is thus limited, as written or construed, the First Amendment values applicable to the States through the Fourteenth Amendment are adequately protected by the ultimate power of appellant courts to conduct an independent review of constitutional claims when necessary.

We emphasize that it is not our function to propose regulatory schemes for the States. That must await their concrete legislative efforts. It is possible, however, to give a few plain examples of what a state statute could define for regulation under part (b) of the standard announced in this opinion, supra:

(a)   Patently offensive representations or descriptions of ultimate sexual acts, normal or perverted, actual or simulated.

(b)   Patently offensive representation or descriptions of masturbation, excretory functions, and lewd exhibition of the genitals.

Sex and nudity may not be exploited without limit by films or pictures exhibited or sold in places of public accommodation any more than live sex and nudity can be exhibited or sold without limit in such public places. At a minimum, prurient, patently offensive depiction or description of sexual conduct must have serious literary, artistic, political, or scientific value to merit First Amendment protection. For example, medical books for the education of physicians and related personnel necessarily use graphic illustrations and descriptions of human anatomy. In resolving the inevitably sensitive questions of fact and law, we must continue to rely on the jury system, accompanied by the safeguards that judges, rules of evidence, presumption of innocence, and other protective features provide, as we do with rape, murder, and a host of other offenses against society and its individual members.

Mr. Justice BRENNAN, author of the opinions of the Court, or the plurality opinions, in Roth v. United States, supra; Jacobellis v. Ohio, supra; Ginzburg v. United States, 383 U.S. 463, 86 S.Ct. 952, 16 L.Ed.2d 31 (1966); Mishkin v. New York, 383 U.S. 502, 86 S.Ct. 958, 16 L.Ed.2d 56 (1966); and Memoiors v. Massachusetts, supra, has abandoned his former position and now maintains that no formulation of this Court, the Congress, or the States can adequately distinguish obscene material unprotected by the First Amendment from protected expression, Paris Adult Theatre

I v. Slaton, 413 U.S. 49, 73, 93 S.Ct. 2628, 2642, 37 L.Ed.2d 446 (Brennan, J., dissenting).

Mr. Justice Brennan also emphasizes 'institutional stress' in justification of his change of view. Noting that '(t)he number of obscenity cases on our docket gives ample testimony to the burden that has been placed upon this Court,' he quite rightly remarks that the examination of contested materials 'is hardly a source of edification to the members of this Court.' Paris Adult Theatre I v. Slaton, supra, 413 U.S., at 92, 93, 93 S.Ct., at 2652. He also notes, and we agree, that 'uncertainty of the standards creates a continuing source of tension between state and federal courts....' 'The problem is ... that one cannot say with certainty that material is obscene until at least five members of this Court, applying inevitably obscure standards, have pronounced it so.'

It is certainly true that the absence, since Roth, of a single majority view of this Court as to proper standards for testing obscenity has placed a strain on both state and federal courts. But today, for the first time since Roth was decided in 1957, a majority of this Court has agreed on concrete guidelines to isolate 'hard core' pornography from expression protected by the First Amendment. Now we may abandon the casual practice of Redrup v. New York, and attempt to provide positive guidance to federal and state courts alike.

Vacated and remanded.

Gregg v. Georgia, 428 U.S. 153 (1976)

Judgment of the Court, and opinion of Mr. Justice Stewart, Mr. Justice Powell, and Mr. Justice Stevens, Announced by Mr. Justice Stewart.

The issue in this case is whether the imposition of the sentence of death for the crime of murder under the law of Georgia violates the Eighth and Fourteenth Amendments.

I

The petitioner, Troy Gregg, was charged with committing armed robbery and murder. In accordance with Georgia procedure in capital cases, the trial was in two stages, a guilt stage and a sentencing stage. The evidence at the guilt trial established that on November 21, 1973, the petitioner and a traveling companion, Floyd Allen, while hitchhiking north in Florida were picked up by Fred Simmons and Bob Moore. Their car broke down, but they continued north after Simmons purchased another vehicle with some of the cash he was carrying. While still in Florida, they picked up another hitchhiker, Dennis Weaver, who rode with them to Atlanta, where he was let out about 11 p. m. A short time later the four men interrupted their journey for a rest stop along the highway. The next morning the bodies of Simmons and Moore were discovered in a ditch nearby.

On November 23, after reading about the shootings in an Atlanta newspaper, Weaver communicated with the Gwinnett County police and related information concerning the journey with the victims, including a description of the car. The next afternoon, the petitioner and Allen, while in Simmons' car, were arrested in Asheville, N. C. In the search incident to the arrest a .25-caliber pistol, later shown to be that used to kill Simmons and Moore, was found in the petitioner's pocket. After receiving the warnings required by Miranda v. Arizona, and signing a written waiver of his rights, the petitioner signed a statement in which he admitted shooting, then robbing Simmons and Moore. He justified the slayings on grounds of self-defense. The next day, while being transferred to Lawrenceville, Ga., the petitioner and Allen were taken to the scene of the shootings. Upon arriving there, Allen recounted the events leading to the slayings. His version of these events was as follows: After Simmons and Moore left the car, the petitioner stated that he intended to rob them. The petitioner then took his pistol in hand and positioned himself on the car to improve his aim. As Simmons and Moore came up an embankment toward the car, the petitioner fired three shots and the two men fell near a ditch. The petitioner, at close range, then fired a shot into the head of each. He robbed them of valuables and drove away with Allen.

A medical examiner testified that Simmons died from a bullet wound in the eye and that Moore died from bullet wounds in the cheek and in the back of the head. He further testified that both men had several bruises and abrasions about the face and head which probably were sustained either from the fall into the ditch or from being dragged or pushed along the embankment. Although Allen did not testify, a police detective recounted the substance of Allen's statements about the slayings and indicated that directly after Allen had made these statements the petitioner had admitted that Allen's account was accurate. The petitioner testified in his own defense. He confirmed that Allen had made the statements described by the detective, but denied their truth or ever having admitted to their accuracy. He indicated that he had shot Simmons and Moore because of fear and in self-defense, testifying they had attacked Allen and him, one wielding a pipe and the other a knife.

The trial judge submitted the murder charges to the jury on both felony-murder and nonfelony-murder theories. He also instructed on the issue of self-defense but declined to instruct on manslaughter. He submitted the robbery case to the jury on both an armed-robbery theory and on the lesser included offense of robbery by intimidation. The jury found the petitioner guilty of two counts of armed robbery and two counts of murder.

At the penalty stage, which took place before the same jury, neither the prosecutor nor the petitioner's lawyer offered any additional evidence. Both counsel, however, made lengthy arguments dealing generally with the propriety of capital punishment under the circumstances and with the weight of the evidence of guilt. The trial judge instructed the jury that it could recommend either a death sentence or a life prison sentence on each count. The judge further charged the jury that in determining what sentence was appropriate the jury was free to consider the facts and circumstances, if any, presented by the parties in mitigation or aggravation.

Finally, the judge instructed the jury that it "would not be authorized to consider (imposing) the penalty of death" unless it first found beyond a reasonable doubt one of these aggravating circumstances:

"One That the offense of murder was committed while the offender was engaged in the commission of two other capital felonies, to-wit the armed robbery of (Simmons and Moore).

"Two That the offender committed the offense of murder for the purpose of receiving money and the automobile described in the indictment.

"Three The offense of murder was outrageously and wantonly vile, horrible and inhuman, in that they (Sic) involved the depravity of (the) mind of the defendant."

Finding the first and second of these circumstances, the jury returned verdicts of death on each count.

The Supreme Court of Georgia affirmed the convictions and the imposition of the death sentences for murder. After reviewing the trial transcript and the record, including the evidence, and comparing the evidence and sentence in similar cases in accordance with the requirements of Georgia law, the court concluded that, considering the nature of the crime and the defendant, the sentences of death had not resulted from prejudice or any other arbitrary factor and were not excessive or disproportionate to the penalty applied in similar cases. The death sentences used for armed robbery, however, were vacated on the grounds that the death penalty had rarely been imposed in Georgia for that offense and that the jury improperly considered the murders as aggravating circumstances for the robberies after having considered the armed robberies as aggravating circumstances for the murders.

We granted the petitioner's application for a writ of certiorari limited to his challenge to the imposition of the death sentences in this case as "cruel and unusual" punishment in violation of the Eighth and the Fourteenth Amendments.

II

Before considering the issues presented it is necessary to understand the Georgia statutory scheme for the imposition of the death penalty. The Georgia statute, as amended after our decision in Furman v. Georgia, 408 U.S. 238 (1972), retains the death penalty for six categories of crime: murder, kidnapping for ransom or where the victim is harmed, armed robbery, rape, treason, and aircraft hijacking. The capital defendant's guilt or innocence is determined in the traditional manner, either by a trial judge or a jury, in the first stage of a bifurcated trial.

If trial is by jury, the trial judge is required to charge lesser included offenses when they are supported by any view of the evidence. After a verdict, finding, or plea of guilty to a capital crime, a presentence hearing is conducted before whoever made the determination of guilt. The sentencing procedures are essentially the same in both bench and jury trials. At the hearing: "(T)he judge (or jury) shall hear additional evidence in extenuation, mitigation, and aggravation of punishment, including the record of any prior criminal convictions and pleas of guilty or pleas of nolo contendere of the defendant, or the absence of any prior conviction and pleas: Provided, however, that only such evidence in aggravation as the State has made known to the defendant prior to his trial shall be admissible. The judge (or jury) shall also hear argument by the defendant or his counsel and the prosecuting attorney ... regarding the punishment to be imposed."

The defendant is accorded substantial latitude as to the types of evidence that he may introduce. Evidence considered during the guilt stage may be considered during the sentencing stage without being resubmitted.

In the assessment of the appropriate sentence to be imposed the judge is also required to consider or to include in his instructions to the jury "any mitigating circumstances or aggravating circumstances otherwise authorized by law and any of (10) statutory aggravating circumstances which may be supported by the evidence...." The scope of the nonstatutory aggravating or mitigating circumstances is not delineated in the statute. Before a convicted defendant may be sentenced to death, however, except in cases of treason or aircraft hijacking, the jury, or the trial judge in cases tried without a jury, must find beyond a reasonable doubt one of the 10 aggravating circumstances specified in the statute. The sentence of death may be imposed only if the jury (or judge) finds one of the statutory aggravating circumstances and then elects to impose that sentence. If the verdict is death, the jury or judge must specify the aggravating circumstance(s) found. In jury cases, the trial judge is bound by the jury's recommended sentence.

In addition to the conventional appellate process available in all criminal cases, provision is made for special expedited direct review by the Supreme Court of Georgia of the appropriateness of imposing the sentence of death in the particular case. The court is directed to consider "the punishment as well as any errors enumerated by way of appeal," and to determine:

"(1) Whether the sentence of death was imposed under the influence of passion, prejudice, or anything arbitrary factor, and

"(2) Whether, in cases other than treason or aircraft hijacking, the evidence supports the jury's or judge's finding of a statutory aggravating circumstance as enumerated in section 27.2534.1(b), and

"(3) Whether the sentence of death is excessive or disproportionate to the penalty imposed in similar cases, considering both the crime and the defendant."

If the court affirms a death sentence, it is required to include in its decision reference to similar cases that it has taken into consideration.

A transcript and complete record of the trial, as well as a separate report by the trial judge, are transmitted to the court for its use in reviewing the sentence. The report is in the form of a 6 ½ page questionnaire, designed to elicit information about the defendant, the crime, and the circumstances of the trial. It requires the trial judge to characterize the trial in several ways designed to test for arbitrariness and disproportionality of sentence. Included in the report are responses to detailed questions concerning the quality of the defendant's representation, whether race played a role in the trial, and, whether, in the trial court's judgment, there was any doubt about the defendant's guilt or the appropriateness of the sentence. A copy of the report is served upon defense counsel. Under its special review authority, the court may either affirm the death sentence or remand the case for resentencing. In cases in which the death sentence is affirmed there remains the possibility of executive clemency.

III

We address initially the basic contention that the punishment of death for the crime of murder is, under all circumstances, "cruel and unusual" in violation of the Eighth and Fourteenth Amendments of the Constitution. In Part IV of this opinion, we will consider the sentence of death imposed under the Georgia statutes at issue in this case.

The Court on a number of occasions has both assumed and asserted the constitutionality of capital punishment. In several cases that assumption provided a necessary foundation for the decision, as the Court was asked to decide whether a particular method of carrying out a capital sentence would be allowed to stand under the Eighth Amendment. But until Furman v. Georgia, 408 U.S. 238 (1972), the Court never confronted squarely the fundamental claim that the punishment of death always, regardless of the enormity of the offense or the procedure followed in imposing the sentence, is cruel and unusual punishment in violation of the Constitution. Although this issue was presented and addressed in *Furman*, it was not resolved by the Court. Four Justices would have held that capital punishment is not unconstitutional *per se*; two Justices would have reached the opposite conclusion; and three Justices, while agreeing that the statutes then before the Court were invalid as applied, left open the question whether such punishment may ever be imposed. We now hold that the punishment of death does not invariably violate the Constitution.

B

Of course, the requirements of the Eighth Amendment must be applied with an awareness of the limited role to be played by the courts. This does not mean that judges have no role to play, for the Eighth Amendment is a restraint upon the exercise of legislative power. "Judicial review by definition, often involves a conflict between judicial and legislative judgment as to what the Constitution means or requires. In this respect, Eighth Amendment cases come to us in no different posture. It seems conceded by all that the Amendment imposes some obligations on the judiciary to judge the constitutionality of punishment and that there are punishments that the Amendment would bar whether legislatively approved or not." Furman v. Georgia, 408 U.S., at 313–314, 92 S.Ct., at 2764 (White, J., concurring). But, while we have an obligation to insure that constitutional bounds are not overreached, we may not act as judges as we might as legislators. "Courts are not representative bodies. They are not designed to be a good reflex of a democratic society. Their judgment is best informed, and therefore most dependable, within narrow limits. Their essential quality is detachment, founded on independence. History teaches that the independence of the judiciary is jeopardized when courts become embroiled in the passions of the day and assume primary responsibility in choosing between competing political, economic and social pressures." Dennis v. United States, 341 U.S. 494, 525, (1951) (Frankfurter, J., concurring in affirmance of judgment). Therefore, in assessing a punishment selected by a democratically elected legislature against the constitutional measure, we presume its validity. We may not require the legislature to select the least severe penalty possible so long as the penalty selected is not cruelly inhumane or disproportionate to the crime involved. And a heavy burden rests on those who would attack the judgment of the representatives of the people.

This is true in part because the constitutional test is intertwined with an assessment of contemporary standards and the legislative judgment weighs heavily in ascertaining such standards. "(I)n a democratic society legislatures, not courts, are constituted to respond to the will and consequently the moral values of the people." *Furman v. Georgia, supra,* 408 U.S., at 383, 92 S.Ct., at 2800 (Burger, C. J., dissenting). The deference we owe to the decisions of the state legislatures under our federal system, is enhanced where the specification of punishments is concerned, for "these are peculiarly questions of legislative policy." A decision that a given punishment is impermissible under the Eighth Amendment cannot be reversed short of a constitutional amendment. The ability of the people to express their preference through the normal democratic processes, as well as through ballot referenda, is shut off. Revisions cannot be made in the light of further experience.

IV

We now consider whether Georgia may impose the death penalty on the petitioner in this case.

A

While Furman did not hold that the infliction of the death penalty Per se violates the Constitution's ban on cruel and unusual punishments, it did recognize that the penalty of death is different in kind from any other punishment imposed under our system of criminal justice. Because of the uniqueness of the death penalty, Furman held that it could not be imposed under sentencing procedures that created a substantial risk that it would be inflicted in an arbitrary and capricious manner. Mr. Justice White concluded that "the death penalty is exacted with great infrequency even for the most atrocious crimes and … there is no meaningful basis for distinguishing the few cases in which it is imposed from the many cases in which it is not." Indeed, the death sentences examined by the Court in Furman were "cruel and unusual in the same way that being struck by lightning is cruel and unusual. For, of all the people convicted of (capital crimes), many just as reprehensible as these, the petitioners (in Furman were) among a capriciously selected random handful upon whom the sentence of death has in fact been imposed. … (T)he Eighth and Fourteenth Amendments cannot tolerate the infliction of a sentence of death under legal systems that permit this unique penalty to be so wantonly and so freakishly imposed."

Furman mandates that where discretion is afforded a sentencing body on a matter so grave as the determination of whether a human life should be taken or spared, that discretion must be suitably directed and limited so as to minimize the risk of wholly arbitrary and capricious action.

Jury sentencing has been considered desirable in capital cases in order "to maintain a link between contemporary community values and the penal system a link without which the determination of punishment could hardly reflect 'the evolving standards of decency that mark the progress of a maturing society.'" But it creates special problems. Much of the information that is relevant to the sentencing decision may have no relevance to the question of guilt, or may even be extremely prejudicial to a fair determination of that question. This problem, however, is scarcely insurmountable. Those who have studied the question suggest that a bifurcated procedure one in which the question of sentence is not considered until the determination of guilt has been made is the best answer.

But the provision of relevant information under fair procedural rules is not alone sufficient to guarantee that the information will be properly used in the imposition of punishment, especially if sentencing is performed by a jury. Since the members of a jury will have had little, if any, previous experience in sentencing, they are unlikely to be skilled in dealing with the information they are given. To the extent that this problem is inherent in jury sentencing, it may not be totally correctible. It seems clear, however, that the problem will be alleviated if the jury is given guidance regarding the factors about the crime and the defendant that the State, representing organized society, deems particularly relevant to the sentencing decision. The idea that a jury should be given guidance in its decisionmaking is also hardly a novel proposition. Juries are invariably given careful instructions on the law and how to apply it before they are authorized to decide the merits of a lawsuit. It would be virtually unthinkable to follow any other course in a legal system that has traditionally operated by following prior precedents and fixed rules of law. When erroneous instructions are given, retrial is often required. It is quite simply a hallmark of our legal system that juries be carefully and adequately guided in their deliberations. While some have suggested that standards to guide a capital jury's sentencing deliberations are impossible to formulate, the fact is that such standards have been developed.

In summary, the concerns expressed in Furman that the penalty of death not be imposed in an arbitrary or capricious manner can be met by a carefully drafted statute that ensures that the sentencing authority is given adequate information and guidance. As a general proposition these concerns are best met by a system that provides for a bifurcated proceeding at which the sentencing authority is apprised of the information relevant to the imposition of sentence and provided with standards to guide its use of the information.

We do not intend to suggest that only the above-described procedures would be permissible under Furman or that any sentencing system constructed along these general lines would inevitably satisfy the concerns of Furman, for each distinct system must be examined on an individual basis. Rather, we have embarked upon this general exposition to make clear that it is possible to construct capital-sentencing systems capable of meeting Furman's constitutional concerns.

B

We now turn to consideration of the constitutionality of Georgia's capital-sentencing procedures. In the wake of Furman, Georgia amended its capital punishment statute, but chose not to narrow the scope of its murder provisions. Thus, now as before Furman, in Georgia "(a) person commits murder when he unlawfully and with malice aforethought, either express or implied, causes the death of another human being." All persons convicted of murder "shall be punished by death or by imprisonment for life."

Georgia did act, however, to narrow the class of murderers subject to capital punishment by specifying 10 statutory aggravating circumstances, one of which must be found by the jury to exist beyond a reasonable doubt before a death sentence can ever be imposed. In addition, the jury is authorized to consider any other appropriate aggravating or mitigating circumstances. The jury is not required to find any mitigating circumstance in order to make a recommendation of mercy that is binding on the trial court, but it must find a *statutory* aggravating circumstance before recommending a sentence of death.

These procedures require the jury to consider the circumstances of the crime and the criminal before it recommends sentence. No longer can a Georgia jury do as Furman's jury did: reach a finding of the defendant's guilt and then, without guidance or direction, decide whether he should live or die. Instead, the jury's attention is directed to the specific circumstances of the crime: Was it committed in the course of another capital felony? Was it committed for money? Was it committed upon a peace officer or judicial officer? Was it committed in a particularly heinous way or in a manner that endangered the lives of many persons? In addition, the jury's attention is focused on the characteristics of the person who committed the crime: Does he have a record of prior convictions for capital offenses? Are there any special facts about this defendant that mitigate against imposing capital punishment (E. g., his youth, the extent of his cooperation with the police, his emotional state at the time of the crime). As a result, while some jury discretion still exists, "the discretion to be exercised is controlled by clear and objective standards so as to produce non-discriminatory application."

As an important additional safeguard against arbitrariness and caprice, the Georgia statutory scheme provides for automatic appeal of all death sentences to the State's Supreme Court. That court is required by statute to review each sentence of death and determine whether it was imposed under the influence of passion or prejudice, whether the evidence supports the jury's finding of a statutory aggravating circumstance, and whether the sentence is disproportionate compared to those sentences imposed in similar cases.

In short, Georgia's new sentencing procedures require as a prerequisite to the imposition of the death penalty, specific jury findings as to the circumstances of the crime or the character of the defendant. Moreover, to guard further against a situation comparable to that presented in Furman, the Supreme Court of Georgia compares each death sentence with the sentences imposed on similarly situated defendants to ensure that the sentence of death in a particular case is not disproportionate. On their face these procedures seem to satisfy the concerns of Furman. No longer should there be "no meaningful basis for distinguishing the few cases in which (the death penalty) is imposed from the many cases in which it is not."

The petitioner contends, however, that the changes in the Georgia sentencing procedures are only cosmetic, that the arbitrariness and capriciousness condemned by Furman continue to exist in Georgia both in traditional practices that still remain and in the new sentencing procedures adopted in response to Furman.

1

First, the petitioner focuses on the opportunities for discretionary action that are inherent in the processing of any murder case under Georgia law. He notes that the state prosecutor has unfettered authority to select those persons whom he wishes to prosecute for a capital offense and to plea bargain with them. Further, at the trial the jury may choose to convict a defendant of a lesser included offense rather than find him guilty of a crime punishable by death, even if the evidence would support a capital verdict. And finally, a defendant who is convicted and sentenced to die may have his sentence commuted by the Governor of the State and the Georgia Board of Pardons and Paroles.

The existence of these discretionary stages is not determinative of the issues before us. At each of these stages an actor in the criminal justice system makes a decision which may remove a defendant from consideration as a candidate for the death penalty. Furman, in contrast, dealt with the decision to impose the death sentence on a specific individual who had been convicted of a capital offense. Nothing in any of our cases suggests that the decision to afford an individual defendant mercy violates the Constitution. Furman held only that, in order to minimize the risk that the death penalty would be imposed on a capriciously selected group of offenders, the decision to impose it had to be guided by standards so that the sentencing authority would focus on the particularized circumstances of the crime and the defendant.

2

The petitioner further contends that the capital-sentencing procedures adopted by Georgia in response to Furman do not eliminate the dangers of arbitrariness and caprice in jury sentencing that were held in Furman to be violative of the Eighth and Fourteenth Amendments. He claims that the statute is so broad and vague as to leave juries free to act as arbitrarily and capriciously as they wish in deciding whether to impose the death penalty. While there is no claim that the jury in this case relied upon a vague or overbroad provision to establish the existence of a statutory aggravating circumstance, the petitioner looks to the sentencing system as a whole (as the Court did in Furman and we do today) and argues that it fails to reduce sufficiently the risk of arbitrary infliction of death sentences. Specifically, Gregg urges that the statutory aggravating circumstances are too broad and too vague, that the sentencing procedure allows for arbitrary grants of mercy, and that the scope of the evidence and argument that can be considered at the presentence hearing is too wide.

The petitioner attacks the seventh statutory aggravating circumstance, which authorizes imposition of the death penalty if the murder was "outrageously or wantonly vile, horrible or inhuman in that it involved torture, depravity of mind, or an aggravated battery to the victim," contending that it is so broad that capital punishment could be imposed in any murder case. It is, of course, arguable that any murder involves depravity of mind or an aggravated battery. But this language need not be construed in this way, and there is no reason to assume that the Supreme Court of Georgia will adopt such an open-ended construction. In only one case has it upheld a jury's decision to sentence a defendant to death when the only statutory aggravating circumstance found was that of the seventh, and that homicide was a horrifying torture-murder.

The petitioner also argues that two of the statutory aggravating circumstances are vague and therefore susceptible of widely differing interpretations, thus creating a substantial risk that the death penalty will be arbitrarily inflicted by Georgia juries. In light of the decisions of the Supreme Court of Georgia we must disagree. First, the petitioner attacks that part of s 27-2534.1(b)(1) that authorizes a jury to consider whether a defendant has a "substantial history of serious assaultive criminal convictions." The Supreme Court of Georgia, however, has demonstrated a concern that the new sentencing procedures provide guidance to juries. It held this provision to be impermissibly vague in Arnold v. State, 236 Ga. 534, 540, 224 S.E.2d 386, 391

(1976), because it did not provide the jury with "sufficiently 'clear and objective standards.'" Second, the petitioner points to s 27-2534.1(b)(3) which speaks of creating a "great risk of death to more than one person." While such a phrase might be susceptible of an overly broad interpretation, the Supreme Court of Georgia has not so construed it. The only case in which the court upheld a conviction in reliance on this aggravating circumstance involved a man who stood up in a church and fired a gun indiscriminately into the audience. On the other hand, the court expressly reversed a finding of great risk when the victim was simply kidnaped in a parking lot.

The petitioner next argues that the requirements of Furman are not met here because the jury has the power to decline to impose the death penalty even if it finds that one or more statutory aggravating circumstances are present in the case. This contention misinterprets Furman. Moreover, it ignores the role of the Supreme Court of Georgia which reviews each death sentence to determine whether it is proportional to other sentences imposed for similar crimes. Since the proportionality requirement on review is intended to prevent caprice in the decision to inflict the penalty, the isolated decision of a jury to afford mercy does not render unconstitutional death sentences imposed on defendants who were sentenced under a system that does not create a substantial risk of arbitrariness or caprice.

The petitioner objects, finally, to the wide scope of evidence and argument allowed at presentence hearings. We think that the Georgia court wisely has chosen not to impose unnecessary restrictions on the evidence that can be offered at such a hearing and to approve open and far-ranging argument. So long as the evidence introduced and the arguments made at the presentence hearing do not prejudice a defendant, it is preferable not to impose restrictions. We think it desirable for the jury to have as much information before it as possible when it makes the sentencing decision.

3

Finally, the Georgia statute has an additional provision designed to assure that the death penalty will not be imposed on a capriciously selected group of convicted defendants. The new sentencing procedures require that the State Supreme Court review every death sentence to determine whether it was imposed under the influence of passion, prejudice, or any other arbitrary factor, whether the evidence supports the findings of a statutory aggravating circumstance, and "(w)hether the sentence of death is excessive or disproportionate to the penalty imposed in similar cases, considering both the crime and the defendant." In performing its sentence-review function, the Georgia court has held that "if the death penalty is only rarely imposed for an act or it is substantially out of line with sentences imposed for other acts it will be set aside as excessive." The court on another occasion stated that "we view it to be our duty under the similarity standard to assure that no death sentence is affirmed unless in similar cases throughout the state the death penalty has been imposed generally...."

The provision for appellate review in the Georgia capital-sentencing system serves as a check against the random or arbitrary imposition of the death penalty. In particular, the proportionality review substantially eliminates the possibility that a person will be sentenced to die by the action of an aberrant jury. If a time comes when juries generally do not impose the death sentence in a certain kind of murder case, the appellate review procedures assure that no defendant convicted under such circumstances will suffer a sentence of death.

V

The basic concern of Furman centered on those defendants who were being condemned to death capriciously and arbitrarily Under the procedures before the Court in that case, sentencing authorities were not directed to give attention to the nature or circumstances of the crime committed or to the character or record of the defendant. Left unguided, juries imposed the death sentence in a way that could only be called freakish. The new Georgia sentencing procedures, by contrast, focus the jury's attention on the particularized nature of the crime and the particularized characteristics of the individual defendant. While the jury is permitted to consider any aggravating or mitigating circumstances, it must find and identify at least one statutory aggravating factor before it may impose a penalty of death. In this way the jury's discretion is channeled. No longer can a jury wantonly and freakishly impose the death sentence; it is always circumscribed by the legislative guidelines. In addition, the review function of the Supreme Court of Georgia affords additional assurance that the concerns that prompted our decision in *Furman* are not present to any significant degree in the Georgia procedure applied here.

For the reasons expressed in this opinion, we hold that the statutory system under which Gregg was sentenced to death does not violate the Constitution. Accordingly, the judgment of the Georgia Supreme Court is affirmed.

It is so ordered.

Craig v. Boren, 429 U.S. 190 (1976)

Mr. Justice Brennan delivered the opinion of the Court.

The interaction of two sections of an Oklahoma statute, Okla.Stat., Tit. 37, ss 241 and 245 (1958 and Supp.1976), prohibits the sale of "nonintoxicating" 3.2% beer to males under the age of 21 and to females under the age of 18. The question to be decided is whether such a gender-based differential constitutes a denial to males 18–20 years of age of the equal protection of the laws in violation of the Fourteenth Amendment.

This action was brought in the District Court for the Western District of Oklahoma on December 20, 1972, by appellant Craig, a male then between 18 and 21 years of age, and by appellant Whitener, a licensed vendor of 3.2% beer. The complaint sought declaratory and injunctive relief against enforcement of the gender-based differential on the ground that it constituted invidious discrimination against males 18–20 years of age. A three-judge court convened under 28 U.S.C. s 2281 sustained the constitutionality of the statutory differential and dismissed the action. 399 F.Supp. 1304 (1975). We noted probable jurisdiction of appellants' appeal, 423 U.S. 1047, 96 S.Ct. 771, 46 L.Ed.2d 635 (1976). We reverse.

II

A

Before 1972, Oklahoma defined the commencement of civil majority at age 18 for females and age 21 for males. Okla.Stat., Tit. 15, s 13 (1972 and Supp.1976). In contrast, females were held criminally responsible as adults at age 18 and males at age 16. Okla.Stat., Tit. 10, s 1101(a) (Supp.1976). After the Court of Appeals for the Tenth Circuit held in 1972, on the authority of Reed v. Reed, 404 U.S. 71, 92 S.Ct. 251, 30 L.Ed. 225 (1971), that the age distinction was unconstitutional for purposes of establishing criminal responsibility as adults, Lamb v. Brown, 456 F.2d 18, the Oklahoma Legislature fixed age 18 as applicable to both males and females. Okla. Stat., Tit. 10, s 1101(a) (Supp.1976). In 1972, 18 also was established as the age of majority for males and females in civil matters, Okla.Stat., Tit. 15, s 13 (1972 and Supp.1976), except that ss 241 and 245 of the 3.2% beer statute were simultaneously codified to create an exception to the gender-free rule.

Analysis may appropriately begin with the reminder that Reed emphasized that statutory classifications that distinguish between males and females are "subject to scrutiny under the Equal Protection Clause." 404 U.S., at 75, 92 S.Ct., at 253. To withstand constitutional challenge, previous cases establish that classifications by gender must serve important governmental objectives and must be substantially related to achievement of those objectives. Thus, in Reed, the objectives of "reducing the workload on probate courts," id., at 76, 92 S.Ct., at 254, and "avoiding intrafamily controversy," id., at 77, 92 S.Ct., at 254, were deemed of insufficient importance to sustain use of an overt gender criterion in the appointment of administrators of intestate decedents' estates. Decisions following Reed similarly have rejected administrative ease and convenience as sufficiently important objectives to justify gender-based classifications. And only two Terms ago, Stanton v. Stanton, 421 U.S. 7, 95 S.Ct. 1373, 43 L.Ed.2d 688 (1975), expressly stating that Reed v. Reed was "controlling," 421 U.S., at 13, 95 S.Ct., at 1377, held that Reed required invalidation of a Utah differential age-of-majority statute, notwithstanding the statute's coincidence with and furtherance of the State's purpose of fostering "old notions" of role typing and preparing boys for their expected performance in the economic and political worlds.

Reed v. Reed has also provided the underpinning for decisions that have invalidated statutes employing gender as an inaccurate proxy for other, more germane bases of classification. Hence, "archaic and overbroad" generalizations, Schlesinger v. Ballard, supra, 419 U.S., at 508, 95 S.Ct., at 577, concerning the financial position of servicewomen, Frontiero v. Richardson, supra, 411 U.S., at 689 n. 23, 93 S.Ct., at 1772, and working women, Weinberger v. Wiesenfeld, 420 U.S. 636, 643, 95 S.Ct. 1225, 1230, 43 L.Ed.2d 514 (1975), could not justify use of a gender line in determining eligibility for certain governmental entitlements. Similarly, increasingly outdated misconceptions concerning the role of females in the home rather than in the "marketplace and world of ideas" were rejected as loose-fitting characterizations incapable of supporting state statutory schemes that were premised upon their accuracy. In light of the weak congruence between gender and the characteristic or trait that gender purported to represent, it was necessary that the legislatures choose either to realign their substantive laws in a gender-neutral fashion, or to adopt procedures for identifying those instances where the sex-centered generalization actually comported with fact.

We turn then to the question whether, under Reed, the difference between males and females with respect to the purchase of 3.2% beer warrants the differential in age drawn by the Oklahoma statute. We conclude that it does not.

B

The District Court recognized that Reed v. Reed was controlling. In applying the teachings of that case, the court found the requisite important governmental objective in the traffic-safety goal proffered by the Oklahoma Attorney General. It then concluded that the statistics introduced by the appellees established that the gender-based distinction was substantially related to achievement of that goal.

C

We accept for purposes of discussion the District Court's identification of the objective underlying ss 241 and 245 as the enhancement of traffic safety. Clearly, the protection of public health and safety represents an important function of state and local governments. However, appellees' statistics in our view cannot support the conclusion that the gender-based distinction closely serves to achieve that objective and therefore the distinction cannot under Reed withstand equal protection challenge.

The appellees introduced a variety of statistical surveys. First, an analysis of arrest statistics for 1973 demonstrated that 18–20-year-old male arrests for "driving under the influence" and "drunkenness" substantially exceeded female arrests for that same age period. Similarly, youths aged 17–21 were found to be overrepresented among those killed or injured in traffic accidents, with males again numerically exceeding females in this regard. Third, a random roadside survey in Oklahoma City revealed that young males were more inclined to drive and drink beer than were their female counterparts. Fourth, Federal Bureau of Investigation nationwide statistics exhibited a notable increase in arrests for "driving under the influence." Finally, statistical evidence gathered in other jurisdictions, particularly Minnesota and Michigan, was offered to corroborate Oklahoma's experience by indicating the pervasiveness of youthful participation in motor vehicle accidents following the imbibing of alcohol. Conceding that "the case is not free from doubt," 399 F.Supp., at 1314, the District Court nonetheless concluded that this statistical showing substantiated "a rational basis for the legislative judgment underlying the challenged classification."

Even were this statistical evidence accepted as accurate, it nevertheless offers only a weak answer to the equal protection question presented here. The most focused and relevant of the statistical surveys, arrests of 18–20-year-olds for alcohol-related driving offenses, exemplifies the ultimate unpersuasiveness of this evidentiary record. Viewed in terms of the correlation between sex and the actual activity that Oklahoma seeks to regulate driving while under the influence of alcohol the statistics broadly establish that .18% of females and 2% of males in that age group were arrested for that offense. While such a disparity is not trivial in a statistical sense, it hardly can form the basis for employment of a gender line as a classifying device. Certainly if maleness is to serve as a proxy for drinking and driving, a correlation of 2% must be considered an unduly tenuous "fit." Indeed, prior cases have consistently rejected the use of sex as a decisionmaking factor even though the statutes in question certainly rested on far more predictive empirical relationships than this.

Moreover, the statistics exhibit a variety of other shortcomings that seriously impugn their value to equal protection analysis. Setting aside the obvious methodological problems, the surveys do not adequately justify the salient features of Oklahoma's gender-based traffic-safety law. None purports to measure the use and dangerousness of 3.2% beer as opposed to alcohol generally, a detail that is of particular importance since, in light of its low alcohol level, Oklahoma apparently considers the 3.2% beverage to be "nonintoxicating." Okla.Stat., Tit. 37, s 163.1 (1958); see State ex rel. Springer v. Bliss, 199 Okl. 198, 185 P.2d 220 (1947). Moreover, many of the studies, while graphically documenting the unfortunate increase in driving while under the influence of alcohol, make no effort to relate their findings to age-sex differentials as involved here. Indeed, the only survey that explicitly centered its attention upon young drivers and their use of beer albeit apparently not of the diluted 3.2% variety reached results that hardly can be viewed as impressive in justifying either a gender or age classification.

There is no reason to belabor this line of analysis. It is unrealistic to expect either members of the judiciary or state officials to be well versed in the rigors of experimental or statistical technique. But this merely illustrates that proving broad sociological propositions by statistics is a dubious business, and one that inevitably is in tension with the normative philosophy that underlies the Equal Protection Clause. Suffice to say that the showing offered by the appellees does not satisfy us that sex represents a legitimate, accurate proxy for the regulation of drinking and driving. In fact, when it is further recognized that Oklahoma's statute prohibits only the selling of 3.2% beer to young males and not their drinking the beverage once acquired (even after purchase by their 18–20-year-old female companions), the relationship between gender and traffic safety becomes far too tenuous to satisfy Reed's requirement that the gender-based difference be substantially related to achievement of the statutory objective.

We hold, therefore, that under Reed, Oklahoma's 3.2% beer statute invidiously discriminates against males 18–20 years of age.

Richmond Newspapers, Inc. v. Virginia, 448 U.S. 555 (1980)

Chief Justice Burger wrote for the Court.

Mr. Justice White and Mr. Justice Stevens filed concurring opinions.

Mr. Justice Brennan filed opinion concurring in judgment in which Mr. Justice Marshall joined. Mr. Justice Stewart and Mr. Justice Blackmun filed opinions concurring in the judgment. Mr. Justice Rehnquist filed a dissenting opinion.

The narrow question presented in this case is whether the right of the public and press to attend criminal trials is guaranteed under the United States Constitution.

I

In March 1976, one Stevenson was indicted for the murder of a hotel manager who had been found stabbed to death on December 2, 1975. Tried promptly in July 1976, Stevenson was convicted of second-degree murder in the Circuit Court of Hanover County, Va. The Virginia Supreme Court reversed the conviction in October 1977, holding that a bloodstained shirt purportedly belonging to Stevenson had been improperly admitted into evidence.

Stevenson was retried in the same court. This second trial ended in a mistrial on May 30, 1978, when a juror asked to be excused after trial had begun and no alternate was available.

A third trial, which began in the same court on June 6, 1978, also ended in a mistrial. It appears that the mistrial may have been declared because a prospective juror had read about Stevenson's previous trials in a newspaper and had told other prospective jurors about the case before the retrial began.

Stevenson was tried in the same court for a fourth time beginning on September 11, 1978. Present in the courtroom when the case was called were appellants Wheeler and McCarthy, reporters for appellant Richmond Newspapers, Inc. Before the trial began, counsel for the defendant moved that it be closed to the public.

The trial judge, who had presided over two of the three previous trials, asked if the prosecution had any objection to clearing the courtroom. The prosecutor stated he had no objection and would leave it to the discretion of the court. Presumably referring to Va.Code § 19.2-266 (Supp.1980), the trial judge then announced: "[T]he statute gives me that power specifically and the defendant has made the motion." He then ordered "that the Courtroom be kept clear of all parties except the witnesses when they testify." The record does not show that any objections to the closure order were made by anyone present at the time, including appellants Wheeler and McCarthy.

Later that same day, however, appellants sought a hearing on a motion to vacate the closure order. The trial judge granted the request and scheduled a hearing to follow the close of the day's proceedings. When the hearing began, the court ruled that the hearing was to be treated as part of the trial; accordingly, he again ordered the reporters to leave the courtroom, and they complied.

At the closed hearing, counsel for appellants observed that no evidentiary findings had been made by the court prior to the entry of its closure order and pointed out that the court had failed to consider any other, less drastic measures within its power to ensure a fair trial. Counsel for appellants argued that constitutional considerations mandated that before ordering closure, the court should first decide that the rights of the defendant could be protected in no other way.

Counsel for defendant Stevenson pointed out that this was the fourth time he was standing trial. He also referred to "difficulty with information between the jurors," and stated that he "didn't want information to leak out," be published by the media, perhaps inaccurately, and then be seen by the jurors. Defense counsel argued that these things, plus the fact that "this is a small community," made this a proper case for closure. The trial judge noted that counsel for the defendant had made similar statements at the morning hearing.

The court denied the motion to vacate and ordered the trial to continue the following morning "with the press and public excluded."

"[I]n the absence of the jury, the defendant by counsel made a Motion that a mis-trial be declared, which motion was taken under advisement.

"At the conclusion of the Commonwealth's evidence, the attorney for the defendant moved the Court to strike the Commonwealth's evidence on grounds stated to the record, which Motion was sustained by the Court.

"And the jury having been excused, the Court doth find the accused NOT GUILTY of Murder, as charged in the Indictment, and he was allowed to depart."

On September 27, 1978, the trial court granted appellants' motion to intervene *nunc pro tunc* in the Stevenson case. Appellants then petitioned the Virginia Supreme Court for writs of mandamus and prohibition and filed an appeal from the trial court's closure order. On July 9, 1979, the Virginia Supreme court dismissed the mandamus and prohibition petitions and, finding no reversible error, denied the petition for appeal.

Appellants then sought review in this Court, invoking both our appellate, 28 U.S.C. § 1257(2), and certiorari jurisdiction, § 1257(3). We postponed further consideration of the question of our jurisdiction to the hearing of the case on the merits. We conclude that jurisdiction by appeal does not lie; however, treating the filed papers as a petition for a writ of certiorari pursuant to 28 U.S.C. § 2103, we grant the petition.

II

We begin consideration of this case by noting that the precise issue presented here has not previously been before this Court for decision. In *Gannett Co. v. DePasquale, supra*, the Court was not required to decide whether a right of access to *trials*, as distinguished from hearings on *pre* trial motions, was constitutionally guaranteed. The Court held that the Sixth Amendment's guarantee to the accused of a public trial gave neither the public nor the press an enforceable right of access to a *pre* trial suppression hearing. One concurring opinion specifically emphasized that "a hearing on a motion before trial to suppress evidence is not a *trial*...." Moreover, the Court did not decide whether the First and Fourteenth Amendments guarantee a right of the public to attend trials.

But here for the first time the Court is asked to decide whether a criminal trial itself may be closed to the public upon the unopposed request of a defendant, without any demonstration that closure is required to protect the defendant's superior right to a fair trial, or that some other overriding consideration requires closure.

A

The origins of the proceeding which has become the modern criminal trial in Anglo-American justice can be traced back beyond reliable historical records. We need not here review all details of its development, but a summary of that history is instructive. What is significant for present purposes is that throughout its evolution, the trial has been open to all who care to observe.

In the days before the Norman Conquest, cases in England were generally brought before moots, such as the local court of the hundred or the county court, which were attended by the freemen of the community. Somewhat like modern jury duty, attendance at these early meetings was compulsory on the part of the freemen, who were called upon to render judgment. With the gradual evolution of the jury system in the years after the Norman Conquest, the duty of all freemen to attend trials to render judgment was relaxed, but there is no indication that criminal trials did not remain public.

We have found nothing to suggest that the presumptive openness of the trial, which English courts were later to call "one of the essential qualities of a court of justice," *Daubney v. Cooper*, 10 B. & C. 237, 240, 109 Eng.Rep. 438, 440 (K. B. 1829), was not also an attribute of the judicial systems of colonial America. In Virginia, for example, such records as there are of early criminal trials indicate that they were open, and nothing to the contrary has been cited.

Other contemporary writings confirm the recognition that part of the very nature of a criminal trial was its openness to those who wished to attend. Perhaps the best indication of this is found in an address to the inhabitants of Quebec which was drafted by a committee consisting of Thomas Cushing, Richard Henry Lee, and John Dickinson and approved by the First Continental Congress on October 26, 1774. 1 Journals of the Continental Congress, 1774–1789, pp. 101, 105 (1904) (Journals). This address, written to explain the position of the Colonies and to gain the support of the people of Quebec, is an "exposition of the fundamental rights of the colonists, as they were understood by a representative assembly chosen from all the colonies." Because it was intended for the inhabitants of Quebec, who had been "educated under another form of government" and had only recently become English subjects, it was thought desirable for the Continental Congress to explain "the inestimable advantages of a free English constitution of government, which it is the privilege of all English subjects to enjoy." 1 Journals 106.

"[One] great right is that of trial by jury. This provides, that neither life, liberty nor property, can be taken from the possessor, until twelve of his unexceptionable countrymen and peers of his vicinage, who from that neighbourhood may reasonably be supposed to be acquainted with his character, and the characters of the witnesses, upon a fair trial, and full enquiry, face to face, *in open Court, before as many of the people as chuse to attend*, shall pass their sentence upon oath against him…

B

As we have shown, and as was shown in both the Court's opinion and the dissent in *Gannett*, 443 U.S., at 384, 386, n. 15, 418–425, the historical evidence demonstrates conclusively that at the time when our organic laws were adopted, criminal trials both here and in England had long been presumptively open. This is no quirk of history; rather, it has long been recognized as an indispensible attribute of an Anglo-American trial.

This observation raises the important point that "[t]he publicity of a judicial proceeding is a requirement of much broader bearing than its mere effect upon the quality of testimony." The early history of open trials in part reflects the widespread acknowledgment, long before there were behavioral scientists, that public trials had significant community therapeutic value. Even without such experts to frame the concept in words, people sensed from experience and observation that, especially in the administration of criminal justice, the means used to achieve justice must have the support derived from public acceptance of both the process and its results. When a shocking crime occurs, a community reaction of outrage and public protest often follows. Thereafter the open processes of justice serve an important prophylactic purpose, providing an outlet for community concern, hostility, and emotion. Without an awareness that society's responses to criminal conduct are underway, natural human reactions of outrage and protest are frustrated and may manifest themselves in some form of vengeful "self-help," as indeed they did regularly in the activities of vigilante "committees" on our frontiers. "The accusation and conviction or acquittal, as much perhaps as the execution of punishment, operat[e] to restore the imbalance which was created by the offense or public charge, to reaffirm the temporarily lost feeling of security and, perhaps, to satisfy that latent 'urge to punish.'" Civilized societies withdraw both from the victim and the vigilante the enforcement of criminal laws, but they cannot erase from people's consciousness the fundamental, natural yearning to see justice done—or even the urge for retribution. The crucial prophylactic aspects of the administration of justice cannot function in the dark; no community catharsis can occur if justice is "done in a corner [or] in any covert manner." It is not enough to say that results alone will satiate the natural community desire for "satisfaction." A result considered untoward may undermine public confidence, and where the trial has been concealed from public view an unexpected outcome can cause a reaction that the system at best has failed and at worst has been corrupted. To work effectively, it is important that society's criminal process "satisfy the appearance of and the appearance of justice can best be provided by allowing people to observe it."

> "The educative effect of public attendance is a material advantage. Not only is respect for the law increased and intelligent acquaintance acquired with the methods of government, but a strong confidence in judicial remedies is secured which could never be inspired by a system of secrecy."

In earlier times, both in England and America, attendance at court was a common mode of "passing the time." With the press, cinema, and electronic media now supplying the representations or reality of the real life drama once available only in the courtroom, attendance at court is no longer a widespread pastime. Yet "[i]t is not unrealistic even in this day to believe that public inclusion affords citizens a form of legal education and hopefully promotes confidence in the fair administration of justice." Instead of acquiring information about trials by firsthand observation or by word of mouth from those who attended, people now acquire it chiefly through the print and electronic media. In a sense, this validates the media claim of functioning as surrogates for the public. While media representatives enjoy the same right of access as the public, they often are provided special seating and priority of entry so that they may report what people in attendance have seen and heard. This "contribute[s] to public understanding of the rule of law and to comprehension of the functioning of the entire criminal justice system...." *Nebraska Press Assn. v. Stuart*, 427 U.S., at 587.

C

From this unbroken, uncontradicted history, supported by reasons as valid today as in centuries past, we are bound to conclude that a presumption of openness inheres in the very nature of a criminal trial under our system of justice. This conclusion is hardly novel; without a direct holding on the issue, the Court has voiced its recognition of it in a variety of contexts over the years.

Despite the history of criminal trials being presumptively open since long before the Constitution, the State presses its contention that neither the Constitution nor the Bill of Rights contains any provision which by its terms guarantees to the public the right to attend criminal trials. Standing alone, this is correct, but there remains the question whether, absent an explicit provision, the Constitution affords protection against exclusion of the public from criminal trials.

III

A

The First Amendment, in conjunction with the Fourteenth, prohibits governments from "abridging the freedom of speech, or of the press; or the right of the people peaceably to assemble, and to petition the Government for a redress of grievances." These expressly guaranteed freedoms share a common core purpose of assuring freedom of communication on matters relating to the functioning of government. Plainly it would be difficult to single out any aspect of government of higher concern and importance to the people than the manner in which criminal trials are conducted; as we have shown, recognition of this pervades the centuries-old history of open trials and the opinions of this Court.

The Bill of Rights was enacted against the backdrop of the long history of trials being presumptively open. Public access to trials was then regarded as an important aspect of the process itself; the conduct of trials "before as many of the people as chuse to attend" was regarded as one of "the inestimable advantages of a free English constitution of government." "[T]he First Amendment goes beyond protection of the press and the self-expression of individuals to prohibit from limiting the stock of information from which members of the public may draw." What this means in the context of trials is that the First Amendment guarantees of speech and press, standing alone, prohibit government from summarily closing courtroom doors which had long been open to the public at the time that Amendment was adopted. "For the First Amendment does not speak equivocally. ... It must be taken as a command of the broadest scope that explicit language, read in the context of a liberty-loving society, will allow."

It is not crucial whether we describe this right to attend criminal trials to hear, see, and communicate observations concerning them as a "right of access," cf. *Gannett, supra*, 443 U.S., at 397; *Saxbe v. Washington Post Co.*, 417 U.S. 843 (1974); *Pell v. Procunier*, 417 U.S. 817 (1974), or a "right to gather information," for we have recognized that "without some protection for seeking out the news, freedom of the press could be eviscerated." The explicit, guaranteed rights to speak and to publish concerning what takes place at a trial would lose much meaning if access to observe the trial could, as it was here, be foreclosed arbitrarily.

B

The State argues that the Constitution nowhere spells out a guarantee for the right of the public to attend trials, and that accordingly no such right is protected. The possibility that such a contention could be made did not escape the notice of the Constitution's draftsmen; they were concerned that some important rights might be thought disparaged because not specifically guaranteed. It was even argued that because of this danger no Bill of Rights should be adopted. See, *e. g.*, The Federalist No. 84 (A. Hamilton). In a letter to Thomas Jefferson in October 1788, James Madison explained why he, although "in favor of a bill of rights," had "not viewed it in an important light" up to that time: "I conceive that in a certain degree ... the rights in question are reserved by the manner in which the federal powers are granted." He went on to state that "there is great reason to fear that a positive declaration of some of the most essential rights could not be obtained in the requisite latitude." 5 Writings of James Madison 271 (G. Hunt ed. 1904).
But arguments such as the State makes have not precluded recognition of important rights not enumerated. Notwithstanding the appropriate caution against reading into the Constitution rights not explicitly defined, the Court has acknowledged that certain unarticulated rights are implicit in enumerated guarantees. For example, the rights of association and of privacy, the right to be presumed innocent, and the right to be judged by a standard of proof beyond a reasonable doubt in a criminal trial, as well as the right to travel, appear nowhere in the Constitution or Bill of Rights. Yet these important but unarticulated rights have nonetheless been found to share constitutional protection in common with explicit guarantees. The concerns expressed by Madison and others have thus been resolved; fundamental rights, even though not expressly guaranteed, have been recognized by the Court as indispensable to the enjoyment of rights explicitly defined.
We hold that the right to attend criminal trials is implicit in the guarantees of the First Amendment; without the freedom to attend such trials, which people have exercised for centuries, important aspects of freedom of speech and "of the press could be eviscerated."
Reversed.

Mr. Justice Powell took no part in the consideration or decision of this case.
Mr. Justice White concurring.

This case would have been unnecessary had *Gannett Co. v. DePasquale*, 443 U.S. 368 (1979), construed the Sixth Amendment to forbid excluding the public from criminal proceedings except in narrowly defined circumstances. But the Court there rejected the submission of four of us to this effect, thus requiring that the First Amendment issue involved here be addressed.

Garcia v. San Antonio Metropolitan Transit Authority, 469 U.S. 528 (1985)

Justice Blackmun delivered the opinion of the Court.

We revisit in these cases an issue raised in *National League of Cities v. Usery*, 426 U.S. 833, (1976). In that litigation, this Court, by a sharply divided vote, ruled that the Commerce Clause does not empower Congress to enforce the minimum-wage and overtime provisions of the Fair Labor Standards Act (FLSA) against the States "in areas of traditional governmental functions." Although *National League of Cities* supplied some examples of "traditional governmental functions," it did not offer a general explanation of how a "traditional" function is to be distinguished from a "nontraditional" one. Since then, federal and state courts have struggled with the task, thus imposed, of identifying a traditional function for purposes of state immunity under the Commerce Clause.

In the present cases, a Federal District Court concluded that municipal ownership and operation of a mass-transit system is a traditional governmental function and thus, under *National League of Cities*, is exempt from the obligations imposed by the FLSA. Faced with the identical question, three Federal Courts of Appeals and one state appellate court have reached the opposite conclusion.

Our examination of this "function" standard applied in these and other cases over the last eight years now persuades us that the attempt to draw the boundaries of state regulatory immunity in terms of "traditional governmental function" is not only unworkable but is also inconsistent with established principles of federalism and, indeed, with those very federalism principles on which *National League of Cities* purported to rest. That case, accordingly, is overruled.

I

The history of public transportation in San Antonio, Tex., is characteristic of the history of local mass transit in the United States generally. Passenger transportation for hire within San Antonio originally was provided on a private basis by a local transportation company. In 1913, the Texas Legislature authorized the State's municipalities to regulate vehicles providing carriage for hire. Two years later, San Antonio enacted an ordinance setting forth franchising, insurance, and safety requirements for passenger vehicles operated for hire. The city continued to rely on such publicly regulated private mass transit until 1959, when it purchased the privately owned San Antonio Transit Company and replaced it with a public authority known as the San Antonio Transit System (SATS). SATS operated until 1978, when the city transferred its facilities and equipment to appellee San Antonio Metropolitan Transit Authority (SAMTA), a public mass-transit authority organized on a countywide basis. SAMTA currently is the major provider of transportation in the San Antonio metropolitan area; between 1978 and 1980 alone, its vehicles traveled over 26 million route miles and carried over 63 million passengers.

The present controversy concerns the extent to which SAMTA may be subjected to the minimum-wage and overtime requirements of the FLSA. When the FLSA was enacted in 1938, its wage and overtime provisions did not apply to local mass-transit employees or, indeed, to employees of state and local governments. In 1961, Congress extended minimum-wage coverage to employees of any private mass-transit carrier whose annual gross revenue was not less than $1 million. Fair Labor Standards Amendments of 1961, Five years later, Congress extended FLSA coverage to state and local-government employees for the first time by withdrawing the minimum-wage and overtime exemptions from public hospitals, schools, and mass-transit carriers whose rates and services were subject to state regulation. Fair Labor Standards Amendments of 1966, §§ 102(a) and (b), 80 Stat. 831. At the same time, Congress eliminated the overtime exemption for all mass-transit employees other than drivers, operators, and conductors. § 206(c), 80 Stat. 836. The application of the FLSA to public schools and hospitals was ruled to be within Congress' power under the Commerce Clause. *Maryland v. Wirtz*, 392 U.S. 183 (1968).

The FLSA obligations of public mass-transit systems like SATS were expanded in 1974 when Congress provided for the progressive repeal of the surviving overtime exemption for mass-transit employees. Fair Labor Standards Amendments of 1974, § 21(b), 88 Stat. 68. Congress simultaneously brought the States and their subdivisions further within the ambit of the FLSA by extending FLSA coverage to virtually all state and local-government employees. §§ 6(a)(1) and (6), 88 Stat. 58, 60, 29 U.S.C. §§ 203(d) and (x). SATS complied with the FLSA's overtime requirements until 1976, when this Court, in *National League of Cities*, overruled *Maryland v. Wirtz*, and held that the FLSA could not be applied constitutionally to the "traditional governmental functions" of state and local governments. Four months after *National League of Cities* was handed down, SATS informed its employees that the decision relieved SATS of its overtime obligations under the FLSA.

Matters rested there until September 17, 1979, when the Wage and Hour Administration of the Department of Labor issued an opinion that SAMTA's operations "are not constitutionally immune from the application of the Fair Labor Standards Act" under *National League of Cities*. Opinion WH-499, 6 LRR 91:1138. On November 21 of that year, SAMTA filed this action against the Secretary of Labor in the United States District Court for the Western District of Texas. It sought a declaratory judgment that, contrary to the Wage and Hour Administration's determination, *National League of Cities* precluded the application of the FLSA's overtime requirements to SAMTA's operations. The Secretary counterclaimed under 29 U.S.C. § 217 for enforcement of the overtime and recordkeeping requirements of the FLSA. On the same day that SAMTA filed its action, appellant Garcia and several other SAMTA employees brought suit against SAMTA in the same District Court for overtime pay under the FLSA. The District Court has stayed that action pending the outcome of these cases, but it allowed Garcia to intervene in the present litigation as a defendant in support of the Secretary. One month after SAMTA brought suit, the Department of Labor formally amended its FLSA interpretive regulations to provide that publicly owned local mass-transit systems are not entitled to immunity under National League of Cities.

On November 17, 1981, the District Court granted SAMTA's motion for summary judgment and denied the Secretary's and Garcia's cross-motion for partial summary judgment. Without further explanation, the District Court ruled that "local public mass transit systems (including [SAMTA]) constitute integral operations in areas of traditional governmental functions" under *National League of Cities*. The Secretary and Garcia both appealed directly to this Court pursuant to 28 U.S.C. § 1252. During the pendency of those appeals, *Transportation Union v. Long Island R. Co.*, 455 U.S. 678 (1982), was decided. In that case, the Court ruled that commuter rail service provided by the state-owned Long Island Rail Road did not constitute a "traditional governmental function" and hence did not enjoy constitutional immunity, under *National League of Cities*, from the requirements of the Railway Labor Act. Thereafter, it vacated the District Court's judgment in the present cases and remanded them for further consideration in the light of *Long Island*.

On remand, the District Court adhered to its original view and again entered judgment for SAMTA.. The court looked first to what it regarded as the "historical reality" of state involvement in mass transit. It recognized that States not always had owned and operated mass-transit systems, but concluded that they had engaged in a longstanding pattern of public regulation, and that this regulatory tradition gave rise to an "inference of sovereignty." The court next looked to the record of federal involvement in the field and concluded that constitutional immunity would not result in an erosion of federal authority with respect to state-owned mass-transit systems, because many federal statutes themselves contain exemptions for States and thus make the withdrawal of federal regulatory power over public mass-transit systems a supervening federal policy. Although the Federal Government's authority over employee wages under the FLSA obviously would be eroded, Congress had not asserted any interest in the wages of public mass-transit employees until 1966 and hence had not established a longstanding federal interest in the field, in contrast to the century-old federal regulatory presence in the railroad industry found significant for the decision in *Long Island*. Finally, the court compared mass transit to the list of functions identified as constitutionally immune in *National League of Cities* and concluded that it did not differ from those functions in any material respect. The court stated: "If transit is to be distinguished from the exempt [*National League of Cities*] functions it will have to be by identifying a traditional state function in the same way pornography is sometimes identified: someone knows it when they see it, but they can't describe it."

The Secretary and Garcia again took direct appeals from the District Court's judgment. We noted probable jurisdiction. After initial argument, the cases were restored to our calendar for reargument, and the parties were requested to brief and argue the following additional question:

"Whether or not the principles of the Tenth Amendment as set forth in *National League of Cities v. Usery*, 426 U.S. 833 (1976), should be reconsidered?"

II

The prerequisites for governmental immunity under *National League of Cities* were summarized by this Court in Hodel. Under that summary, four conditions must be satisfied before a state activity may be deemed immune from a particular federal regulation under the Commerce Clause. First, it is said that the federal statute at issue must regulate "the 'States as States.'" Second, the statute must "address matters that are indisputably 'attribute[s] of state sovereignty.'" Third, state compliance with the federal obligation must "directly impair [the States'] ability 'to structure integral operations in areas of traditional governmental functions.'" Finally, the relation of state and federal interests must not be such that "the nature of the federal interest ... justifies state submission." 452 U.S., at 287–288, and n. 29, 101 S.Ct., at 2365–2366, and n. 29, quoting *National League of Cities*, 426 U.S., at 845, 852. The controversy in the present cases has focused on the third *Hodel* requirement— that the challenged federal statute trench on "traditional governmental functions." The District Court voiced a common concern: "Despite the abundance of adjectives, identifying which particular state functions are immune remains difficult." Just how troublesome the task has been is revealed by the results reached in other federal cases. Thus, courts have held that regulating ambulance services, licensing automobile drivers, operating a municipal airport, performing solid waste disposal, and operating a highway authority, are functions *protected* under *National League of Cities*. At the same time, courts have held that issuance of industrial development bonds, regulation of intrastate natural gas sales, regulation of traffic on public roads, regulation of air transportation, operation of a telephone system, leasing and sale of natural gas, operation of a mental health facility, and provision of in-house domestic services for the aged and handicapped, are *not* entitled to immunity. We find it difficult, if not impossible, to identify an organizing principle that places each of the cases in the first group on one side of a line and each of the cases in the second group on the other side. The constitutional distinction between licensing drivers and regulating traffic, for example, or between operating a highway authority and operating a mental health facility, is elusive at best.

Thus far, this Court itself has made little headway in defining the scope of the governmental functions deemed protected under *National League of Cities*. In that case the Court set forth examples of protected and unprotected functions, but provided no explanation of how those examples were identified. The only other case in which the Court has had occasion to address the problem is *Long Island*. We there observed: "The determination of whether a federal law impairs a state's authority with respect to 'areas of traditional [state] functions' may at times be a difficult one." quoting *National League of Cities*, 426 U.S., at 852. The accuracy of that statement is demonstrated by this Court's own difficulties in *Long Island* in developing a workable standard for "traditional governmental functions." We relied in large part there on "the *historical reality* that the operation of railroads is not among the functions *traditionally* performed by state and local governments," but we simultaneously disavowed "a static historical view of state functions generally immune from federal regulation." 455 U.S., at 686, 102 S.Ct., at 1355 (first emphasis added; second emphasis in original). We held that the inquiry into a particular function's "traditional" nature was merely a means of determining whether the federal statute at issue unduly handicaps "basic state prerogatives," but we did not offer an explanation of what makes one state function a "basic prerogative" and another function not basic. Finally, having disclaimed a rigid reliance on the historical pedigree of state involvement in a particular area, we nonetheless found it appropriate to emphasize the extended historical record of *federal* involvement in the field of rail transportation.

Many constitutional standards involve "undoubte[d] … gray areas," and, despite the difficulties that this Court and other courts have encountered so far, it normally might be fair to venture the assumption that case-by-case development would lead to a workable standard for determining whether a particular governmental function should be immune from federal regulation under the Commerce Clause. A further cautionary note is sounded, however, by the Court's experience in the related field of state immunity from federal taxation. In *South Carolina v. United States*, 199 U.S. 437, (1905), the Court held for the first time that the state tax immunity recognized in *Collector v. Day*, 11 Wall. 113, 20 L.Ed. 122 (1871), extended only to the "ordinary" and "strictly governmental" instrumentalities of state governments and not to instrumentalities "used by the State in the carrying on of an ordinary private business." While the Court applied the distinction outlined in *South Carolina* for the following 40 years, at no time during that period did the Court develop a consistent formulation of the kinds of governmental functions that were entitled to immunity. The Court identified the protected functions at various times as "essential," "usual," "traditional," or "strictly governmental." While "these differences in phraseology … must not be too literally contradistinguished," they reflect an inability to specify precisely what aspects of a governmental function made it necessary to the "unimpaired existence" of the States. Indeed, the Court ultimately chose "not, by an attempt to formulate any general test, [to] risk embarrassing the decision of cases [concerning] activities of a different kind which may arise in the future.

If these tax-immunity cases had any common thread, it was in the attempt to distinguish between "governmental" and "proprietary" functions. To say that the distinction between "governmental" and "proprietary" proved to be stable, however, would be something of an overstatement. In 1911, for example, the Court declared that the provision of a municipal water supply "is no part of the essential governmental functions of a State." Twenty-six years later, without any intervening change in the applicable legal standards, the Court simply rejected its earlier position and decided that the provision of a municipal water supply *was* immune from federal taxation as an essential governmental function, even though municipal water-works long had been operated for profit by private industry. At the same time that the Court was holding a municipal water supply to be immune from federal taxes, it had held that a state-run commuter rail system was *not* immune. Justice Black, in *Helvering v. Gerhardt*, 304 U.S. 405, 427, (1938), was moved to observe: "An implied constitutional distinction which taxes income of an officer of a state-operated transportation system and exempts income of the manager of a municipal water works system manifests the uncertainty created by the 'essential' and 'non-essential' test" (concurring opinion). It was this uncertainty and instability that led the Court shortly thereafter, in *New York v. United States*, 326 U.S. 572 (1946), unanimously to conclude that the distinction between "governmental" and "proprietary" functions was "untenable" and must be abandoned.

The distinction the Court discarded as unworkable in the field of tax immunity has proved no more fruitful in the field of regulatory immunity under the Commerce Clause. Neither do any of the alternative standards that might be employed to distinguish between protected and unprotected governmental functions appear manageable. We rejected the possibility of making immunity turn on a purely historical standard of "tradition" in *Long Island*, and properly so. The most obvious defect of a historical approach to state immunity is that it prevents a court from accommodating changes in the historical functions of States, changes that have resulted in a number of once-private functions like education being assumed by the States and their subdivisions. At the same time, the only apparent virtue of a rigorous historical standard, namely, its promise of a reasonably objective measure for state immunity, is illusory. Reliance on history as an organizing principle results in line-drawing of the most arbitrary sort; the genesis of state governmental functions stretches over a historical continuum from before the Revolution to the present, and courts would have to decide by fiat precisely how longstanding a pattern of state involvement had to be for federal regulatory authority to be defeated.

A nonhistorical standard for selecting immune governmental functions is likely to be just as unworkable as is a historical standard. The goal of identifying "uniquely" governmental functions, for example, has been rejected by the Court in the field of governmental tort liability in part because the notion of a "uniquely" governmental function is unmanageable.

We believe, however, that there is a more fundamental problem at work here, a problem that explains why the Court was never able to provide a basis for the governmental/proprietary distinction in the intergovernmental tax-immunity cases and why an attempt to draw similar distinctions with respect to federal regulatory authority under *National League of Cities* is unlikely to succeed regardless of how the distinctions are phrased. The problem is that neither the governmental/proprietary distinction nor any other that purports to separate out important governmental functions can be faithful to the role of federalism in a democratic society. The essence of our federal system is that within the realm of authority left open to them under the Constitution, the States must be equally free to engage in any activity that their citizens choose for the common weal, no matter how unorthodox or unnecessary anyone else—including the judiciary—deems state involvement to be. Any rule of state immunity that looks to the "traditional," "integral," or "necessary" nature of governmental functions inevitably invites an unelected federal judiciary to make decisions about which state policies it favors and which ones it dislikes. We therefore now reject, as unsound in principle and unworkable in practice, a rule of state immunity from federal regulation that turns on a judicial appraisal of whether a particular governmental function is "integral" or "traditional." Any such rule leads to inconsistent results at the same time that it disserves principles of democratic self-governance, and it breeds inconsistency precisely because it is divorced from those principles. If there are to be limits on the Federal Government's power to interfere with state functions—as undoubtedly there are—we must look elsewhere to find them. We accordingly return to the underlying issue that confronted this Court in *National League of Cities*—the manner in which the Constitution insulates States from the reach of Congress' power under the Commerce Clause.

III

The central theme of *National League of Cities* was that the States occupy a special position in our constitutional system and that the scope of Congress' authority under the Commerce Clause must reflect that position. Of course, the Commerce Clause by its specific language does not provide any special limitation on Congress' actions with respect to the States. It is equally true, however, that the text of the Constitution provides the beginning rather than the final answer to every inquiry into questions of federalism, for "[b]ehind the words of the constitutional provisions are postulates which limit and control." *National League of Cities* reflected the general conviction that the Constitution precludes "the National Government [from] devour[ing] the essentials of state sovereignty." In order to be faithful to the underlying federal premises of the Constitution, courts must look for the "postulates which limit and control."

What has proved problematic is not the perception that the Constitution's federal structure imposes limitations on the Commerce Clause, but rather the nature and content of those limitations. One approach to defining the limits on Congress' authority to regulate the States under the Commerce Clause is to identify certain underlying elements of political sovereignty that are deemed essential to the States' "separate and independent existence." This approach obviously underlay the Court's use of the "traditional governmental function" concept in *National League of Cities*. It also has led to the separate requirement that the challenged federal statute "address matters that are indisputably 'attribute[s]' of state sovereignty.'" In *National League of Cities* itself, for example, the Court concluded that decisions by a State concerning the wages and hours of its employees are an "undoubted attribute of state sovereignty." The opinion did not explain what aspects of such decisions made them such an "undoubted attribute," and the Court since then has remarked on the uncertain scope of the concept. The point of the inquiry, however, has remained to single out particular features of a State's internal governance that are deemed to be intrinsic parts of state sovereignty.

We doubt that courts ultimately can identify principled constitutional limitations on the scope of Congress' Commerce Clause powers over the States merely by relying on *a priori* definitions of state sovereignty. In part, this is because of the elusiveness of objective criteria for "fundamental" elements of state sovereignty, a problem we have witnessed in the search for "traditional governmental functions." There is, however, a more fundamental reason: the sovereignty of the States is limited by the Constitution itself. A variety of sovereign powers, for example, are withdrawn from the States by Article I, § 10. Section 8 of the same Article works an equally sharp contraction of state sovereignty by authorizing Congress to exercise a wide range of legislative powers and (in conjunction with the Supremacy Clause of Article VI) to displace contrary state legislation. By providing for final review of questions of federal law in this Court, Article III curtails the sovereign power of the States' judiciaries to make authoritative determinations of law. See *Martin v. Hunter's Lessee,* 1 Wheat. 304, 4 L.Ed. 97 (1816). Finally, the developed application, through the Fourteenth Amendment, of the greater part of the Bill of Rights to the States limits the sovereign authority that States otherwise would possess to legislate with respect to their citizens and to conduct their own affairs.

It is so ordered.

Justice Powell, with Whom the Chief Justice, Justice Rehnquist, and Justice O'Connor Join, Dissenting.

The Court today, in its 5–4 decision, overrules *National League of Cities v. Usery,* a case in which we held that Congress lacked authority to impose the requirements of the Fair Labor Standards Act on state and local governments. Because I believe this decision substantially alters the federal system embodied in the Constitution, I dissent.

I

There are, of course, numerous examples over the history of this Court in which prior decisions have been reconsidered and overruled. There have been few cases, however, in which the principle of *stare decisis* and the rationale of recent decisions were ignored as abruptly as we now witness.

Although the doctrine is not rigidly applied to constitutional questions, "any departure from the doctrine of *stare decisis* demands special justification." *Arizona v. Rumsey,* 467 U.S. 203, 212 (1984). In the present cases, the five Justices who compose the majority today participated in *National League of Cities* and the cases reaffirming it. The stability of judicial decision, and with it respect for the authority of this Court, are not served by the precipitate overruling of multiple precedents that we witness in these cases.

Whatever effect the Court's decision may have in weakening the application of *stare decisis,* it is likely to be less important than what the Court has done to the Constitution itself. A unique feature of the United States is the *federal* system of government guaranteed by the Constitution and implicit in the very name of our country. Despite some genuflecting in the Court's opinion to the concept of federalism, today's decision effectively reduces the Tenth Amendment to meaningless rhetoric when Congress acts pursuant to the Commerce Clause. The Court holds that the Fair Labor Standards Act (FLSA) "contravened no affirmative limit on Congress' power under the Commerce Clause" to determine the wage rates and hours of employment of all state and local employees.

To leave no doubt about its intention, the Court renounces its decision in *National League of Cities* because it "inevitably invites an unelected federal judiciary to make decisions about which state policies it favors and which ones it dislikes." In other words, the extent to which the States may exercise their authority, when Congress purports to act under the Commerce Clause, henceforth is to be determined from time to time by political decisions made by members of the Federal Government, decisions the Court says will not be subject to judicial review. I note that it does not seem to have occurred to the Court that *it*—an unelected majority of five Justices—today rejects almost 200 years of the understanding of the constitutional status of federalism. In doing so, there is only a single passing reference to the Tenth Amendment. Nor is so much as a dictum of any court cited in support of the view that the role of the States in the federal system may depend upon the grace of elected federal officials, rather than on the Constitution as interpreted by this Court.

4.   The Rehnquist Court

INTRODUCTION

William Rehnquist was supposed to be one of President Richard Nixon's Justices. In many ways he fulfilled that promise.

Chapter 3 described how Richard Nixon in 1968 ran as a law and order president, playing upon the middle-class anxieties over the demonstrations and protests associated with the anti-war and civil rights movements. He decried many Warren Court decisions that he and other conservatives viewed as being soft on crime or hamstringing the ability of the police to do their job. The exclusionary rule from *Mapp v. Ohio*[1] and the *Miranda* warnings from *Miranda v. Arizona*[2] were two decisions specifically that he and other law and order people pointed to as tipping the balance away from the police and to the defendant.

Nixon hoped that he could shift the balance of the Court with the appointment of Justices. He was given his first opportunity in 1969, when he was able to replace Earl Warren with Warren Burger as Chief Justice. Nixon had three more appointees, Harry Blackmun in 1970 (–1994), Lewis Powell in 1971 (–1987), and then William Rehnquist in 1972 (–2005). Rehnquist was an Assistant Attorney General for Nixon, and reliably conservative politically, and presumably with his appointment to the Supreme Court he would push it to the right and reverse many of the Warren Court decisions he and Nixon disliked. The Burger Court did reverse many precedents, as discussed in Chapter 3. But because of the holdover of several of the Warren Court liberal stalwarts, such as William Brennan, and because it is not easy simply to overturn a precedent at will, the Burger Court's legacy was more mixed in terms of how successfully it moved the Court to the right on legal issues.

But in 1986 things changed. Warren Burger retired and Ronald Reagan nominated Rehnquist to become the Chief Justice. Earlier in 1981 Potter Stewart (1958–1981) retired and was replaced by Sandra Day O'Connor (1981–2006), Antonin Scalia (1986–2016) replaced Rehnquist as an Associate

---

[1]   367 U.S. 643 (1961).
[2]   384 U.S. 436 (1966).

Justice, and Lewis Powell was eventually replaced by Anthony Kennedy (1988–2018) after President Reagan was unsuccessful in elevating Court of Appeals Judge Robert Bork to the Supreme Court. Add to this the appointments in 1990 and 1991 by George H.W. Bush respectively of David Souter (1990–2009) and Clarence Thomas (1991–) and it looked like the Court that conservatives hoped to have had under Chief Justice Burger would now occur under Rehnquist.

The Rehnquist Court did deliver on many of the hopes that legal and political conservatives had. It was a Court that supported the death penalty, carved holes in the exclusionary rule of Fourth Amendment search warrant requirements, defended states' rights and property rights. It also had to address racial, gender, and LGBTQ civil rights or discrimination issues. In many areas of the law the Court cut new ground and therefore did not actually have to address or reverse precedent, such as with voting rights or eminent domain; it could distinguish precedents or the law without actually overturning past decisions. But it did overturn 30 constitutional precedents, two fewer than the Warren and Burger Courts each, but at a slightly higher level of reversal than the Burger Court. Some noted this pattern, suggesting that changing personnel on the Court, who may be less bound by precedent than existing Justices, accounted for this.[3]

But what was notable about the Rehnquist Court was the self-awareness that it was overturning precedents, and the need to articulate a theory or set of criteria to consider when do that.[4] Specifically, up to the time of the Rehnquist Court, the constitutional precedents the Court overturned were generally done with less of a theoretical discussion of the basis for why they were rejecting them. In decisions such as *U.S. v. Darby*[5] or *Brown v. Board of Education*[6] the Court was explicit in overturning *Plessy v. Ferguson*[7] and *Hammer v. Dagenhart*[8] respectively. The Court made clear in the former decisions why it thought the latter were incorrect. Even under the Burger Court, when it overturned its own past precedents, such as in *Garcia v. San Antonio Metropolitan Transit Authority*,[9] when it overturned *National League of Cities v. Usery*,[10] the

---

3   Powell, Lewis F. Jr. 1990. *Stare Decisis and Judicial Restraint*, 47 Wash. & Lee L. Rev. 28.
4   Maltz, Earl L. 1994. *No Rules in a Knife Fight: Chief Justice Rehnquist and the Doctrine of Stare Decisis*, 25 Rutgers L.J. 669.
5   312 U.S. 100 (1941).
6   347 U.S. 483 (1954).
7   163 U.S. 537 (1896).
8   247 U.S. 251 (1918).
9   469 U.S. 528 (1985).
10   426 U.S. 833 (1976).

majority explained why it found the previous precedent unworkable, but it did not engage in a broader theoretical discussion of precedent and when it should be adhered to or rejected. That begins to change with the Rehnquist Court.

Starting especially with Chief Justice Rehnquist in *Payne v. Tennessee*,[11] one will begin to hear the phrase "*Stare decisis* is not an inexorable command; [rather, it 'is a principle of policy and not a mechanical formula of adherence to the latest decision.']" Beginning with the Rehnquist Court and continuing into the Roberts Court, the Justices often engage in a very open and conscious discussion of why they are overturning a precedent and the conditions under which precedent should prevail or be abandoned. One will begin quite explicitly to see references to arguments about precedent that were highlighted and discussed in the Introduction of this book, such as reliance interests and appeals to consistency or uniformity. In effect, the Court almost seems to be seeking a theory of precedent.

Why might that be? There are several possible answers. One is simply to claim that the Court is principled, looking for a theory of precedent, and the facts and cases before them afford the Justices the opportunity to do that. A second possible answer is the Court's awareness that the precedent it is overturning is significant and it enjoys a lot of legal and perhaps popular support. For example, consider *Planned Parenthood v. Casey*.[12] This was a heavily publicized and anticipated case where there was an expectation that the Court would overturn *Roe v. Wade*. It did not. Moreover, there was an anticipation that three recent appointments to the Court, Justices O'Connor, Kennedy, and Souter, would vote to overturn *Roe*. They did not. Instead, they wrote the majority opinion, explaining why *Roe* was still good law and why as a precedent it should be followed. Their opinion heavily relies upon a discussion of reliance interests of women.

Similarly, in *Dickerson v. U.S.*,[13] the Court was expected to overturn *Miranda v. Arizona*.[14] It did not and, to the surprise of nearly everyone, Chief Justice Rehnquist wrote the opinion upholding the latter. He again quotes the "inexorable command" language and then proceeds to explain how *Miranda*, whether right or wrong, was settled law, and therefore there had to be some good reason to reject it, which he did not find.

The conscious and overt discussion of when precedent can or should be rejected (from a more theoretical basis) uniquely begins with the Rehnquist Court. It now seems to almost be required going forward, with the Roberts Court

---

[11] 501 U.S. 808 (1991).
[12] 505 U.S. 833 (1992).
[13] 530 U.S. 428 (2000).
[14] 384 U.S. 436 (1966).

similarly compelled to engage in that discussion. As suggested above, perhaps a sign of the Justices becoming more sophisticated in discussing precedent or perhaps a political or legal tool employed to explain or justify why they are overturning or upholding a significant or perhaps apparent "super precedent." Whatever the reason, think of *Payne v. Tennessee* as a precedent for cases challenging constitutional precedents. By that, if *Ashwander v. TVA*[15] articulated basic rules regarding how the Court would approach decision-making and constitutional questions, *Payne* seems to provide a groundwork for how the Court will address precedent. It is a precedent for addressing precedent.

Finally, *Casey* and *Dickerson* are important decisions in a couple of other ways. One is that they point to how, despite the expected political orientations of specific Justices, legal precedent seemed to limit their ability to reject it. This might speak to the power of precedent in terms of how it does constrain decision-making. Two, these two decisions also reveal the ways that the Rehnquist Court did not always decide in ways that were anticipated, in that pure politics or ideology did not always prevail. Three, look at *Casey*, *Dickerson*, and other decisions where precedent is discussed. What types of reliance interests, for example, are favored? How does the Court weigh reliance against settling the law versus getting the decision right? How do specific Justices weigh these factors? All these are important considerations as one thinks about how precedent is being approached by the Court.

Payne v. Tennessee, 501 U.S. 808 (1991)

Chief Justice Rehnquist delivered the opinion of the Court.

> Payne and his *amicus* argue that despite these numerous infirmities in the rule created by *Booth* and *Gathers*, we should adhere to the doctrine of *stare decisis* and stop short of overruling those cases. *Stare decisis* is the preferred course because it promotes the evenhanded, predictable, and consistent development of legal principles, fosters reliance on judicial decisions, and contributes to the actual and perceived integrity of the judicial process. See *Vasquez v. Hillery*, 474 U.S. 254, 265–266, 106 S.Ct. 617, 624–625, 88 L.Ed.2d 598 (1986). Adhering to precedent "is usually the wise policy, because in most matters it is more important that the applicable rule of law be settled than it be settled right." *Burnet v. Coronado Oil & Gas Co.*, 285 U.S. 393, 406, 52 S.Ct. 443, 447, 76 L.Ed. 815 (1932) (Brandeis, J., dissenting). Nevertheless, when governing decisions are unworkable or are badly reasoned, "this Court has never felt constrained to follow precedent." *Smith v. Allwright*, 321 U.S. 649, 665, 64 S.Ct. 757, 765, 88 L.Ed. 987 (1944). *Stare decisis* is not an inexorable command; rather, it "is a principle of policy and not a mechanical formula of adherence to the latest decision." Helvering v. Hallock, 309 U.S. 106, 119, 60 S.Ct. 444, 451, 84 L.Ed. 604 (1940). This is particularly true in

---

[15]   297 U.S. 288 (1936).

constitutional cases, because in such cases "correction through legislative action is practically impossible." *Burnet v. Coronado Oil & Gas Co., supra*, 285 U.S., at 407, 52 S.Ct., at 447 (Brandeis, J., dissenting). Considerations in favor of *stare decisis* are at their acme in cases involving property and contract rights, where reliance interests are involved, see *Swift & Co. v. Wickham*, 382 U.S. 111, 116, 86 S.Ct. 258, 261–262, 15 L.Ed.2d 194 (1965); *Oregon ex rel. State Land Bd. v. Corvallis Sand & Gravel Co.*, 429 U.S. 363, 97 S.Ct. 582, 50 L.Ed.2d 550 (1977); *Burnet v. Coronado Oil & Gas Co., supra*, 285 U.S., at 405–411, 52 S.Ct., at 446–449 (Brandeis, J., dissenting); *United States v. Title Ins. & Trust Co.*, 265 U.S. 472, 44 S.Ct. 621, 68 L.Ed. 1110 (1924); *The Genesee Chief v. Fitzhugh*, 12 How. 443, 458, 13 L.Ed. 1058 (1852); the opposite is true in cases such as the present one involving procedural and evidentiary rules.

Applying these general principles, the Court has during the past 20 Terms overruled in whole or in part 33 of its previous constitutional decisions. *Booth* and *Gathers* were decided by the narrowest of margins, over spirited dissents challenging the basic underpinnings of those decisions. They have been questioned by Members of the Court in later decisions, and have defied consistent application by the lower courts. See *Gathers*, 490 U.S., at 813, 109 S.Ct., at 2212 (O'CONNOR, J., dissenting); *Mills v. Maryland*, 486 U.S. 367, 395–396, 108 S.Ct. 1860, 1875–1876, 100 L.Ed.2d 384 (1988) (REHNQUIST, C.J., dissenting). Reconsidering these decisions now, we conclude, for the reasons heretofore stated, that they were wrongly decided and should be, and now are, overruled. We accordingly affirm the judgment of the Supreme Court of Tennessee.

Planned Parenthood of Southeastern Pennsylvania v. Casey, 505 U.S. 833 (1992)

III

A

The obligation to follow precedent begins with necessity, and a contrary necessity marks its outer limit. With Cardozo, we recognize that no judicial system could do society's work if it eyed each issue afresh in every case that raised it. See B. Cardozo, The Nature of the Judicial Process 149 (1921). Indeed, the very concept of the rule of law underlying our own Constitution requires such continuity over time that a respect for precedent is, by definition, indispensable. At the other extreme, a different necessity would make itself felt if a prior judicial ruling should come to be seen so clearly as error that its enforcement was for that very reason doomed.

Even when the decision to overrule a prior case is not, as in the rare, latter instance, virtually foreordained, it is common wisdom that the rule of *stare decisis* is not an "inexorable command," and certainly it is not such in every constitutional case, see *Burnet v. Coronado Oil & Gas Co.*, 285 U.S. 393, 405–411, 52 S.Ct. 443, 446–449, 76 L.Ed. 815 (1932) (Brandeis, J., dissenting). See also *Payne v. Tennessee*, 501 U.S. 808, 842, 111 S.Ct. 2597, 2617–2618, 115 L.Ed.2d 720 (1991). Rather, when this Court reexamines a prior holding, its judgment is customarily informed by a series of prudential and pragmatic considerations designed to test the consistency of overruling a prior decision with the ideal of the rule of law, and to gauge the respective costs of reaffirming and overruling a prior case. Thus, for example, we may ask whether the rule has proven to be intolerable simply in defying practical workability, *Swift & Co. v. Wickham*, 382 U.S. 111, 116, 86 S.Ct. 258, 261, 15 L.Ed.2d 194 (1965); whether the rule is subject to a kind of reliance that would lend a special hardship to the consequences of overruling and add inequity to the cost of repudiation, *e.g., United States v. Title Ins. & Trust Co.*, 265 U.S. 472, 486, 44 S.Ct. 621, 623, 68 L.Ed. 1110 (1924); whether related principles of law have so far developed as to have left the old rule no more than a remnant of abandoned doctrine, see *Patterson v. McLean Credit Union*, 491 U.S. 164, 173–174, 109 S.Ct. 2363, 2370–2371, 105 L.Ed.2d 132 (1989); or whether facts have so changed, or come to be seen so differently, as to have robbed the old rule of significant application or justification, *e.g., Burnet, supra*, 285 U.S., at 412, 52 S.Ct., at 449 (Brandeis, J., dissenting).

So in this case we may enquire whether *Roe*'s central rule has been found unworkable; whether the rule's limitation on state power could be removed without serious inequity to those who have relied upon it or significant damage to the stability of the society governed by it; whether the law's growth in the intervening years has left *Roe*'s central rule a doctrinal anachronism discounted by society; and whether *Roe*'s premises of fact have so far changed in the ensuing two decades as to render its central holding somehow irrelevant or unjustifiable in dealing with the issue it addressed.

1

Although *Roe* has engendered opposition, it has in no sense proven "unworkable." While *Roe* has, of course, required judicial assessment of state laws affecting the exercise of the choice guaranteed against government infringement, and although the need for such review will remain as a consequence of today's decision, the required determinations fall within judicial competence.

2

The inquiry into reliance counts the cost of a rule's repudiation as it would fall on those who have relied reasonably on the rule's continued application. Since the classic case for weighing reliance heavily in favor of following the earlier rule occurs in the commercial context, see *Payne v. Tennessee, supra*, 501 U.S., at 828, 111 S.Ct., at 2609–2610, where advance planning of great precision is most obviously a necessity, it is no cause for surprise that some would find no reliance worthy of consideration in support of *Roe*.

While neither respondents nor their *amici* in so many words deny that the abortion right invites some reliance prior to its actual exercise, one can readily imagine an argument stressing the dissimilarity of this case to one involving property or contract. Abortion is customarily chosen as an unplanned response to the consequence of unplanned activity or to the failure of conventional birth control, and except on the assumption that no intercourse would have occurred but for *Roe*'s holding, such behavior may appear to justify no reliance claim. Even if reliance could be claimed on that unrealistic assumption, the argument might run, any reliance interest would be *de minimis*. This argument would be premised on the hypothesis that reproductive planning could take virtually immediate account of any sudden restoration of state authority to ban abortions.

To eliminate the issue of reliance that easily, however, one would need to limit cognizable reliance to specific instances of sexual activity. But to do this would be simply to refuse to face the fact that for two decades of economic and social developments, people have organized intimate relationships and made choices that define their views of themselves and their places in society, in reliance on the availability of abortion in the event that contraception should fail. The ability of women to participate equally in the economic and social life of the Nation has been facilitated by their ability to control their reproductive lives. The Constitution serves human values, and while the effect of reliance on *Roe* cannot be exactly measured, neither can the certain cost of overruling *Roe* for people who have ordered their thinking and living around that case be dismissed.

3

No evolution of legal principle has left *Roe*'s doctrinal footings weaker than they were in 1973. No development of constitutional law since the case was decided has implicitly or explicitly left *Roe* behind as a mere survivor of obsolete constitutional thinking.

It will be recognized, of course, that *Roe* stands at an intersection of two lines of decisions, but in whichever doctrinal category one reads the case, the result for present purposes will be the same. The *Roe* Court itself placed its holding in the succession of cases most prominently exemplified by *Griswold v. Connecticut*, 381 U.S. 479, 85 S.Ct. 1678, 14 L.Ed.2d 510 (1965). See *Roe*, 410 U.S., at 152–153, 93 S.Ct., at 726. When it is so seen, *Roe* is clearly in no jeopardy, since subsequent constitutional developments have neither disturbed, nor do they threaten to diminish, the scope of recognized protection accorded to the liberty relating to intimate relationships, the family, and decisions about whether or not to beget or bear a child. See, *e.g., Carey v. Population Services International*, 431 U.S. 678, 97 S.Ct. 2010, 52 L.Ed.2d 675 (1977); *Moore v. East Cleveland*, 431 U.S. 494, 97 S.Ct. 1932, 52 L.Ed.2d 531 (1977).

Roe, however, may be seen not only as an exemplar of *Griswold* liberty but as a rule (whether or not mistaken) of personal autonomy and bodily integrity, with doctrinal affinity to cases recognizing limits on governmental power to mandate medical treatment or to bar its rejection. If so, our cases since *Roe* accord with *Roe*'s view that a State's interest in the protection of life falls short of justifying any plenary override of individual liberty claims.

Finally, one could classify *Roe* as *sui generis*. If the case is so viewed, then there clearly has been no erosion of its central determination. The original holding resting on the concurrence of seven Members of the Court in 1973 was expressly affirmed by a majority of six in 1983, see *Akron v. Akron Center for Reproductive Health, Inc.*, 462 U.S. 416, 103 S.Ct. 2481, 76 L.Ed.2d 687 (*Akron I*), and by a majority of five in 1986, see *Thornburgh v. American College of Obstetricians and Gynecologists*, 476 U.S. 747, 106 S.Ct. 2169, 90 L.Ed.2d 779, expressing adherence to the constitutional ruling despite legislative efforts in some States to test its limits. More recently, in *Webster v. Reproductive Health Services*, 492 U.S. 490, 109 S.Ct. 3040, 106 L.Ed.2d 410 (1989), although two of the present authors questioned the trimester framework in a way consistent with our judgment today, see *id.*, at 518,

109 S.Ct., at 3056 (REHNQUIST, C.J., joined by WHITE and KENNEDY, JJ.); *id.*, at 529, 109 S.Ct., at 3063 (O'CONNOR, J., concurring in part and concurring in judgment), a majority of the Court either decided to reaffirm or declined to address the constitutional validity of the central holding of *Roe*. See *Webster*, 492 U.S., at 521, 109 S.Ct., at 3058 (REHNQUIST, C.J., joined by WHITE and KENNEDY, JJ.); *id.*, at 525–526, 109 S.Ct., at 3060–3061 (O'CONNOR, J., concurring in part and concurring in judgment); *id.*, at 537, 553, 109 S.Ct., at 3067, 3075 (BLACKMUN, J., joined by Brennan and Marshall, JJ., concurring in part and dissenting in part); *id.*, at 561–563, 109 S.Ct., at 3079–3081 (STEVENS, J., concurring in part and dissenting in part).

Nor will courts building upon *Roe* be likely to hand down erroneous decisions as a consequence. Even on the assumption that the central holding of *Roe* was in error, that error would go only to the strength of the state interest in fetal protection, not to the recognition afforded by the Constitution to the woman's liberty. The latter aspect of the decision fits comfortably within the framework of the Court's prior decisions, including *Skinner v. Oklahoma ex rel. Williamson*, 316 U.S. 535, 62 S.Ct. 1110, 86 L.Ed. 1655 (1942); *Griswold, supra*; *Loving v. Virginia*, 388 U.S. 1, 87 S.Ct. 1817, 18 L.Ed.2d 1010 (1967); and *Eisenstadt v. Baird*, 405 U.S. 438, 92 S.Ct. 1029, 31 L.Ed.2d 349 (1972), the holdings of which are "not a series of isolated points," but mark a "rational continuum." *Poe v. Ullman*, 367 U.S., at 543, 81 S.Ct., at 1777 (Harlan, J., dissenting). As we described in *Carey v. Population Services International, supra*, the liberty which encompasses those decisions "includes 'the interest in independence in making certain kinds of important decisions.' While the outer limits of this aspect of [protected liberty] have not been marked by the Court, it is clear that among the decisions that an individual may make without unjustified government interference are personal decisions 'relating to marriage, procreation, contraception, family relationships, and child rearing and education.'" 431 U.S., at 684–685, 97 S.Ct., at 2016 (citations omitted).

The soundness of this prong of the *Roe* analysis is apparent from a consideration of the alternative. If indeed the woman's interest in deciding whether to bear and beget a child had not been recognized as in *Roe*, the State might as readily restrict a woman's right to choose to carry a pregnancy to term as to terminate it, to further asserted state interests in population control, or eugenics, for example. Yet *Roe* has been sensibly relied upon to counter any such suggestions. *E.g., Arnold v. Board of Education of Escambia County, Ala.*, 880 F.2d 305, 311 (CA11 1989) (relying upon *Roe* and concluding that government officials violate the Constitution by coercing a minor to have an abortion); *Avery v. County of Burke*, 660 F.2d 111, 115 (CA4 1981) (county agency inducing teenage girl to undergo unwanted sterilization on the basis of misrepresentation that she had sickle cell trait); see also *In re Quinlan*, 70 N.J. 10, 355 A.2d 647 (relying on *Roe* in finding a right to terminate medical treatment, cert. denied *sub nom. Garger v. New Jersey*, 429 U.S. 922, 97 S.Ct. 319, 50 L.Ed.2d 289 (1976)). In any event, because *Roe*'s scope is confined by the fact of its concern with postconception potential life, a concern otherwise likely to be implicated only by some forms of contraception protected independently under *Griswold* and later cases, any error in *Roe* is unlikely to have serious ramifications in future cases.

4

We have seen how time has overtaken some of *Roe*'s factual assumptions: advances in maternal health care allow for abortions safe to the mother later in pregnancy than was true in 1973, and advances in neonatal care have advanced viability to a point somewhat earlier. But these facts go only to the scheme of time limits on the realization of competing interests, and the divergences from the factual premises of 1973 have no bearing on the validity of *Roe*'s central holding, that viability marks the earliest point at which the State's interest in fetal life is constitutionally adequate to justify a legislative ban on nontherapeutic abortions. The soundness or unsoundness of that constitutional judgment in no sense turns on whether viability occurs at approximately 28 weeks, as was usual at the time of *Roe*, at 23 to 24 weeks, as it sometimes does today, or at some moment even slightly earlier in pregnancy, as it may if fetal respiratory capacity can somehow be enhanced in the future. Whenever it may occur, the attainment of viability may continue to serve as the critical fact, just as it has done since *Roe* was decided; which is to say that no change in *Roe*'s factual underpinning has left its central holding obsolete, and none supports an argument for overruling it.

5

The sum of the precedential enquiry to this point shows *Roe*'s underpinnings unweakened in any way affecting its central holding. While it has engendered disapproval, it has not been unworkable. An entire generation has come of age free to assume *Roe*'s concept of liberty in defining the capacity of women to act in society, and to make reproductive decisions; no erosion of principle going to liberty or personal autonomy has left *Roe*'s central holding a doctrinal remnant; *Roe* portends no developments at odds with other precedent for the analysis of personal liberty; and no changes of fact have rendered viability more or less appropriate as the point at which the balance of interests tips. Within the bounds of normal *stare decisis* analysis, then, and subject to the considerations on which it customarily turns, the stronger argument is for affirming *Roe*'s central holding, with whatever degree of personal reluctance any of us may have, not for overruling it.

Adarand Constructors, Inc. v. Pen, 515 U.S. 200 (1995)

Justice O'Connor announced the judgment of the Court.

I

In 1989, the Central Federal Lands Highway Division (CFLHD), which is part of the United States Department of Transportation (DOT), awarded the prime contract for a highway construction project in Colorado to Mountain Gravel & Construction Company. Mountain Gravel then solicited bids from subcontractors for the guardrail portion of the contract. Adarand, a Colorado-based highway construction company specializing in guardrail work, submitted the low bid. Gonzales Construction Company also submitted a bid.

The prime contract's terms provide that Mountain Gravel would receive additional compensation if it hired subcontractors certified as small businesses controlled by "socially and economically disadvantaged individuals," Gonzales is certified as such a business; Adarand is not. Mountain Gravel awarded the subcontract to Gonzales, despite Adarand's low bid, and Mountain Gravel's Chief Estimator has submitted an affidavit stating that Mountain Gravel would have accepted Adarand's bid, had it not been for the additional payment it received by hiring Gonzales instead. Federal law requires that a subcontracting clause similar to the one used here must appear in most federal agency contracts, and it also requires the clause to state that "[t]he contractor shall presume that socially and economically disadvantaged individuals include Black Americans, Hispanic Americans, Native Americans, Asian Pacific Americans, and other minorities, or any other individual found to be disadvantaged by the [Small Business] Administration pursuant to section 8(a) of the Small Business Act." Adarand claims that the presumption set forth in that statute discriminates on the basis of race in violation of the Federal Government's Fifth Amendment obligation not to deny anyone equal protection of the laws.

These fairly straightforward facts implicate a complex scheme of federal statutes and regulations, to which we now turn.

The operative clause in the contract in this case reads as follows:

"*Subcontracting.* This subsection is supplemented to include a Disadvantaged Business Enterprise (DBE) Development and Subcontracting Provision as follows:

"Monetary compensation is offered for awarding subcontracts to small business concerns owned and controlled by socially and economically disadvantaged individuals...

II

Adarand, in addition to its general prayer for "such other and further relief as to the Court seems just and equitable," specifically seeks declaratory and injunctive relief against any *future* use of subcontractor compensation clauses.

III

Respondents urge that "[t]he Subcontracting Compensation Clause program is ... a program based on *disadvantage*, not on race," and thus that it is subject only to "the most relaxed judicial scrutiny." To the extent that the statutes and regulations involved in this case are race neutral, we agree. Respondents concede, however, that "the race-based rebuttable presumption used in some certification determinations under the Subcontracting Compensation Clause" is subject to some heightened level of scrutiny. The parties disagree as to what that level should be. (We note, incidentally, that this case concerns only classifications based explicitly on race, and presents none of the additional difficulties posed by laws that, although facially race neutral, result in racially disproportionate impact and are motivated by a racially discriminatory purpose.)

Adarand's claim arises under the Fifth Amendment to the Constitution, which provides that "No person shall ... be deprived of life, liberty, or property, without due process of law." Although this Court has always understood that Clause to provide some measure of protection against *arbitrary* treatment by the Federal Government, it is not as explicit a guarantee of *equal* treatment as the Fourteenth Amendment, which provides that "No *State* shall ... deny to any person within its jurisdiction the equal protection of the laws" (emphasis added). Our cases have accorded varying degrees of significance to the difference in the language of those two Clauses. We think it necessary to revisit the issue here.

B

In 1978, the Court confronted the question whether race-based governmental action designed to *benefit* such groups should also be subject to "the most rigid scrutiny." *Regents of Univ. of Cal. v. Bakke*, 438 U.S. 265, involved an equal protection challenge to a state-run medical school's practice of reserving a number of spaces in its entering class for minority students. The petitioners argued that "strict scrutiny" should apply only to "classifications that disadvantage 'discrete and insular minorities.'" *Bakke* did not produce an opinion for the Court, but Justice Powell's opinion announcing the Court's judgment rejected the argument. In a passage joined by Justice White, Justice Powell wrote that "[t]he guarantee of equal protection cannot mean one thing when applied to one individual and something else when applied to a person of another color." He concluded that "[r]acial and ethnic distinctions of any sort are inherently suspect and thus call for the most exacting judicial examination." On the other hand, four Justices in *Bakke* would have applied a less stringent standard of review to racial classifications "designed to further remedial purposes." And four Justices thought the case should be decided on statutory grounds.

Two years after *Bakke*, the Court faced another challenge to remedial race-based action, this time involving action undertaken by the Federal Government. In *Fullilove v. Klutznick*, 448 U.S. 448,(1980), the Court upheld Congress' inclusion of a 10% set-aside for minority-owned businesses in the Public Works Employment Act of 1977. As in *Bakke*, there was no opinion for the Court. Chief Justice Burger, in an opinion joined by Justices White and Powell, observed that "[a]ny preference based on racial or ethnic criteria must necessarily receive a most searching examination to make sure that it does not conflict with constitutional guarantees." That opinion, however, "d[id] not adopt, either expressly or implicitly, the formulas of analysis articulated in such cases as [*Bakke*]." It employed instead a two-part test which asked, first, "whether the *objectives* of th[e] legislation are within the power of Congress," and second, "whether the limited use of racial and ethnic criteria, in the context presented, is a constitutionally permissible *means* for achieving the congressional objectives." It then upheld the program under that test, adding at the end of the opinion that the program also "would survive judicial review under either 'test' articulated in the several *Bakke* opinions."

In *Wygant v. Jackson Bd. of Ed.*, 476 U.S. 267 (1986), the Court considered a Fourteenth Amendment challenge to another form of remedial racial classification. The issue in *Wygant* was whether a school board could adopt race-based preferences in determining which teachers to lay off. Justice Powell's plurality opinion observed that "the level of scrutiny does not change merely because the challenged classification operates against a group that historically has not been subject to governmental discrimination," and stated the two-part inquiry as "whether the layoff provision is supported by a compelling state purpose and whether the means chosen to accomplish that purpose are narrowly tailored." In other words, "racial classifications of any sort must be subjected to 'strict scrutiny.'" The plurality then concluded that the school board's interest in "providing minority role models for its minority students, as an attempt to alleviate the effects of societal discrimination," was not a compelling interest that could justify the use of a racial classification. It added that "[s]ocietal discrimination, without more, is too amorphous a basis for imposing a racially classified and insisted instead that 'a public employer ... must ensure that, before it embarks on an affirmative-action program, it has convincing evidence that remedial action is warranted.'"

The Court's failure to produce a majority opinion in *Bakke, Fullilove,* and *Wygant* left unresolved the proper analysis for remedial race-based governmental action. The Court resolved the issue, at least in part, in 1989. *Richmond v. J.A. Croson Co.,* 488 U.S. 469 (1989), concerned a city's determination that 30% of its contracting work should go to minority-owned businesses. A majority of the Court in *Croson* held that "the standard of review under the Equal Protection Clause is not dependent on the race of those burdened or benefited by a particular classification," and that the single standard of review for racial classifications should be "strict scrutiny."

With *Croson,* the Court finally agreed that the Fourteenth Amendment requires strict scrutiny of all race-based action by state and local governments. But *Croson* of course had no occasion to declare what standard of review the Fifth Amendment requires for such action taken by the Federal Government. *Croson* observed simply that the Court's "treatment of an exercise of congressional power in *Fullilove* cannot be dispositive here," because *Croson*'s facts did not implicate Congress' broad power under § 5 of the Fourteenth Amendment.

A year later, however, the Court took a surprising turn. *Metro Broadcasting, Inc. v. FCC,* involved a Fifth Amendment challenge to two race-based policies of the Federal Communications Commission (FCC). In *Metro Broadcasting,* the Court repudiated the long-held notion that "it would be unthinkable that the same Constitution would impose a lesser duty on the Federal Government" than it does on a State to afford equal protection of the laws. It did so by holding that "benign" federal racial classifications need only satisfy intermediate scrutiny, even though *Croson* had recently concluded that such classifications enacted by a State must satisfy strict scrutiny.

Applying this test, the Court first noted that the FCC policies at issue did not serve as a remedy for past discrimination. Proceeding on the assumption that the policies were nonetheless "benign," it concluded that they served the "important governmental objective" of "enhancing broadcast diversity," and that they were "substantially related" to that objective. It therefore upheld the policies.

By adopting intermediate scrutiny as the standard of review for congressionally mandated "benign" racial classifications, *Metro Broadcasting* departed from prior cases in two significant respects. First, it turned its back on *Croson*'s explanation of why strict scrutiny of all governmental racial classifications is essential.

Second, *Metro Broadcasting* squarely rejected one of the three propositions established by the Court's earlier equal protection cases, namely, congruence between the standards applicable to federal and state racial classifications, and in so doing also undermined the other two—skepticism of all racial classifications and consistency of treatment irrespective of the race of the burdened or benefited group. Under *Metro Broadcasting,* certain racial classifications ("benign" ones enacted by the Federal Government) should be treated less skeptically than others; and the race of the benefited group is critical to the determination of which standard of review to apply. *Metro Broadcasting* was thus a significant departure from much of what had come before it.

The three propositions undermined by *Metro Broadcasting* all derive from the basic principle that the Fifth and Fourteenth Amendments to the Constitution protect *persons*, not *groups*. It follows from that principle that all governmental action based on race—a *group* classification long recognized as "in most circumstances irrelevant and therefore prohibited," *[and]* should be subjected to detailed judicial inquiry to ensure that the *personal* right to equal protection of the laws has not been infringed. These ideas have long been central to this Court's understanding of equal protection, and holding "benign" state and federal racial classifications to different standards does not square with them. "[A] free people whose institutions are founded upon the doctrine of equality," should tolerate no retreat from the principle that government may treat people differently because of their race only for the most compelling reasons. Accordingly, we hold today that all racial classifications, imposed by whatever federal, state, or local governmental actor, must be analyzed by a reviewing court under strict scrutiny. In other words, such classifications are constitutional only if they are narrowly tailored measures that further compelling governmental interests. To the extent that *Metro Broadcasting* is inconsistent with that holding, it is overruled.

C

"Although adherence to precedent is not rigidly required in constitutional cases, any departure from the doctrine of *stare decisis* demands special justification." *Arizona v. Rumsey*, 467 U.S. 203, 212, (1984). In deciding whether this case presents such justification, we recall Justice Frankfurter's admonition that "*stare decisis* is a principle of policy and not a mechanical formula of adherence to the latest decision, however recent and questionable, when such adherence involves collision with a prior doctrine more embracing in its scope, intrinsically sounder, and verified by experience." *Helvering v. Hallock*, 309 U.S. 106 (1940). Remaining true to an "intrinsically sounder" doctrine established in prior cases better serves the values of *stare decisis* than would following a more recently decided case inconsistent with the decisions that came before it; the latter course would simply compound the recent error and would likely make the unjustified break from previously established doctrine complete. In such a situation, "special justification" exists to depart from the recently decided case.

As we have explained, *Metro Broadcasting* undermined important principles of this Court's equal protection jurisprudence, established in a line of cases stretching back over 50 years. Those principles together stood for an "embracing" and "intrinsically soun[d]" understanding of equal protection "verified by experience," namely, that the Constitution imposes upon federal, state, and local governmental actors the same obligation to respect the personal right to equal protection of the laws. This case therefore presents precisely the situation described by Justice Frankfurter in *Helvering*: We cannot adhere to our most recent decision without colliding with an accepted and established doctrine. We also note that *Metro Broadcasting*'s application of different standards of review to federal and state racial classifications has been consistently criticized by commentators.

It is worth pointing out the difference between the applications of *stare decisis* in this case and in *Planned Parenthood of Southeastern Pa. v. Casey*, 505 U.S. 833

(1992). *Casey* explained how considerations of *stare decisis* inform the decision whether to overrule a long-established precedent that has become integrated into the fabric of the law. Overruling precedent of that kind naturally may have consequences for "the ideal of the rule of law." In addition, such precedent is likely to have engendered substantial reliance, as was true in *Casey* itself. But in this case, as we have explained, we do not face a precedent of that kind, because *Metro Broadcasting* itself *departed* from our prior cases—and did so quite recently. By refusing to follow *Metro Broadcasting*, then, we do not depart from the fabric of the law; we restore it. We also note that reliance on a case that has recently departed from precedent is likely to be minimal, particularly where, as here, the rule set forth in that case is unlikely to affect primary conduct in any event.

Justice Stevens, with whom Justice Ginsburg joins, dissenting.

Instead of deciding this case in accordance with controlling precedent, the Court today delivers a disconcerting lecture about the evils of governmental racial classifications. For its text the Court has selected three propositions, represented by the bywords "skepticism," "consistency," and "congruence." I shall comment on each of these propositions, then add a few words about *stare decisis*, and finally explain why I believe this Court has a duty to affirm the judgment of the Court of Appeals. The Court's concept of *stare decisis* treats some of the language we have used in explaining our decisions as though it were more important than our actual holdings. In my opinion that treatment is incorrect.

This is the third time in the Court's entire history that it has considered the constitutionality of a federal affirmative-action program. On each of the two prior occasions, the first in 1980, *Fullilove v. Klutznick*, and the second in 1990, *Metro Broadcasting, Inc. v. FCC*, the Court upheld the program. Today the Court explicitly overrules *Metro Broadcasting* (at least in part), and undermines *Fullilove* by recasting the standard on which it rested and by calling even its holding into question. By way of explanation, Justice O'CONNOR advises the federal agencies and private parties that have made countless decisions in reliance on those cases that "we do not depart from the fabric of the law; we restore it." A skeptical observer might ask whether this pronouncement is a faithful application of the doctrine of *stare decisis.* A brief comment on each of the two ailing cases may provide the answer.

In the Court's view, our decision in *Metro Broadcasting* was inconsistent with the rule announced in *Richmond v. J.A. Croson Co.* But two decisive distinctions separate those two cases. First, *Metro Broadcasting* involved a federal program, whereas *Croson* involved a city ordinance. *Metro Broadcasting* thus drew primary support from *Fullilove*, which predated *Croson* and which *Croson* distinguished on the grounds of the federal-state dichotomy that the majority today discredits. Although Members of today's majority trumpeted the importance of that distinction in *Croson*, they now reject it in the name of "congruence." It is therefore quite wrong for the Court to suggest today that overruling *Metro Broadcasting* merely restores the *status quo ante*, for the law at the time of that decision was entirely open to the result the Court reached. *Today's* decision is an unjustified departure from settled law.

Second, *Metro Broadcasting*'s holding rested on more than its application of "intermediate scrutiny." Indeed, I have always believed that, labels notwithstanding, the Federal Communications Commission (FCC) program we upheld in that case would have satisfied any of our various standards in affirmative-action cases—including the one the majority fashions today. What truly distinguishes *Metro Broadcasting* from our other affirmative-action precedents is the distinctive goal of the federal program in that case. Instead of merely seeking to remedy past discrimination, the FCC program was intended to achieve future benefits in the form of broadcast diversity. Reliance on race as a legitimate means of achieving diversity was first endorsed by Justice Powell in *Regents of Univ. of Cal. v. Bakke.* Later, in *Wygant v. Jackson Bd. of Ed.*, I also argued that race is not always irrelevant to governmental decisionmaking.

Thus, prior to *Metro Broadcasting*, the interest in diversity had been mentioned in a few opinions, but it is perfectly clear that the Court had not yet decided whether that interest had sufficient magnitude to justify a racial classification. *Metro Broadcasting*, of course, answered that question in the affirmative. The majority today overrules *Metro Broadcasting* only insofar as it is "inconsistent with [the] holding" that strict scrutiny applies to "benign" racial classifications promulgated by the Federal Government. The proposition that fostering diversity may provide a sufficient interest to justify such a program is *not* inconsistent with the Court's holding today—indeed, the question is not remotely presented in this case—and I do not take the Court's opinion to diminish that aspect of our decision in *Metro Broadcasting.*

Dickerson v. U.S., 530 U.S. 428 (2000)

Chief Justice Rehnquist delivered the opinion of the Court.

In Miranda v. Arizona, 384 U.S. 436 (1966), we held that certain warnings must be given before a suspect's statement made during custodial interrogation could be admitted in evidence. In the wake of that decision, Congress enacted 18 U.S.C. § 3501, which in essence laid down a rule that the admissibility of such statements should turn only on whether or not they were voluntarily made. We hold that Miranda, being a constitutional decision of this Court, may not be in effect overruled by an Act of Congress, and we decline to overrule Miranda ourselves. We therefore hold that Miranda and its progeny in this Court govern the admissibility of statements made during custodial interrogation in both state and federal courts.

The law in this area is clear. This Court has supervisory authority over the federal courts, and we may use that authority to prescribe rules of evidence and procedure that are binding in those tribunals. Carlisle v. United States, 517 U.S. 416, 426, 116 S.Ct. 1460, 134 L.Ed.2d 613 (1996). However, the power to judicially create and enforce nonconstitutional "rules of procedure and evidence for the federal courts exists only in the absence of a relevant Act of Congress." Palermo v. United States, 360 U.S. 343, 353, n. 11, 79 S.Ct. 1217, 3 L.Ed.2d 1287 (1959) (citing Funk v. United States, 290 U.S. 371, 382, 54 S.Ct. 212, 78 L.Ed. 369 (1933), and Gordon v. United States, 344 U.S. 414, 418, 73 S.Ct. 369, 97 L.Ed. 447 (1953). Congress retains the ultimate authority to modify or set aside any judicially created rules of evidence and procedure that are not required by the Constitution.

But Congress may not legislatively supersede our decisions interpreting and applying the Constitution. This case therefore turns on whether the Miranda Court announced a constitutional rule or merely exercised its supervisory authority to regulate evidence in the absence of congressional direction. Recognizing this point, the

Court of Appeals surveyed Miranda and its progeny to determine the constitutional status of the Miranda decision. Relying on the fact that we have created several exceptions to Miranda's warnings requirement and that we have repeatedly referred to the Miranda warnings as "prophylactic," [T]he Court of Appeals concluded that the protections announced in Miranda are not constitutionally required.

Whether or not we would agree with Miranda's reasoning and its resulting rule, were we addressing the issue in the first instance, the principles of stare decisis weigh heavily against overruling it now. While "stare decisis is not an inexorable command," State Oil Co. v. Khan, 522 U.S. 3, 20, 118 S.Ct. 275, 139 L.Ed.2d 199 (1997) (quoting Payne v. Tennessee, 501 U.S. 808, 828, 111 S.Ct. 2597, 115 L.Ed.2d 720 (1991)), particularly when we are interpreting the Constitution, Agostini v. Felton, 521 U.S. 203, 235, 117 S.Ct. 1997, 138 L.Ed.2d 391 (1997), "even in constitutional cases, the doctrine carries such persuasive force that we have always required a departure from precedent to be supported by some 'special justification.'" United States v. International Business Machines Corp., 517 U.S. 843, 856, 116 S.Ct. 1793, 135 L.Ed.2d 124 (1996) (quoting Payne, supra, at 842, 111 S.Ct. 2597 (SOUTER, J., concurring), in turn quoting Arizona v. Rumsey, 467 U.S. 203, 212, 104 S.Ct. 2305, 81 L.Ed.2d 164 (1984)).

We do not think there is such justification for overruling Miranda. Miranda has become embedded in routine police practice to the point where the warnings have become part of our national culture. See Mitchell v. United States, 526 U.S. 314, 331–332, 119 S.Ct. 1307, 143 L.Ed.2d 424 (1999) (SCALIA, J., dissenting) (stating that the fact that a rule has found "wide acceptance in the legal culture" is "adequate reason not to overrule" it). While we have overruled our precedents when subsequent cases have undermined their doctrinal underpinnings, see, e.g., Patterson v. McLean Credit Union, 491 U.S. 164, 173, 109 S.Ct. 2363, 105 L.Ed.2d 132 (1989), we do not believe that this has happened to the Miranda decision. If anything, our subsequent cases have reduced the impact of the Miranda rule on legitimate law enforcement while reaffirming the decision's core ruling that unwarned statements may not be used as evidence in the prosecution's case in chief.

The disadvantage of the Miranda rule is that statements which may be by no means involuntary, made by a defendant who is aware of his "rights," may nonetheless be excluded and a guilty defendant go free as a result. But experience suggests that the totality-of-the-circumstances test which § 3501 seeks to revive is more difficult than Miranda for law enforcement officers to conform to, and for courts to apply in a consistent manner. See, e.g., Haynes v. Washington, 373 U.S., at 515, 83 S.Ct. 1336 ("The line between proper and permissible police conduct and techniques and methods offensive to due process is, at best, a difficult one to draw"). The requirement that Miranda warnings be given does not, of course, dispense with the voluntariness inquiry. But as we said in Berkemer v. McCarty, 468 U.S. 420, 104 S.Ct. 3138, 82 L.Ed.2d 317 (1984), "[c]ases in which a defendant can make a colorable argument that a self-incriminating statement was 'compelled' despite the fact that the law enforcement authorities adhered to the dictates of Miranda are rare."

In sum, we conclude that Miranda announced a constitutional rule that Congress may not supersede legislatively. Following the rule of stare decisis, we decline to overrule Miranda ourselves. The judgment of the Court of Appeals is therefore Reversed.

Lawrence v. Texas, 539 U.S. 558 (2003)

Justice Kennedy delivered the opinion of the Court.

Liberty protects the person from unwarranted government intrusions into a dwelling or other private places. In our tradition the State is not omnipresent in the home. And there are other spheres of our lives and existence, outside the home, where the State should not be a dominant presence. Freedom extends beyond spatial bounds. Liberty presumes an autonomy of self that includes freedom of thought, belief, expression, and certain intimate conduct. The instant case involves liberty of the person both in its spatial and in its more transcendent dimensions.

I

The question before the Court is the validity of a Texas statute making it a crime for two persons of the same sex to engage in certain intimate sexual conduct.

In Houston, Texas, officers of the Harris County Police Department were dispatched to a private residence in response to a reported weapons disturbance. They entered an apartment where one of the petitioners, John Geddes Lawrence, resided. The right of the police to enter does not seem to have been questioned. The officers observed Lawrence and another man, Tyron Garner, engaging in a sexual act. The two petitioners were arrested, held in custody overnight, and charged and convicted before a Justice of the Peace.

The complaints described their crime as "deviate sexual intercourse, namely anal sex, with a member of the same sex (man)." The applicable state law is Tex. Penal Code Ann. § 21.06(a) (2003). It provides: "A person commits an offense if he engages in deviate sexual intercourse with another individual of the same sex."

The Court of Appeals for the Texas Fourteenth District considered the petitioners' federal constitutional arguments under both the Equal Protection and Due Process Clauses of the Fourteenth Amendment. After hearing the case en banc the court, in a divided opinion, rejected the constitutional arguments and affirmed the convictions. The majority opinion indicates that the Court of Appeals considered our decision in *Bowers v. Hardwick*, 478 U.S. 186, (1986), to be controlling on the federal due process aspect of the case. *Bowers* then being authoritative, this was proper.

We granted certiorari, to consider three questions:

1. Whether petitioners' criminal convictions under the Texas 'Homosexual Conduct' law—which criminalizes sexual intimacy by same-sex couples, but not identical behavior by different-sex couples—violate the Fourteenth Amendment guarantee of equal protection of the laws.

2. Whether petitioners' criminal convictions for adult consensual sexual intimacy in the home violate their vital interests in liberty and privacy protected by the Due Process Clause of the Fourteenth Amendment.

3. Whether *Bowers v. Hardwick*, *supra*, should be overruled.

The petitioners were adults at the time of the alleged offense. Their conduct was in private and consensual.

II

We conclude the case should be resolved by determining whether the petitioners were free as adults to engage in the private conduct in the exercise of their liberty under the Due Process Clause of the Fourteenth Amendment to the Constitution. For this inquiry we deem it necessary to reconsider the Court's holding in *Bowers*. There are broad statements of the substantive reach of liberty under the Due Process Clause in earlier cases, including *Pierce v. Society of Sisters*, 268 U.S. 510 (1925), and *Meyer v. Nebraska*, 262 U.S. 39 (1923); but the most pertinent beginning point is our decision in *Griswold v. Connecticut*, 381 U.S. 479 (1965).

In *Griswold* the Court invalidated a state law prohibiting the use of drugs or devices of contraception and counseling or aiding and abetting the use of contraceptives. The Court described the protected interest as a right to privacy and placed emphasis on the marriage relation and the protected space of the marital bedroom.

After *Griswold* it was established that the right to make certain decisions regarding sexual conduct extends beyond the marital relationship. In *Eisenstadt v. Baird*, 405 U.S. 438 (1972), the Court invalidated a law prohibiting the distribution of contraceptives to unmarried persons. The case was decided under the Equal Protection Clause, but with respect to unmarried persons, the Court went on to state the fundamental proposition that the law impaired the exercise of their personal rights,

The opinions in *Griswold* and *Eisenstadt* were part of the background for the decision in *Roe v. Wade*, 410 U.S. 113 (1973). As is well known, the case involved a challenge to the Texas law prohibiting abortions, but the laws of other States were affected as well. Although the Court held the woman's rights were not absolute, her right to elect an abortion did have real and substantial protection as an exercise of her liberty under the Due Process Clause. The Court cited cases that protect spatial freedom and cases that go well beyond it. *Roe* recognized the right of a woman to make certain fundamental decisions affecting her destiny and confirmed once more that the protection of liberty under the Due Process Clause has a substantive dimension of fundamental significance in defining the rights of the person.

In *Carey v. Population Services Int'l*, 431 U.S. 678,(1977), the Court confronted a New York law forbidding sale or distribution of contraceptive devices to persons under 16 years of age. Although there was no single opinion for the Court, the law was invalidated. Both *Eisenstadt* and *Carey*, as well as the holding and rationale in *Roe*, confirmed that the reasoning of *Griswold* could not be confined to the protection of rights of married adults. This was the state of the law with respect to some of the most relevant cases when the Court considered *Bowers v. Hardwick*.

The facts in *Bowers* had some similarities to the instant case. A police officer, whose right to enter seems not to have been in question, observed Hardwick, in his own bedroom, engaging in intimate sexual conduct with another adult male. The conduct was in violation of a Georgia statute making it a criminal offense to engage in sodomy. One difference between the two cases is that the Georgia statute prohibited the conduct whether or not the participants were of the same sex, while the Texas statute, as we have seen, applies only to participants of the same sex. Hardwick was not prosecuted, but he brought an action in federal court to declare the state statute invalid. He alleged he was a practicing homosexual and that the criminal prohibition violated rights guaranteed to him by the Constitution. The Court, in an opinion by Justice White, sustained the Georgia law. Chief Justice Burger and Justice Powell joined the opinion of the Court and filed separate, concurring opinions. Four Justices dissented.

The Court began its substantive discussion in *Bowers* as follows: "The issue presented is whether the Federal Constitution confers a fundamental right upon homosexuals to engage in sodomy and hence invalidates the laws of the many States that still make such conduct illegal and have done so for a very long time." That statement, we now conclude, discloses the Court's own failure to appreciate the extent of the liberty at stake. To say that the issue in *Bowers* was simply the right to engage in certain sexual conduct demeans the claim the individual put forward, just as it would demean a married couple were it to be said marriage is simply about the right to have sexual intercourse. The laws involved in *Bowers* and here are, to be sure, statutes that purport to do no more than prohibit a particular sexual act. Their penalties and purposes, though, have more far-reaching consequences, touching upon the most private human conduct, sexual behavior, and in the most private of places, the home. The statutes do seek to control a personal relationship that, whether or not entitled to formal recognition in the law, is within the liberty of persons to choose without being punished as criminals.

This, as a general rule, should counsel against attempts by the State, or a court, to define the meaning of the relationship or to set its boundaries absent injury to a person or abuse of an institution the law protects. It suffices for us to acknowledge that adults may choose to enter upon this relationship in the confines of their homes and their own private lives and still retain their dignity as free persons. When sexuality finds overt expression in intimate conduct with another person, the conduct can be but one element in a personal bond that is more enduring. The liberty protected by the Constitution allows homosexual persons the right to make this choice.

Having misapprehended the claim of liberty there presented to it, and thus stating the claim to be whether there is a fundamental right to engage in consensual sodomy, the *Bowers* Court said: "Proscriptions against that conduct have ancient roots." In academic writings, and in many of the scholarly *amicus* briefs filed to assist the Court in this case, there are fundamental criticisms of the historical premises relied upon by the majority and concurring opinions.

At the outset it should be noted that there is no longstanding history in this country of laws directed at homosexual conduct as a distinct matter. Beginning in colonial times there were prohibitions of sodomy derived from the English criminal laws passed in the first instance by the Reformation Parliament of 1533. The English prohibition was understood to include relations between men and women as well as relations between men and men.

Laws prohibiting sodomy do not seem to have been enforced against consenting adults acting in private. A substantial number of sodomy prosecutions and convictions for which there are surviving records were for predatory acts against those who could not or did not consent, as in the case of a minor or the victim of an assault. As to these, one purpose for the prohibitions was to ensure there would be no lack of coverage if a predator committed a sexual assault that did not constitute rape as defined by the criminal law.

To the extent that there were any prosecutions for the acts in question, 19th-century evidence rules imposed a burden that would make a conviction more difficult to obtain even taking into account the problems always inherent in prosecuting consensual acts committed in private. Under then-prevailing standards, a man could not be convicted of sodomy based upon testimony of a consenting partner, because the partner was considered an accomplice. A partner's testimony, however, was admissible if he or she had not consented to the act or was a minor, and therefore incapable of consent.

It was not until the 1970s that any State singled out same-sex relations for criminal prosecution, and only nine States have done so. Post-*Bowers* even some of these States did not adhere to the policy of suppressing homosexual conduct. Over the course of the last decades, States with same-sex prohibitions have moved toward abolishing them.

In summary, the historical grounds relied upon in *Bowers* are more complex than the majority opinion and the concurring opinion by Chief Justice Burger indicate. Their historical premises are not without doubt and, at the very least, are overstated. It must be acknowledged, of course, that the Court in *Bowers* was making the broader point that for centuries there have been powerful voices to condemn homosexual conduct as immoral. The condemnation has been shaped by religious beliefs, conceptions of right and acceptable behavior, and respect for the traditional family. For many persons these are not trivial concerns but profound and deep convictions accepted as ethical and moral principles to which they aspire and which thus determine the course of their lives. These considerations do not answer the question before us, however. The issue is whether the majority may use the power of the State to enforce these views on the whole society through operation of the criminal law. This emerging recognition should have been apparent when *Bowers* was decided.

In *Bowers* the Court referred to the fact that before 1961 all 50 States had outlawed sodomy, and that at the time of the Court's decision 24 States and the District of Columbia had sodomy laws. Justice Powell pointed out that these prohibitions often were being ignored, however. Georgia, for instance, had not sought to enforce its law for decades.

The sweeping references by Chief Justice Burger to the history of Western civilization and to Judeo–Christian moral and ethical standards did not take account of other authorities pointing in an opposite direction. A committee advising the British Parliament recommended in 1957 repeal of laws punishing homosexual conduct. The Wolfenden Report: Report of the Committee on Homosexual Offenses and Prostitution (1963). Parliament enacted the substance of those recommendations 10 years later.

Of even more importance, almost five years before *Bowers* was decided the European Court of Human Rights considered a case with parallels to *Bowers* and to today's case. An adult male resident in Northern Ireland alleged he was a practicing homosexual who desired to engage in consensual homosexual conduct. The laws of Northern Ireland forbade him that right. He alleged that he had been questioned, his home had been searched, and he feared criminal prosecution. The court held that the laws proscribing the conduct were invalid under the European Convention on Human Rights. *Dudgeon v. United Kingdom*, 45 Eur. Ct. H.R. (1981) & ¶ 52. Authoritative in all countries that are members of the Council of Europe (21 nations then, 45 nations now), the decision is at odds with the premise in *Bowers* that the claim put forward was insubstantial in our Western civilization.

In our own constitutional system the deficiencies in *Bowers* became even more apparent in the years following its announcement. The 25 States with laws prohibiting the relevant conduct referenced in the *Bowers* decision are reduced now to 13, of which 4 enforce their laws only against homosexual conduct. In those States where sodomy is still proscribed, whether for same-sex or heterosexual conduct, there is a pattern of nonenforcement with respect to consenting adults acting in private. The

State of Texas admitted in 1994 that as of that date it had not prosecuted anyone under those circumstances.

Two principal cases decided after *Bowers* cast its holding into even more doubt. In *Planned Parenthood of Southeastern Pa. v. Casey*, 505 U.S. 833 (1992), the Court reaffirmed the substantive force of the liberty protected by the Due Process Clause. The *Casey* decision again confirmed that our laws and tradition afford constitutional protection to personal decisions relating to marriage, procreation, contraception, family relationships, child rearing, and education.

The second post-*Bowers* case of principal relevance is *Romer v. Evans*, 517 U.S. 620 (1996). There the Court struck down class-based legislation directed at homosexuals as a violation of the Equal Protection Clause. *Romer* invalidated an amendment to Colorado's Constitution which named as a solitary class persons who were homosexuals, lesbians, or bisexual either by "orientation, conduct, practices or relationships," and deprived them of protection under state antidiscrimination laws. We concluded that the provision was "born of animosity toward the class of persons affected" and further that it had no rational relation to a legitimate governmental purpose.

As an alternative argument in this case, counsel for the petitioners and some *amici* contend that *Romer* provides the basis for declaring the Texas statute invalid under the Equal Protection Clause. That is a tenable argument, but we conclude the instant case requires us to address whether *Bowers* itself has continuing validity. Were we to hold the statute invalid under the Equal Protection Clause some might question whether a prohibition would be valid if drawn differently, say, to prohibit the conduct both between same-sex and different-sex participants.

Equality of treatment and the due process right to demand respect for conduct protected by the substantive guarantee of liberty are linked in important respects, and a decision on the latter point advances both interests. If protected conduct is made criminal and the law which does so remains unexamined for its substantive validity, its stigma might remain even if it were not enforceable as drawn for equal protection reasons. When homosexual conduct is made criminal by the law of the State, that declaration in and of itself is an invitation to subject homosexual persons to discrimination both in the public and in the private spheres. The central holding of *Bowers* has been brought in question by this case, and it should be addressed. Its continuance as precedent demeans the lives of homosexual persons.

The foundations of *Bowers* have sustained serious erosion from our recent decisions in *Casey* and *Romer*. When our precedent has been thus weakened, criticism from other sources is of greater significance. In the United States criticism of *Bowers* has been substantial and continuing, disapproving of its reasoning in all respects, not just as to its historical assumptions.

The doctrine of *stare decisis* is essential to the respect accorded to the judgments of the Court and to the stability of the law. It is not, however, an inexorable command. *Payne v. Tennessee*, 501 U.S. 808, 828 (1991) ("*Stare decisis* is not an inexorable command; rather, it 'is a principle of policy and not a mechanical formula of adherence to the latest decision'" (quoting *Helvering v. Hallock*, 309 U.S. 106, 119, 60 S.Ct. 444, 84 L.Ed. 604 (1940))). In *Casey* we noted that when a court is asked to overrule a precedent recognizing a constitutional liberty interest, individual or societal reliance on the existence of that liberty cautions with particular strength against reversing course.

The holding in *Bowers*, however, has not induced detrimental reliance comparable to some instances where recognized individual rights are involved. Indeed, there has been no individual or societal reliance on *Bowers* of the sort that could counsel against overturning its holding once there are compelling reasons to do so. *Bowers* itself causes uncertainty, for the precedents before and after its issuance contradict its central holding.

The rationale of *Bowers* does not withstand careful analysis. In his dissenting opinion in Bowers Justice STEVENS came to these conclusions:

"Our prior cases make two propositions abundantly clear. First, the fact that the governing majority in a State has traditionally viewed a particular practice as immoral is not a sufficient reason for upholding a law prohibiting the practice; neither history nor tradition could save a law prohibiting miscegenation from constitutional attack. Second, individual decisions by married persons, concerning the intimacies of their physical relationship, even when not intended to produce offspring, are a form of 'liberty' protected by the Due Process Clause of the Fourteenth Amendment. Moreover, this protection extends to intimate choices by unmarried as well as married persons."

Bowers was not correct when it was decided, and it is not correct today. It ought not to remain binding precedent. *Bowers v. Hardwick* should be and now is overruled.

5.   The Roberts Court

INTRODUCTION

The Roberts Supreme Court as of 2020 could be described as one with at least three phases or periods. The first was from the time John Roberts became Chief Justice in 2005 until the retirement of Justice Anthony Kennedy in 2018. This was a period when the Supreme Court was arguably split 4–1–4. By that, there were four Justices, including Roberts, who were aligned or inclined to vote more conservatively, four who tended liberal, and Kennedy, who was considered a swing Justice whose vote generally determined the outcome of a case. To underscore Kennedy's importance, consider that during the 2006 term there were 24 opinions decided by 5–4. In every one of those cases Kennedy was in the majority. His vote was decisive in 33% of the opinions handed down that year.

The second phase of the Roberts Court occurred after Kennedy left and was replaced by Brett Kavanaugh in 2018. At that point the Supreme Court was no longer split 4–1–4 but arguably had swung more decisively in a 5–4 conservative majority. However, at this point Chief Justice Roberts assumed a more swing role on the Court. Roberts was overall in the majority 97% of the time, he was in the majority 92% of the time in 5–4 opinions, and he wrote the most 5–4 opinions.

The third phase came in 2020 when Ruth Bader Ginsburg died and was replaced by Amy Coney Barrett. Arguably this shifted the Court in a 6–3 direction or, if one still considered the Chief Justice a swing vote, the court moved to 5–1–3, with five of the Justices considered conservative. The five justices—Clarence Thomas, Samuel Alito, Neil Gorsuch, Brett Kavanaugh, and Amy Coney Barrett—had sufficient votes to move on issues without the votes of the Chief Justice or any of the other Justice on the Court.

The ideological makeup of the Court is important for understanding constitutional precedent. We have seen from earlier chapters that having an ideological majority is no guarantee that a precedent will be overturned. The Burger and Rehnquist Courts disappointed many conservatives, who expected them to overturn more liberal rulings, including those on criminal due process and specifically *Roe v. Wade*. Precedent does seem to constrain ideological voting and often dictates how a Justice will approach an issue. Yet it takes five votes to overturn an existing constitutional precedent. Even though there is no guarantee that Justices of the same ideological orientation will always vote together, there is a greater likelihood they may view a precedent similarly and may be more inclined to agree on when it should be rejected or upheld. Whether as of 2020 a Roberts Court leaning heavily conservative will overturn or affirm *Roe* will be a test both of the strength of that case as precedent and how it (or a majority) view the various factors articulated in *Payne v. Tennessee* and followed in subsequent decisions when weighing when precedent should be upheld.

Through the end of the 2020 term the Roberts Court has overturned 15 constitutional precedents. Its overturn rate is greater than the Burger Court and less than the Warren, but the rates for the three are nearly identical. The Roberts Court has not overturned precedent at the same rate as the Warren Court. In its approach to precedent, it has continued the approach set by the Rehnquist Court in that in major or important cases overturning precedent, it has engaged in a detailed discussion regarding when it should or should not. The Court continues to quote the line from *Payne v. Tennessee* that "*Stare decisis* is not an inexorable command," suggesting that it too feels constrained by precedent when approaching cases.

Under the Roberts Court there seems to be several factors or approaches to precedent. One is that which is exemplified in *Citizens United v. Federal Election Commission*.[1] Here the Court seems to say that the finality of deciding a case and adhering to it as a precedent is important, but only to the extent that the original decision was decided correctly. Here the Court weighs in on saying that cases that were wrongly decided initially, or which have faulty or insufficient reasoning or analysis to support them, should be rejected. Rejection on precedent is appropriate as an error correction tool.

A second approach is found in *South Dakota v. Wayfair*.[2] Here the Court examined the continued constitutional prohibition on states requiring out-of-state companies to collect a sales or use tax on goods sold there even if the companies have no physical presence. Justice Kennedy wrote that the empirical conditions had so much changed in the last 25 years (prior to *Wayfair*) that these changes have undermined the original precedent.

A third approach, as found in *Janus v. American Federation of State, County, and Municipal Employees Council Number 31*,[3] is that subsequent cases since the original precedent had altered the legal landscape, rendering the original decision less firm and viable than it had once been. The third approach

---

[1]   558 U.S. 310 (2010).
[2]   138 S.Ct. 2080 (2018).
[3]   138 S.Ct. 2448 (2018).

is when the text, or the Framers' historical intent of it, comes into conflict with the precedent. An example of this is *Ramos v. Louisiana*,[4] where the Court argued that the historical understanding or intent of unanimous criminal jury verdicts outweighs the value of the precedent.

While none of the above cases solely overturned precedent based on one approach, they do highlight the factors the Court is taking into account now when it comes to addressing constitutional precedent. How the Court will continue in the future to address constitutional precedent, and whether it will follow the rules it has articulated, remains to be seen.

The factors considering when precedent should be followed or rejected are many, and the exact weighing process, as noted in the Introduction, is not mathematical, thereby allowing specific Justices to use their own judgment when deciding. As Justice Chief Justice Roberts declared in *June Medical Services L. L. C. v. Russo*,[5] when he concurred in a judgment to strike down a Louisiana abortion law he personally supported: "The constraint of precedent distinguishes the judicial method and philosophy from those of the political and legislative process."[6]

Finally, consider *Trump v. Hawaii*,[7] which upheld the Trump administration's travel ban from countries with large Muslim majorities. In doing so the Court in passing note overturned *Korematsu v. United States*.[8] At the highpoint of World War II the Supreme Court in *Korematsu v. United States* upheld the internment of more than 120,000 Japanese-Americans out of security concerns, even though there was no indication of individualized suspicion of disloyalty. The case is also famous for the Court declaring that any classification of individuals based on race was inherently suspect. Chief Justice Roberts declares in *Trump v. Hawaii* that *Korematsu* has been overruled by the court of history. What does that mean? Is *Korematsu* actually overruled and, if so, what part? The constitutionality of the internment camps, or the use of strict scrutiny to examine racial classifications?

Citizens United v. Federal Election Commission, 558 U.S. 310 (2010)

Chief Justice Roberts, with whom Justice Alito joins, concurring.

The Government urges us in this case to uphold a direct prohibition on political speech. It asks us to embrace a theory of the First Amendment that would allow

---

[4] 140 S.Ct. 1390 (2020).
[5] 140 S.Ct. 2103 (2020).
[6] *Id.* at 2134.
[7] 138 S. Ct. 923 (2018).
[8] 323 U.S. 214 (1944).

censorship not only of television and radio broadcasts, but of pamphlets, posters, the Internet, and virtually any other medium that corporations and unions might find useful in expressing their views on matters of public concern. Its theory, if accepted, would empower the Government to prohibit newspapers from running editorials or opinion pieces supporting or opposing candidates for office, so long as the newspapers were owned by corporations—as the major ones are. First Amendment rights could be confined to individuals, subverting the vibrant public discourse that is at the foundation of our democracy.

The Court properly rejects that theory, and I join its opinion in full. The First Amendment protects more than just the individual on a soapbox and the lonely pamphleteer. I write separately to address the important principles of judicial restraint and *stare decisis* implicated in this case.

I

Judging the constitutionality of an Act of Congress is "the gravest and most delicate duty that this Court is called upon to perform." Because the stakes are so high, our standard practice is to refrain from addressing constitutional questions except when necessary to rule on particular claims before us. See *Ashwander v. TVA*, 297 U.S. 288, 346–348, (1936) (Brandeis, J., concurring).

It is only because the majority rejects Citizens United's statutory claim that it proceeds to consider the group's various constitutional arguments, beginning with its narrowest claim (that *Hillary* is not the functional equivalent of express advocacy) and proceeding to its broadest claim (that *Austin v. Michigan Chamber of Commerce*, 494 U.S. 652, 110 S.Ct. 1391, 108 L.Ed.2d 652 (1990) should be overruled). This is the same order of operations followed by the controlling opinion in *Federal Election Comm'n v. Wisconsin Right to Life, Inc.* There the appellant was able to prevail on its narrowest constitutional argument because its broadcast ads did not qualify as the functional equivalent of express advocacy; there was thus no need to go on to address the broader claim that *McConnell v. Federal Election Comm'n* should be overruled. This case is different—not, as the dissent suggests, because the approach taken in *WRTL* has been deemed a "failure," but because, in the absence of any valid narrower ground of decision, there is no way to avoid Citizens United's broader constitutional argument.

The dissent advocates an approach to addressing Citizens United's claims that I find quite perplexing. It presumably agrees with the majority that Citizens United's narrower statutory and constitutional arguments lack merit—otherwise its conclusion that the group should lose this case would make no sense. Despite agreeing that these narrower arguments fail, however, the dissent argues that the majority should nonetheless latch on to one of them in order to avoid reaching the broader constitutional question of whether *Austin* remains good law. It even suggests that the Court's failure to adopt one of these concededly meritless arguments is a sign that the majority is not "serious about judicial restraint."

Because it is necessary to reach Citizens United's broader argument that *Austin* should be overruled, the debate over whether to consider this claim on an as-applied or facial basis strikes me as largely beside the point. Citizens United has standing— it is being injured by the Government's enforcement of the Act. Citizens United has a constitutional claim—the Act violates the First Amendment, because it prohibits political speech. The Government has a defense—the Act may be enforced, consistent with the First Amendment, against corporations. Whether the claim or the defense prevails is the question before us.

II

The text and purpose of the First Amendment point in the same direction: Congress may not prohibit political speech, even if the speaker is a corporation or union. What makes this case difficult is the need to confront our prior decision in *Austin*.

A

Fidelity to precedent—the policy of *stare decisis*—is vital to the proper exercise of the judicial function. "*Stare decisis* is the preferred course because it promotes the evenhanded, predictable, and consistent development of legal principles, fosters reliance on judicial decisions, and contributes to the actual and perceived integrity of the judicial process." For these reasons, we have long recognized that departures from precedent are inappropriate in the absence of a "special justification."

At the same time, *stare decisis* is neither an "inexorable command," *Lawrence v. Texas*, 539 U.S. 558, 577, 123 S.Ct. 2472, 156 L.Ed.2d 508 (2003), nor "a mechanical formula of adherence to the latest decision," *Helvering v. Hallock*, 309 U.S. 106, 119, 60 S.Ct. 444, 84 L.Ed. 604 (1940), especially in constitutional cases. If it were, segregation would be legal, minimum wage laws would be unconstitutional, and the Government could wiretap ordinary criminal suspects without first obtaining warrants. As the dissent properly notes, none of us has viewed *stare decisis* in such absolute terms.

Stare decisis is instead a "principle of policy." When considering whether to reexamine a prior erroneous holding, we must balance the importance of having constitutional questions *decided* against the importance of having them *decided right*.

In conducting this balancing, we must keep in mind that *stare decisis* is not an end in itself. Its greatest purpose is to serve a constitutional ideal—the rule of law. It follows that in the unusual circumstance when fidelity to any particular precedent does more to damage this constitutional ideal than to advance it, we must be more willing to depart from that precedent.

Thus, for example, if the precedent under consideration itself departed from the Court's jurisprudence, returning to the "'intrinsically sounder' doctrine established in prior cases" may "better serv[e] the values of *stare decisis* than would following [the] more recently decided case inconsistent with the decisions that came before it." Abrogating the errant precedent, rather than reaffirming or extending it, might better preserve the law's coherence and curtail the precedent's disruptive effects.

Likewise, if adherence to a precedent actually impedes the stable and orderly adjudication of future cases, its *stare decisis* effect is also diminished. This can happen in a number of circumstances, such as when the precedent's validity is so hotly contested that it cannot reliably function as a basis for decision in future cases, when its rationale threatens to upend our settled jurisprudence in related areas of law, and when the precedent's underlying reasoning has become so discredited that the Court cannot keep the precedent alive without jury-rigging new and different justifications to shore up the original mistake.

Justice Stevens, with whom Justice Ginsburg, Justice Breyer, and Justice Sotomayor join, concurring in part and dissenting in part.

In his landmark concurrence in *Ashwander v. TVA*, Justice Brandeis stressed the importance of adhering to rules the Court has "developed ... for its own governance" when deciding constitutional questions.

The final principle of judicial process that the majority violates is the most transparent: *stare decisis*. I am not an absolutist when it comes to *stare decisis*, in the campaign finance area or in any other. No one is. But if this principle is to do any meaningful work in supporting the rule of law, it must at least demand a significant justification, beyond the preferences of five Justices, for overturning settled doctrine. "[A] decision to overrule should rest on some special reason over and above the belief that a prior case was wrongly decided." No such justification exists in this case, and to the contrary there are powerful prudential reasons to keep faith with our precedents.

The Court's central argument for why *stare decisis* ought to be trumped is that it does not like *Austin*. The opinion "was not well reasoned," our colleagues assert, and it conflicts with First Amendment principles. This, of course, is the Court's merits argument, the many defects in which we will soon consider. I am perfectly willing to concede that if one of our precedents were dead wrong in its reasoning or irreconcilable with the rest of our doctrine, there would be a compelling basis for revisiting it.

Perhaps in recognition of this point, the Court supplements its merits case with a smattering of assertions. The Court proclaims that "Austin is undermined by experience since its announcement." This is a curious claim to make in a case that lacks a developed record. The majority has no empirical evidence with which to substantiate the claim; we just have its *ipse dixit* that the real world has not been kind to *Austin*. Nor does the majority bother to specify in what sense *Austin* has been "undermined."

The majority also contends that the Government's hesitation to rely on *Austin*'s antidistortion rationale "diminishe[s]" "the principle of adhering to that precedent." Why it diminishes the value of *stare decisis* is left unexplained. We have never thought fit to overrule a precedent because a litigant has taken any particular tack. Nor should we. Our decisions can often be defended on multiple grounds, and a litigant may have strategic or case-specific reasons for emphasizing only a subset of them. Members of the public, moreover, often rely on our bottom-line holdings far more than our precise legal arguments; surely this is true for the legislatures that have been regulating corporate electioneering since *Austin*. The task of evaluating the continued viability of precedents falls to this Court, not to the parties.

Although the majority opinion spends several pages making these surprising arguments, it says almost nothing about the standard considerations we have used to determine *stare decisis* value, such as the antiquity of the precedent, the workability of its legal rule, and the reliance interests at stake.

We have recognized that "*[s]tare decisis* has special force when legislators or citizens 'have acted in reliance on a previous decision, for in this instance overruling the decision would dislodge settled rights and expectations or require an extensive legislative response.'" *Stare decisis* protects not only personal rights involving property or contract but also the ability of the elected branches to shape their laws in an effective and coherent fashion. Today's decision takes away a power that we have long permitted these branches to exercise. State legislatures have relied on their authority to regulate corporate electioneering, confirmed in *Austin*, for more than a century. The Federal Congress has relied on this authority for a comparable stretch of time, and it specifically relied on *Austin* throughout the years it spent developing and debating BCRA. The total record it compiled was *100,000 pages* long. Pulling out the rug beneath Congress after affirming the constitutionality of § 203 six years ago shows great disrespect for a coequal branch.

Beyond the reliance interests at stake, the other *stare decisis* factors also cut against the Court. Considerations of antiquity are significant for similar reasons. *McConnell* is only six years old, but *Austin* has been on the books for two decades, and many of the statutes called into question by today's opinion have been on the books for a half-century or more. The Court points to no intervening change in circumstances that warrants revisiting *Austin*. Certainly nothing relevant has changed since we decided *WRTL* two Terms ago. And the Court gives no reason to think that *Austin* and *McConnell* are unworkable.

Obergefell v. Hodges, 576 U.S. 644 (2015)

Justice Kennedy delivered the opinion of the Court.

The Constitution promises liberty to all within its reach, a liberty that includes certain specific rights that allow persons, within a lawful realm, to define and express their identity. The petitioners in these cases seek to find that liberty by marrying someone of the same sex and having their marriages deemed lawful on the same terms and conditions as marriages between persons of the opposite sex.

I

These cases come from Michigan, Kentucky, Ohio, and Tennessee, States that define marriage as a union between one man and one woman. The petitioners are 14 same-sex couples and two men whose same-sex partners are deceased. The respondents are state officials responsible for enforcing the laws in question. The petitioners claim the respondents violate the Fourteenth Amendment by denying them the right to marry or to have their marriages, lawfully performed in another State, given full recognition.

Petitioners filed these suits in United States District Courts in their home States. Each District Court ruled in their favor. The Court of Appeals held that a State has no constitutional obligation to license same-sex marriages or to recognize same-sex marriages performed out of State.

The petitioners sought certiorari. This Court granted review, limited to two questions. The first, presented by the cases from Michigan and Kentucky, is whether the Fourteenth Amendment requires a State to license a marriage between two people of the same sex. The second, presented by the cases from Ohio, Tennessee, and, again, Kentucky, is whether the Fourteenth Amendment requires a State to recognize a same-sex marriage licensed and performed in a State which does grant that right.

II

Before addressing the principles and precedents that govern these cases, it is appropriate to note the history of the subject now before the Court.

A

Recounting the circumstances of three of these cases illustrates the urgency of the petitioners' cause from their perspective. Petitioner James Obergefell, a plaintiff in the Ohio case, met John Arthur over two decades ago. They fell in love and started a life together, establishing a lasting, committed relation. In 2011, however, Arthur was diagnosed with amyotrophic lateral sclerosis, or ALS. This debilitating disease is progressive, with no known cure. Two years ago, Obergefell and Arthur decided to commit to one another, resolving to marry before Arthur died. To fulfill their mutual promise, they traveled from Ohio to Maryland, where same-sex marriage was legal. It was difficult for Arthur to move, and so the couple were wed inside a medical transport plane as it remained on the tarmac in Baltimore. Three months later, Arthur died. Ohio law does not permit Obergefell to be listed as the surviving spouse on Arthur's death certificate. By statute, they must remain strangers even in death, a state-imposed separation Obergefell deems "hurtful for the rest of time." He brought suit to be shown as the surviving spouse on Arthur's death certificate.

B

The ancient origins of marriage confirm its centrality, but it has not stood in isolation from developments in law and society. The history of marriage is one of both continuity and change. That institution—even as confined to opposite-sex relations—has evolved over time.

This dynamic can be seen in the Nation's experiences with the rights of gays and lesbians. Until the mid-20th century, same-sex intimacy long had been condemned as immoral by the state itself in most Western nations, a belief often embodied in the criminal law. For this reason, among others, many persons did not deem homosexuals to have dignity in their own distinct identity. A truthful declaration by same-sex couples of what was in their hearts had to remain unspoken.

This Court first gave detailed consideration to the legal status of homosexuals in *Bowers v. Hardwick*, 478 U.S. 186 (1986). There it upheld the constitutionality of a Georgia law deemed to criminalize certain homosexual acts. Ten years later, in *Romer v. Evans*, 517 U.S. 620 (1996), the Court invalidated an amendment to Colorado's Constitution that sought to foreclose any branch or political subdivision of the State from protecting persons against discrimination based on sexual orientation. Then, in 2003, the Court overruled Bowers, holding that laws making same-sex intimacy a crime "demea[n] the lives of homosexual persons." *Lawrence v. Texas*, 539 U.S. 558, 575.

Against this background, the legal question of same-sex marriage arose. In 1993, the Hawaii Supreme Court held Hawaii's law restricting marriage to opposite-sex couples constituted a classification on the basis of sex and was therefore subject to strict scrutiny under the Hawaii Constitution. *Baehr v. Lewin*, 74 Haw. 530, 852 P.2d 44. Although this decision did not mandate that same-sex marriage be allowed, some States were concerned by its implications and reaffirmed in their laws that marriage is defined as a union between opposite-sex partners. So too in 1996, Congress passed the Defense of Marriage Act (DOMA), defining marriage for all federal-law purposes as "only a legal union between one man and one woman as husband and wife."

The new and widespread discussion of the subject led other States to a different conclusion. In 2003, the Supreme Judicial Court of Massachusetts held the State's Constitution guaranteed same-sex couples the right to marry. See *Goodridge v. Department of Public Health*, 440 Mass. 309, 798 N.E.2d 941 (2003). After that ruling, some additional States granted marriage rights to same-sex couples, either through judicial or legislative processes. These decisions and statutes are cited in Appendix B, *infra*. Two Terms ago, in *United States v. Windsor*, 570 U.S. 744, 133 S.Ct. 2675 (2013), this Court invalidated DOMA to the extent it barred the Federal Government from treating same-sex marriages as valid even when they were lawful in the State where they were licensed. DOMA, the Court held, impermissibly disparaged those same-sex couples "who wanted to affirm their commitment to one another before their children, their family, their friends, and their community."

Numerous cases about same-sex marriage have reached the United States Courts of Appeals in recent years. In accordance with the judicial duty to base their decisions on principled reasons and neutral discussions, without scornful or disparaging commentary, courts have written a substantial body of law considering all sides of these issues. That case law helps to explain and formulate the underlying principles this Court now must consider. With the exception of the opinion here under review and one other, see *Citizens for Equal Protection v. Bruning*, 455 F.3d 859, 864–868 (C.A.8 2006), the Courts of Appeals have held that excluding same-sex couples from marriage violates the Constitution.

III

Under the Due Process Clause of the Fourteenth Amendment, no State shall "deprive any person of life, liberty, or property, without due process of law." The fundamental liberties protected by this Clause include most of the rights enumerated in the Bill of Rights. In addition these liberties extend to certain personal choices central to individual dignity and autonomy, including intimate choices that define personal identity and beliefs.

The identification and protection of fundamental rights is an enduring part of the judicial duty to interpret the Constitution. That responsibility, however, "has not been reduced to any formula." Rather, it requires courts to exercise reasoned judgment in identifying interests of the person so fundamental that the State must accord them its respect. That process is guided by many of the same considerations relevant to analysis of other constitutional provisions that set forth broad principles rather than specific requirements. History and tradition guide and discipline this inquiry but do not set its outer boundaries.

The nature of injustice is that we may not always see it in our own times. The generations that wrote and ratified the Bill of Rights and the Fourteenth Amendment did not presume to know the extent of freedom in all of its dimensions, and so they entrusted to future generations a charter protecting the right of all persons to enjoy liberty as we learn its meaning. When new insight reveals discord between the

Constitution's central protections and a received legal stricture, a claim to liberty must be addressed.

Applying these established tenets, the Court has long held the right to marry is protected by the Constitution. In *Loving v. Virginia*, 388 U.S. 1 (1967) which invalidated bans on interracial unions, a unanimous Court held marriage is "one of the vital personal rights essential to the orderly pursuit of happiness by free men." The Court reaffirmed that holding in *Zablocki v. Redhail*, 434 U.S. 374, 384 (1978), which held the right to marry was burdened by a law prohibiting fathers who were behind on child support from marrying. The Court again applied this principle in *Turner v. Safley*, 482 U.S. 78, 95 (1987), which held the right to marry was abridged by regulations limiting the privilege of prison inmates to marry. Over time and in other contexts, the Court has reiterated that the right to marry is fundamental under the Due Process Clause.

It cannot be denied that this Court's cases describing the right to marry presumed a relationship involving opposite-sex partners. The Court, like many institutions, has made assumptions defined by the world and time of which it is a part. This was evident in *Baker v. Nelson*, 409 U.S. 810, 93 S.Ct. 37, 34 L.Ed.2d 65, a one-line summary decision issued in 1972, holding the exclusion of same-sex couples from marriage did not present a substantial federal question.

This analysis compels the conclusion that same-sex couples may exercise the right to marry. The four principles and traditions to be discussed demonstrate that the reasons marriage is fundamental under the Constitution apply with equal force to same-sex couples.

A first premise of the Court's relevant precedents is that the right to personal choice regarding marriage is inherent in the concept of individual autonomy.

A second principle in this Court's jurisprudence is that the right to marry is fundamental because it supports a two-person union unlike any other in its importance to the committed individuals.

A third basis for protecting the right to marry is that it safeguards children and families and thus draws meaning from related rights of childrearing, procreation, and education.

Excluding same-sex couples from marriage thus conflicts with a central premise of the right to marry. Without the recognition, stability, and predictability marriage offers, their children suffer the stigma of knowing their families are somehow lesser. Fourth and finally, this Court's cases and the Nation's traditions make clear that marriage is a keystone of our social order.

The States have contributed to the fundamental character of the marriage right by placing that institution at the center of so many facets of the legal and social order. There is no difference between same- and opposite-sex couples with respect to this principle. Yet by virtue of their exclusion from that institution, same-sex couples are denied the constellation of benefits that the States have linked to marriage.

The limitation of marriage to opposite-sex couples may long have seemed natural and just, but its inconsistency with the central meaning of the fundamental right to marry is now manifest. With that knowledge must come the recognition that laws excluding same-sex couples from the marriage right impose stigma and injury of the kind prohibited by our basic charter.

The right to marry is fundamental as a matter of history and tradition, but rights come not from ancient sources alone. They rise, too, from a better informed understanding of how constitutional imperatives define a liberty that remains urgent in our own era. Many who deem same-sex marriage to be wrong reach that conclusion based on decent and honorable religious or philosophical premises, and neither they nor their beliefs are disparaged here. But when that sincere, personal opposition becomes enacted law and public policy, the necessary consequence is to put the imprimatur of the State itself on an exclusion that soon demeans or stigmatizes those whose own liberty is then denied. Under the Constitution, same-sex couples seek in marriage the same legal treatment as opposite-sex couples, and it would disparage their choices and diminish their personhood to deny them this right.

The right of same-sex couples to marry that is part of the liberty promised by the Fourteenth Amendment is derived, too, from that Amendment's guarantee of the equal protection of the laws. The Due Process Clause and the Equal Protection Clause are connected in a profound way, though they set forth independent principles. Rights implicit in liberty and rights secured by equal protection may rest on different precepts and are not always co-extensive, yet in some instances each may be instructive as to the meaning and reach of the other. In any particular case one Clause may be thought to capture the essence of the right in a more accurate and comprehensive way, even as the two Clauses may converge in the identification and definition of the right.

These considerations lead to the conclusion that the right to marry is a fundamental right inherent in the liberty of the person, and under the Due Process and Equal Protection Clauses of the Fourteenth Amendment couples of the same-sex may not be deprived of that right and that liberty. The Court now holds that same-sex couples may exercise the fundamental right to marry. No longer may this liberty be denied to them. *Baker v. Nelson* must be and now is overruled, and the State laws challenged by Petitioners in these cases are now held invalid to the extent they exclude same-sex couples from civil marriage on the same terms and conditions as opposite-sex couples.

The judgment of the Court of Appeals for the Sixth Circuit is reversed.

It is so ordered.

Chief Justice ROBERTS, with whom Justice SCALIA and Justice THOMAS join, dissenting.

Petitioners make strong arguments rooted in social policy and considerations of fairness. They contend that same-sex couples should be allowed to affirm their love and commitment through marriage, just like opposite-sex couples. That position has undeniable appeal; over the past six years, voters and legislators in eleven States and the District of Columbia have revised their laws to allow marriage between two people of the same sex.

But this Court is not a legislature. Whether same-sex marriage is a good idea should be of no concern to us. Under the Constitution, judges have power to say what the law is, not what it should be. The people who ratified the Constitution authorized courts to exercise "neither force nor will but merely judgment." The Federalist No. 78, p. 465 (C. Rossiter ed. 1961) (A. Hamilton) (capitalization altered).

Trump v. Hawaii, 138 S. Ct. 2392 (2018)

Justice Roberts wrote for the majority.

Under the Immigration and Nationality Act, foreign nationals seeking entry into the United States undergo a vetting process to ensure that they satisfy the numerous requirements for admission. The Act also vests the President with authority to restrict the entry of aliens whenever he finds that their entry "would be detrimental to the interests of the United States." Relying on that delegation, the President concluded that it was necessary to impose entry restrictions on nationals of countries that do not share adequate information for an informed entry determination, or that otherwise present national security risks. Presidential Proclamation No. 9645, 82 Fed. Reg. 45161 (2017) (Proclamation). The plaintiffs in this litigation, respondents here, challenged the application of those entry restrictions to certain aliens abroad. We now decide whether the President had authority under the Act to issue the Proclamation, and whether the entry policy violates the Establishment Clause of the First Amendment.

IV

A

We now turn to plaintiffs' claim that the Proclamation was issued for the unconstitutional purpose of excluding Muslims.

B

The First Amendment provides, in part, that "Congress shall make no law respecting an establishment of religion, or prohibiting the free exercise thereof." Our cases recognize that "[t]he clearest command of the Establishment Clause is that one religious denomination cannot be officially preferred over another." Plaintiffs believe that the Proclamation violates this prohibition by singling out Muslims for disfavored treatment. The entry suspension, they contend, operates as a "religious gerrymander," in part because most of the countries covered by the Proclamation have Muslim-majority populations. And in their view, deviations from the information-sharing baseline criteria suggest that the results of the multi-agency review were "foreordained." Relying on Establishment Clause precedents concerning laws and policies applied domestically, plaintiffs allege that the primary purpose of the Proclamation was religious animus and that the President's stated concerns about vetting protocols and national security were but pretexts for discriminating against Muslims.

At the heart of plaintiffs' case is a series of statements by the President and his advisers casting doubt on the official objective of the Proclamation. For example, while a candidate on the campaign trail, the President published a "Statement on Preventing Muslim Immigration" that called for a "total and complete shutdown of Muslims entering the United States until our country's representatives can figure out what is going on." That statement remained on his campaign website until May 2017. Then-candidate Trump also stated that "Islam hates us" and asserted that the United States was "having problems with Muslims coming into the country."

Shortly after being elected, when asked whether violence in Europe had affected his plans to "ban Muslim immigration," the President replied, "You know my plans. All along, I've been proven to be right."

One week after his inauguration, the President issued EO-1. In a television interview, one of the President's campaign advisers explained that when the President "first announced it, he said, 'Muslim ban.' He called me up. He said, 'Put a commission together. Show me the right way to do it legally.'" The adviser said he assembled a group of Members of Congress and lawyers that "focused on, instead of religion, danger... [The order] is based on places where there [is] substantial evidence that people are sending terrorists into our country."

Plaintiffs also note that after issuing EO-2 to replace EO-1, the President expressed regret that his prior order had been "watered down" and called for a "much tougher version" of his "Travel Ban." Shortly before the release of the Proclamation, he stated that the "travel ban ... should be far larger, tougher, and more specific," but "stupidly that would not be politically correct." More recently, on November 29, 2017, the President retweeted links to three anti-Muslim propaganda videos. In response to questions about those videos, the President's deputy press secretary denied that the President thinks Muslims are a threat to the United States, explaining that "the President has been talking about these security issues for years now, from the campaign trail to the White House" and "has addressed these issues with the travel order that he issued earlier this year and the companion proclamation."

Plaintiffs argue that this President's words strike at fundamental standards of respect and tolerance, in violation of our constitutional tradition. But the issue before us is not whether to denounce the statements. It is instead the significance of those statements in reviewing a Presidential directive, neutral on its face, addressing a matter within the core of executive responsibility. In doing so, we must consider not only the statements of a particular President, but also the authority of the Presidency itself.

The case before us differs in numerous respects from the conventional Establishment Clause claim. Unlike the typical suit involving religious displays or school prayer, plaintiffs seek to invalidate a national security directive regulating the entry of aliens abroad. Their claim accordingly raises a number of delicate issues regarding the scope of the constitutional right and the manner of proof. The Proclamation, moreover, is facially neutral toward religion. Plaintiffs therefore ask the Court to probe the sincerity of the stated justifications for the policy by reference to extrinsic statements—many of which were made before the President took the oath of office. These various aspects of plaintiffs' challenge inform our standard of review.

C

For more than a century, this Court has recognized that the admission and exclusion of foreign nationals is a "fundamental sovereign attribute exercised by the Government's political departments largely immune from judicial control." Because decisions in these matters may implicate "relations with foreign powers," or involve "classifications defined in the light of changing political and economic circumstances," such judgments "are frequently of a character more appropriate to either the Legislature or the Executive."

The upshot of our cases in this context is clear: "Any rule of constitutional law that would inhibit the flexibility" of the President "to respond to changing world conditions should be adopted only with the greatest caution," and our inquiry into matters of entry and national security is highly constrained. We need not define the precise contours of that inquiry in this case. For our purposes today, we assume that we may look behind the face of the Proclamation to the extent of applying rational basis review. That standard of review considers whether the entry policy is plausibly related to the Government's stated objective to protect the country and improve vetting processes. As a result, we may consider plaintiffs' extrinsic evidence, but will uphold the policy so long as it can reasonably be understood to result from a justification independent of unconstitutional grounds.

D

Given the standard of review, it should come as no surprise that the Court hardly ever strikes down a policy as illegitimate under rational basis scrutiny. On the few occasions where we have done so, a common thread has been that the laws at issue lack any purpose other than a "bare ... desire to harm a politically unpopular group." The Proclamation is expressly premised on legitimate purposes: preventing entry of nationals who cannot be adequately vetted and inducing other nations to improve their practices. The text says nothing about religion. Plaintiffs and the dissent nonetheless emphasize that five of the seven nations currently included in the Proclamation have Muslim-majority populations. Yet that fact alone does not support an inference of religious hostility, given that the policy covers just 8% of the world's Muslim population and is limited to countries that were previously designated by Congress or prior administrations as posing national security risks.

The Proclamation, moreover, reflects the results of a worldwide review process undertaken by multiple Cabinet officials and their agencies.

Three additional features of the entry policy support the Government's claim of a legitimate national security interest. First, since the President introduced entry restrictions in January 2017, three Muslim-majority countries—Iraq, Sudan, and Chad—have been removed from the list of covered countries.

Second, for those countries that remain subject to entry restrictions, the Proclamation includes significant exceptions for various categories of foreign nationals. The policy permits nationals from nearly every covered country to travel to the United States on a variety of nonimmigrant visas.

Third, the Proclamation creates a waiver program open to all covered foreign nationals seeking entry as immigrants or nonimmigrants.

Finally, the dissent invokes *Korematsu v. United States.* Whatever rhetorical advantage the dissent may see in doing so, *Korematsu* has nothing to do with this case. The forcible relocation of U.S. citizens to concentration camps, solely and explicitly on the basis of race, is objectively unlawful and outside the scope of Presidential authority. But it is wholly inapt to liken that morally repugnant order to a facially neutral policy denying certain foreign nationals the privilege of admission. The entry suspension is an act that is well within executive authority and could have been taken by any other President—the only question is evaluating the actions of this particular President in promulgating an otherwise valid Proclamation.

The dissent's reference to *Korematsu*, however, affords this Court the opportunity to make express what is already obvious: *Korematsu* was gravely wrong the day it was decided, has been overruled in the court of history, and—to be clear—"has no place in law under the Constitution."

South Dakota v. Wayfair, 138 S.Ct. 2080 (2018)

Justice Kennedy delivered the opinion of the Court.

IV

"Although we approach the reconsideration of our decisions with the utmost caution, *stare decisis* is not an inexorable command." *Pearson v. Callahan*, 555 U.S. 223, 233, 129 S.Ct. 808, 172 L.Ed.2d 565 (2009) (quoting *State Oil Co. v. Khan*, 522 U.S. 3, 20, 118 S.Ct. 275, 139 L.Ed.2d 199 (1997); alterations and internal quotation marks omitted). Here, *stare decisis* can no longer support the Court's prohibition of a valid exercise of the States' sovereign power.

If it becomes apparent that the Court's Commerce Clause decisions prohibit the States from exercising their lawful sovereign powers in our federal system, the Court should be vigilant in correcting the error. While it can be conceded that Congress has the authority to change the physical presence rule, Congress cannot change the constitutional default rule. It is inconsistent with the Court's proper role to ask Congress to address a false constitutional premise of this Court's own creation. Courts have acted as the front line of review in this limited sphere; and hence it is important that their principles be accurate and logical, whether or not Congress can or will act in response. It is currently the Court, and not Congress, that is limiting the lawful prerogatives of the States.

Further, the real world implementation of Commerce Clause doctrines now makes it manifest that the physical presence rule as defined by *Quill* must give way to the "far-reaching systemic and structural changes in the economy" and "many other societal dimensions" caused by the Cyber Age. *Direct Marketing*, 575 U.S., at ——, 135 S.Ct., at 1135 (KENNEDY, J., concurring). Though *Quill* was wrong on its own terms when it was decided in 1992, since then the Internet revolution has made its earlier error all the more egregious and harmful.

The *Quill* Court did not have before it the present realities of the interstate marketplace. In 1992, less than 2 percent of Americans had Internet access. Today that number is about 89 percent. When it decided *Quill*, the Court could not have envisioned a world in which the world's largest retailer would be a remote seller.

The Internet's prevalence and power have changed the dynamics of the national economy. In 1992, mail-order sales in the United States totaled $180 billion. Last year, e-commerce retail sales alone were estimated at $453.5 billion. Dept. of Commerce, U.S. Census Bureau News, Quarterly Retail E-Commerce Sales: 4th Quarter 2017 (CB18-21, Feb. 16, 2018). Combined with traditional remote sellers, the total exceeds half a trillion dollars. Since the Department of Commerce first began tracking e-commerce sales, those sales have increased tenfold from 0.8 percent to 8.9 percent of total retail sales in the United States. And it is likely that this percentage will increase. Last year, e-commerce grew at four times the rate of traditional retail, and it shows no sign of any slower pace.

This expansion has also increased the revenue shortfall faced by States seeking to collect their sales and use taxes. In 1992, it was estimated that the States were losing between $694 million and $3 billion per year in sales tax revenues as a result of the physical presence rule. Now estimates range from $8 to $33 billion. The South

Dakota Legislature has declared an emergency, S.B. 106, § 9, which again demonstrates urgency of overturning the physical presence rule.

The argument, moreover, that the physical presence rule is clear and easy to apply is unsound. Attempts to apply the physical presence rule to online retail sales are proving unworkable. States are already confronting the complexities of defining physical presence in the Cyber Age. For example, Massachusetts proposed a regulation that would have defined physical presence to include making apps available to be downloaded by in-state residents and placing cookies on in-state residents' web browsers. Ohio recently adopted a similar standard. Some States have enacted so-called "click through" nexus statutes, which define nexus to include out-of-state sellers that contract with in-state residents who refer customers for compensation. Others still, like Colorado, have imposed notice and reporting requirements on out-of-state retailers that fall just short of actually collecting and remitting the tax. Statutes of this sort are likely to embroil courts in technical and arbitrary disputes about what counts as physical presence.

Reliance interests are a legitimate consideration when the Court weighs adherence to an earlier but flawed precedent. See *Kimble v. Marvel Entertainment, LLC*, 576 U.S. 446, 135 S.Ct. 2401, 2410–2411 (2015). But even on its own terms, the physical presence rule as defined by *Quill* is no longer a clear or easily applicable standard, so arguments for reliance based on its clarity are misplaced. And, importantly, *stare decisis* accommodates only "legitimate reliance interest[s]." *United States v. Ross*, 456 U.S. 798, 824, 102 S.Ct. 2157, 72 L.Ed.2d 572 (1982). Here, the tax distortion created by *Quill* exists in large part because consumers regularly fail to comply with lawful use taxes. Some remote retailers go so far as to advertise sales as tax free. A business "is in no position to found a constitutional right on the practical opportunities for tax avoidance." *Nelson v. Sears, Roebuck & Co.*, 312 U.S. 359, (1941).

Finally, other aspects of the Court's Commerce Clause doctrine can protect against any undue burden on interstate commerce, taking into consideration the small businesses, startups, or others who engage in commerce across state lines. For example, the United States argues that tax-collection requirements should be analyzed under the balancing framework of *Pike v. Bruce Church, Inc.*, 397 U.S. 137. Others have argued that retroactive liability risks a double tax burden in violation of the Court's apportionment jurisprudence because it would make both the buyer and the seller legally liable for collecting and remitting the tax on a transaction intended to be taxed only once. Complex state tax systems could have the effect of discriminating against interstate commerce. Concerns that complex state tax systems could be a burden on small business are answered in part by noting that, as discussed below, there are various plans already in place to simplify collection; and since in-state businesses pay the taxes as well, the risk of discrimination against out-of-state sellers is avoided. And, if some small businesses with only *de minimis* contacts seek relief from collection systems thought to be a burden, those entities may still do so under other theories. These issues are not before the Court in the instant case; but their potential to arise in some later case cannot justify retaining this artificial, anachronistic rule that deprives States of vast revenues from major businesses.

For these reasons, the Court concludes that the physical presence rule of *Quill* is unsound and incorrect. The Court's decisions in *Quill Corp. v. North Dakota*, 504 U.S. 298, 112 S.Ct. 1904, 119 L.Ed.2d 91 (1992), and *National Bellas Hess, Inc. v. Department of Revenue of Ill.*, 386 U.S. 753, 87 S.Ct. 1389, 18 L.Ed.2d 505 (1967), should be, and now are, overruled.

Janus v. American Federation of State, County, and Municipal Employees Council Number 31, **138 S.Ct. 2448 (2018)**

Justice Alito delivered the opinion of the Court.

Under Illinois law, public employees are forced to subsidize a union, even if they choose not to join and strongly object to the positions the union takes in collective bargaining and related activities. We conclude that this arrangement violates the free speech rights of nonmembers by compelling them to subsidize private speech on matters of substantial public concern.

We upheld a similar law in *Abood v. Detroit Bd. of Ed.*, 431 U.S. 209, 261 (1977), and we recognize the importance of following precedent unless there are strong reasons for not doing so. But there are very strong reasons in this case. Fundamental free speech rights are at stake. *Abood* was poorly reasoned. It has led to practical problems and abuse. It is inconsistent with other First Amendment cases and has been undermined by more recent decisions. Developments since *Abood* was handed down have shed new light on the issue of agency fees, and no reliance interests on the part of public-sector unions are sufficient to justify the perpetuation of the free speech violations that *Abood* has countenanced for the past 41 years. *Abood* is therefore overruled.

III

In *Abood*, the Court upheld the constitutionality of an agency-shop arrangement like the one now before us, 431 U.S., at 232, 97 S.Ct. 1782, but in more recent cases we have recognized that this holding is "something of an anomaly," *Knox v. Service Employees*, 567 U.S. 298, 311, 132 S.Ct. 2277, 183 L.Ed.2d 281 (2012), and that *Abood*'s "analysis is questionable on several grounds," *Harris*, 573 U.S., at ——, 134 S.Ct., at 2632; see *id.*, at —— – ——, 134 S.Ct., at 2632–2634 (discussing flaws in *Abood*'s reasoning). We have therefore refused to extend *Abood* to situations where it does not squarely control, see *Harris, supra*, at —— – ——, 134 S.Ct., at 2638–2639, while leaving for another day the question whether *Abood* should be overruled.

VI

For the reasons given above, we conclude that public-sector agency-shop arrangements violate the First Amendment, and *Abood* erred in concluding otherwise. There remains the question whether *stare decisis* nonetheless counsels against overruling *Abood*. It does not.

"*Stare decisis* is the preferred course because it promotes the evenhanded, predictable, and consistent development of legal principles, fosters reliance on judicial decisions, and contributes to the actual and perceived integrity of the judicial process." *Payne v. Tennessee*, 501 U.S. 808, 827, 111 S.Ct. 2597, 115 L.Ed.2d 720 (1991). We will not overturn a past decision unless there are strong grounds for doing so. *United States v. International Business Machines Corp.*, 517 U.S. 843, 855–856 (1996); *Citizens United*, 558 U.S., at 377, 130 S.Ct. 876 (ROBERTS, C.J., concurring). But as we have often recognized, *stare decisis* is "'not an inexorable command.'" *Pearson v. Callahan*, 555 U.S. 223, 233 (2009); see also *Lawrence v. Texas*, 539 U.S. 558, 577, 123 S.Ct. 2472, 156 L.Ed.2d 508 (2003); *Payne, supra*, at 828, 111 S.Ct. 2597.

The doctrine "is at its weakest when we interpret the Constitution because our interpretation can be altered only by constitutional amendment or by overruling our prior decisions." And *stare decisis* applies with perhaps least force of all to decisions that wrongly denied First Amendment rights: "This Court has not hesitated to overrule decisions offensive to the First Amendment (a fixed star in our constitutional constellation, if there is one)." *Federal Election Comm'n v. Wisconsin Right to Life, Inc.*, 551 U.S. 449, 500, 127 S.Ct. 2652, 168 L.Ed.2d 329 (2007) (Scalia, J., concurring in part and concurring in judgment) (internal quotation marks omitted); see also *Citizens United, supra*, at 362–365, 130 S.Ct. 876 (overruling *Austin*, 494 U.S. 652, 110 S.Ct. 1391, 108 L.Ed.2d 652); *Barnette*, 319 U.S., at 642, 63 S.Ct. 1178 (overruling *Minersville School Dist. v. Gobitis*, 310 U.S. 586, 60 S.Ct. 1010, 84 L.Ed. 1375 (1940)).

Our cases identify factors that should be taken into account in deciding whether to overrule a past decision. Five of these are most important here: the quality of *Abood*'s reasoning, the workability of the rule it established, its consistency with other related decisions, developments since the decision was handed down, and reliance on the decision. After analyzing these factors, we conclude that *stare decisis* does not require us to retain *Abood*.

A

An important factor in determining whether a precedent should be overruled is the quality of its reasoning, see *Citizens United*, 558 U.S., at 363–364, 130 S.Ct. 876; *id.*, at 382–385, 130 S.Ct. 876 (ROBERTS, C.J., concurring); *Lawrence*, 539 U.S., at 577–578, 123 S.Ct. 2472, and as we explained in *Harris*, *Abood* was poorly reasoned.

Abood went wrong at the start when it concluded that two prior decisions, *Railway Employees v. Hanson*, 351 U.S. 225, 76 S.Ct. 714, 100 L.Ed. 1112 (1956), and *Machinists v. Street*, 367 U.S. 740, 81 S.Ct. 1784, 6 L.Ed.2d 1141 (1961), "appear[ed] to require validation of the agency-shop agreement before [the Court]." Properly understood, those decisions did no such thing. Both cases involved Congress's "*bare authorization*" of *private-sector* union shops under the Railway Labor Act. *Street*, *Abood* failed to appreciate that a very different First Amendment question arises when a State *requires* its employees to pay agency fees.

Abood's unwarranted reliance on *Hanson* and *Street* appears to have contributed to another mistake: *Abood* judged the constitutionality of public-sector agency fees under a deferential standard that finds no support in our free speech cases. *Abood* did not independently evaluate the strength of the government interests that were said to support the challenged agency-fee provision; nor did it ask how well that provision actually promoted those interests or whether they could have been adequately served without impinging so heavily on the free speech rights of nonmembers. Rather, *Abood* followed *Hanson* and *Street*, which it interpreted as having deferred to "*the legislative assessment* of the important contribution of the union shop to the system of labor relations established by Congress." But *Hanson* deferred to that judgment in deciding the Commerce Clause and substantive due process questions that were the focus of the case. Such deference to legislative judgments is inappropriate in deciding free speech issues.

Abood also did not sufficiently take into account the difference between the effects of agency fees in public- and private-sector collective bargaining. The challengers in *Abood* argued that collective bargaining with a government employer, unlike collective bargaining in the private sector, involves "inherently 'political'" speech. The Court did not dispute that characterization, and in fact conceded that "decisionmaking by a public employer is above all a political process" driven more by policy concerns than economic ones. But (again invoking *Hanson*), the *Abood* Court asserted that public employees do not have "weightier First Amendment interest[s]" against compelled speech than do private employees. That missed the point. Assuming for the sake of argument that the First Amendment applies at all to private-sector agency-shop arrangements, the individual interests at stake still differ. "In the public sector, core issues such as wages, pensions, and benefits are important political issues, but that is generally not so in the private sector."

Overlooking the importance of this distinction, "*Abood* failed to appreciate the conceptual difficulty of distinguishing in public-sector cases between union expenditures that are made for collective-bargaining purposes and those that are made to achieve political ends." Likewise, "*Abood* does not seem to have anticipated the magnitude of the practical administrative problems that would result in attempting to classify public-sector union expenditures as either 'chargeable' ... or nonchargeable." *Ibid.* Nor did *Abood* "foresee the practical problems that would face objecting nonmembers."

In sum, as detailed in *Harris*, *Abood* was not well reasoned.

B

Another relevant consideration in the *stare decisis* calculus is the workability of the precedent in question, *Montejo v. Louisiana*, 556 U.S. 778, 792, 129 S.Ct. 2079, 173 L.Ed.2d 955 (2009), and that factor also weighs against *Abood*.

1

Abood's line between chargeable and nonchargeable union expenditures has proved to be impossible to draw with precision. We tried to give the line some definition in *Lehnert*. There, a majority of the Court adopted a three-part test requiring that chargeable expenses (1) be "germane" to collective bargaining, (2) be "justified" by the government's labor-peace and free-rider interests, and (3) not add "significantly" to the burden on free speech, 500 U.S., at 519, 111 S.Ct. 1950, but the Court splintered over the application of this test. That division was not surprising. As the *Lehnert* dissenters aptly observed, each part of the majority's test "involves a substantial judgment call," *id.*, at 551, 111 S.Ct. 1950 (opinion of Scalia, J.), rendering the test "altogether malleable" and "no[t] principled."

Justice Scalia presciently warned that *Lehnert*'s amorphous standard would invite "perpetua[l] give-it-a-try litigation," and the Court's experience with union lobbying expenses illustrates the point. The *Lehnert* plurality held that money spent on lobbying for increased education funding was not chargeable. But Justice Marshall—applying the same three-prong test—reached precisely the opposite conclusion. And *Lehnert* failed to settle the matter; States and unions have continued to "give it a try" ever since.

2

Abood is also an "anomaly" in our First Amendment jurisprudence, as we recognized in *Harris* and *Knox*. This is not an altogether new observation. In *Abood* itself, Justice Powell faulted the Court for failing to perform the "exacting scrutiny" applied in other cases involving significant impingements on First Amendment rights. Our later cases involving compelled speech and association have also employed exacting scrutiny, if not a more demanding standard. And we have more recently refused, even in agency-fee cases, to extend *Abood* beyond circumstances where it directly controls.

Abood particularly sticks out when viewed against our cases holding that public employees generally may not be required to support a political party. The Court reached that conclusion despite a "long tradition" of political patronage in government. *Rutan, supra,* at 95, 110 S.Ct. 2729 (Scalia, J., dissenting); see also *Elrod,* 427 U.S., at 353, 96 S.Ct. 2673 (plurality opinion); *id.,* at 377–378, 96 S.Ct. 2673 (Powell, J., dissenting). It is an odd feature of our First Amendment cases that political patronage has been deemed largely unconstitutional, while forced subsidization of union speech (which has no such pedigree) has been largely permitted. As Justice Powell observed: "I am at a loss to understand why the State's decision to adopt the agency shop in the public sector should be worthy of *greater* deference, when challenged on First Amendment grounds, than its decision to adhere to the *tradition* of political patronage." *Abood, supra,* at 260, n. 14, 97 S.Ct. 1782 (opinion concurring in judgment) (citing *Elrod, supra,* at 376–380, 382–387, 96 S.Ct. 2673 (Powell, J., dissenting); emphasis added). We have no occasion here to reconsider our political patronage decisions, but Justice Powell's observation is sound as far as it goes. By overruling *Abood,* we end the oddity of privileging compelled union support over compelled party support and bring a measure of greater coherence to our First Amendment law.

D

In some cases, reliance provides a strong reason for adhering to established law, see, e.g., *Hilton v. South Carolina Public Railways Comm'n,* 502 U.S. 197, 202–203 (1991), and this is the factor that is stressed most strongly by respondents, their *amici,* and the dissent. They contend that collective-bargaining agreements now in effect were negotiated with agency fees in mind and that unions may have given up other benefits in exchange for provisions granting them such fees. In this case, however, reliance does not carry decisive weight.

For one thing, it would be unconscionable to permit free speech rights to be abridged in perpetuity in order to preserve contract provisions that will expire on their own in a few years' time. "The fact that [public-sector unions] may view [agency fees] as an entitlement does not establish the sort of reliance interest that could outweigh the countervailing interest that [nonmembers] share in having their constitutional rights fully protected."

For another, *Abood* does not provide "a clear or easily applicable standard, so arguments for reliance based on its clarity are misplaced."

This is especially so because public-sector unions have been on notice for years regarding this Court's misgivings about *Abood.* In *Knox,* decided in 2012, we described *Abood* as a First Amendment "anomaly." Two years later in *Harris,* we were asked to overrule *Abood,* and while we found it unnecessary to take that step, we cataloged *Abood*'s many weaknesses. We granted a petition for certiorari asking us to review a decision that sustained an agency-fee arrangement under *Abood. Friedrichs v. California Teachers Assn.,* 576 U.S. ——, 136 S.Ct. 2545, 195 L.Ed.2d 880 (2016). After exhaustive briefing and argument on the question whether *Abood* should be overruled, we affirmed the decision below by an equally divided vote. 578 U.S. ——, 136 S.Ct. 1083, 194 L.Ed.2d 255 (2016) (*per curiam*). During this period of time, any public-sector union seeking an agency-fee provision in a collective-bargaining agreement must have understood that the constitutionality of such a provision was uncertain.

Ramos v. Louisiana, 140 S. Ct. 1390 (2020)

Justice Gorsuch wrote the opinion in which Justices Ginsburg, Breyer, and Sotomayor joined with respect to Parts II-B, IV-B-2, and V. Justices Ginsburg and Breyer joined with respect to Part IV-A. Justice Sotomayor filed an opinion concurring as to all but Part IV-A. Justice Kavanaugh filed an opinion concurring in part. Justice Thomas filed an opinion concurring in the judgment. Justice Alito filed a dissenting opinion, in which Chief Justice Roberts joined and in which Justice Kagan.

Justice Gorsuch:

Accused of a serious crime, Evangelisto Ramos insisted on his innocence and invoked his right to a jury trial. Eventually, 10 jurors found the evidence against him persuasive. But a pair of jurors believed that the State of Louisiana had failed to prove Mr. Ramos's guilt beyond reasonable doubt; they voted to acquit.

In 48 States and federal court, a single juror's vote to acquit is enough to prevent a conviction. But not in Louisiana. Along with Oregon, Louisiana has long punished people based on 10-to-2 verdicts like the one here. So instead of the mistrial he would have received almost anywhere else, Mr. Ramos was sentenced to life in prison without the possibility of parole.

Why do Louisiana and Oregon allow nonunanimous convictions? Though it's hard to say why these laws persist, their origins are clear. Louisiana first endorsed nonunanimous verdicts for serious crimes at a constitutional convention in 1898. According to one committee chairman, the avowed purpose of that convention was to "establish the supremacy of the white race," and the resulting document included many of the trappings of the Jim Crow era: a poll tax, a combined literacy and property ownership test, and a grandfather clause that in practice exempted white residents from the most onerous of these requirements.

Nor was it only the prospect of African-Americans voting that concerned the delegates. Just a week before the convention, the U.S. Senate passed a resolution calling for an investigation into whether Louisiana was systemically excluding African-Americans from juries. Seeking to avoid unwanted national attention, and aware that this Court would strike down any policy of overt discrimination against African-American jurors as a violation of the Fourteenth Amendment, the delegates sought to undermine African-American participation on juries in another way. With a careful eye on racial demographics, the convention delegates sculpted a "facially race-neutral" rule permitting 10-to-2 verdicts in order "to ensure that African-American juror service would be meaningless."

Adopted in the 1930s, Oregon's rule permitting nonunanimous verdicts can be similarly traced to the rise of the Ku Klux Klan and efforts to dilute "the influence of racial, ethnic, and religious minorities on Oregon juries." In fact, no one before us contests any of this; courts in both Louisiana and Oregon have frankly acknowledged that race was a motivating factor in the adoption of their States' respective nonunanimity rules.

We took this case to decide whether the Sixth Amendment right to a jury trial—as incorporated against the States by way of the Fourteenth Amendment—requires a unanimous verdict to convict a defendant of a serious offense. Louisiana insists that this Court has never definitively passed on the question and urges us to find its practice consistent with the Sixth Amendment. By contrast, the dissent doesn't try to defend Louisiana's law on Sixth or Fourteenth Amendment grounds; tacitly, it seems to admit that the Constitution forbids States from using nonunanimous juries. Yet, unprompted by Louisiana, the dissent suggests our precedent requires us to rule for the State anyway. What explains all this? To answer the puzzle, it's necessary to say a bit more about the merits of the question presented, the relevant precedent, and, at last, the consequences that follow from saying what we know to be true.

I

The Sixth Amendment promises that "[i]n all criminal prosecutions, the accused shall enjoy the right to a speedy and public trial, by an impartial jury of the State and district wherein the crime shall have been committed, which district shall have been previously ascertained by law." The Amendment goes on to preserve other rights for criminal defendants but says nothing else about what a "trial by an impartial jury" entails.

Still, the promise of a jury trial surely meant *something*—otherwise, there would have been no reason to write it down. Nor would it have made any sense to spell out the places from which jurors should be drawn if their powers as jurors could be freely abridged by statute. Imagine a constitution that allowed a "jury trial" to mean nothing but a single person rubberstamping convictions without hearing any evidence—but simultaneously insisting that the lone juror come from a specific judicial district "previously ascertained by law." And if that's not enough, imagine a constitution that included the same hollow guarantee *twice*—not only in the Sixth Amendment, but also in Article III. No: The text and structure of the Constitution clearly suggest that the term "trial by an impartial jury" carried with it *some* meaning about the content and requirements of a jury trial.

One of these requirements was unanimity. Wherever we might look to determine what the term "trial by an impartial jury trial" meant at the time of the Sixth Amendment's adoption—whether it's the common law, state practices in the founding era, or opinions and treatises written soon afterward—the answer is unmistakable. A jury must reach a unanimous verdict in order to convict.

The requirement of juror unanimity emerged in 14th century England and was soon accepted as a vital right protected by the common law. As Blackstone explained, no person could be found guilty of a serious crime unless "the truth of every accusation ... should ... be confirmed by the unanimous suffrage of twelve of his equals and neighbors, indifferently chosen, and superior to all suspicion." A "verdict, taken from eleven, was no verdict" at all.

This same rule applied in the young American States. Six State Constitutions explicitly required unanimity. Another four preserved the right to a jury trial in more general terms. But the variations did not matter much; consistent with the common law, state courts appeared to regard unanimity as an essential feature of the jury trial. It was against this backdrop that James Madison drafted and the States ratified the Sixth Amendment in 1791. By that time, unanimous verdicts had been required for about 400 years. If the term "trial by an impartial jury" carried any meaning at all, it surely included a requirement as long and widely accepted as unanimity.

Influential, postadoption treatises confirm this understanding. For example, in 1824, Nathan Dane reported as fact that the U.S. Constitution required unanimity in criminal jury trials for serious offenses. A few years later, Justice Story explained in his Commentaries on the Constitution that "in common cases, the law not only presumes every man innocent, until he is proved guilty; but unanimity in the verdict of the jury is indispensable." Similar statements can be found in American legal treatises throughout the 19th century

Nor is this a case where the original public meaning was lost to time and only recently recovered. This Court has, repeatedly and over many years, recognized that the Sixth Amendment requires unanimity. As early as 1898, the Court said that a defendant enjoys a "constitutional right to demand that his liberty should not be taken from him except by the joint action of the court and the unanimous verdict of a jury of twelve persons." A few decades later, the Court elaborated that the Sixth Amendment affords a right to "a trial by jury as understood and applied at common law, ... includ[ing] all the essential elements as they were recognized in this country and England when the Constitution was adopted." And, the Court observed, this includes a requirement "that the verdict should be unanimous." In all, this Court has commented on the Sixth Amendment's unanimity requirement no fewer than 13 times over more than 120 years.

There can be no question either that the Sixth Amendment's unanimity requirement applies to state and federal criminal trials equally. This Court has long explained that the Sixth Amendment right to a jury trial is "fundamental to the American scheme of justice" and incorporated against the States under the Fourteenth Amendment.

II

A

How, despite these seemingly straightforward principles, have Louisiana's and Oregon's laws managed to hang on for so long? It turns out that the Sixth Amendment's otherwise simple story took a strange turn in 1972. That year, the Court confronted these States' unconventional schemes for the first time—in *Apodaca v. Oregon* and a companion case, *Johnson v. Louisiana*. Ultimately, the Court could do no more than issue a badly fractured set of opinions. Four dissenting Justices would not have hesitated to strike down the States' laws, recognizing that the Sixth Amendment requires unanimity and that this guarantee is fully applicable against the States under the Fourteenth Amendment. But a four-Justice plurality took a very different view of the Sixth Amendment. These Justices declared that the real question before them was whether unanimity serves an important "function" in "contemporary society." Then, having reframed the question, the plurality wasted few words before concluding that unanimity's costs outweigh its benefits in the modern era, so the Sixth Amendment should not stand in the way of Louisiana or Oregon.

The ninth Member of the Court adopted a position that was neither here nor there. On the one hand, Justice Powell agreed that, as a matter of "history and precedent, … the Sixth Amendment requires a unanimous jury verdict to convict." But, on the other hand, he argued that the Fourteenth Amendment does not render this guarantee against the federal government fully applicable against the States. In this way, Justice Powell doubled down on his belief in "dual-track" incorporation—the idea that a single right can mean two different things depending on whether it is being invoked against the federal or a state government.

Justice Powell acknowledged that his argument for dual-track incorporation came "late in the day." Late it was. The Court had already, nearly a decade earlier, "rejected the notion that the Fourteenth Amendment applies to the States only a 'watered-down, subjective version of the individual guarantees of the Bill of Rights.'" It's a point we've restated many times since, too, including as recently as last year. Still, Justice Powell frankly explained, he was "unwillin[g]" to follow the Court's precedents. So he offered up the essential fifth vote to uphold Mr. Apodaca's conviction—if based only on a view of the Fourteenth Amendment that he knew was (and remains) foreclosed by precedent.

B

In the years following *Apodaca*, both Louisiana and Oregon chose to continue allowing nonunanimous verdicts. But their practices have always stood on shaky ground. After all, while Justice Powell's vote secured a favorable judgment for the States in *Apodaca*, it's never been clear what rationale could support a similar result in future cases. Only two possibilities exist: Either the Sixth Amendment allows nonunanimous verdicts, or the Sixth Amendment's guarantee of a jury trial applies with less force to the States under the Fourteenth Amendment. Yet, as we've seen, both bear their problems. In *Apodaca* itself, a majority of Justices—including Justice Powell—recognized that the Sixth Amendment demands unanimity, just as our cases have long said. And this Court's precedents, both then and now, prevent the Court from applying the Sixth Amendment to the States in some mutated and diminished form under the Fourteenth Amendment. So what could we possibly describe as the "holding" of *Apodaca*?

Really, no one has found a way to make sense of it. In later cases, this Court has labeled *Apodaca* an "exception," "unusual," and in any event "not an endorsement" of Justice Powell's view of incorporation. At the same time, we have continued to recognize the historical need for unanimity.

IV

B

1

There's another obstacle the dissent must overcome. Even if we accepted the premise that *Apodaca* established a precedent, no one on the Court today is prepared to say it was rightly decided, and *stare decisis* isn't supposed to be the art of methodically ignoring what everyone knows to be true. Of course, the precedents of this Court warrant our deep respect as embodying the considered views of those who have come before. But *stare decisis* has never been treated as "an inexorable command." And the doctrine is "at its weakest when we interpret the Constitution" because a mistaken judicial interpretation of that supreme law is often "practically impossible" to correct through other means. To balance these considerations, when it revisits a precedent this Court has traditionally considered "the quality of the decision's reasoning; its consistency with related decisions; legal developments since the decision; and reliance on the decision." In this case, each factor points in the same direction.

Start with the quality of the reasoning. Whether we look to the plurality opinion or Justice Powell's separate concurrence, *Apodaca* was gravely mistaken; again, no Member of the Court today defends either as rightly decided. Without repeating what we've already explained in detail, it's just an implacable fact that the plurality spent almost no time grappling with the historical meaning of the Sixth Amendment's jury trial right, this Court's long-repeated statements that it demands unanimity, or the racist origins of Louisiana's and Oregon's laws. Instead, the plurality subjected the Constitution's jury trial right to an incomplete functionalist analysis of its own creation for which it spared one paragraph. And, of course, five Justices expressly rejected the plurality's conclusion that the Sixth Amendment does not require unanimity. Meanwhile, Justice Powell refused to follow this Court's incorporation precedents. Nine Justices (including Justice Powell) recognized this for what it was; eight called it an error.

Looking to *Apodaca*'s consistency with related decisions and recent legal developments compounds the reasons for concern. *Apodaca* sits uneasily with 120 years of preceding case law. Given how unmoored it was from the start, it might seem unlikely that later developments could have done more to undermine the decision. Yet they have. While Justice Powell's dual-track theory of incorporation was already foreclosed in 1972, some at that time still argued that it might have a role to play outside the realm of criminal procedure. Since then, the Court has held otherwise. Until recently, dual-track incorporation attracted at least a measure of support in dissent. But this Court has now roundly rejected it.

When it comes to reliance interests, it's notable that neither Louisiana nor Oregon claims anything like the prospective economic, regulatory, or social disruption litigants seeking to preserve precedent usually invoke. No one, it seems, has signed a contract, entered a marriage, purchased a home, or opened a business based on the expectation that, should a crime occur, at least the accused may be sent away by a 10-to-2 verdict. Nor does anyone suggest that nonunanimous verdicts have "become part of our national culture." It would be quite surprising if they had, given that nonunanimous verdicts are insufficient to convict in 48 States and federal court. Instead, the only reliance interests that might be asserted here fall into two categories. The first concerns the fact Louisiana and Oregon may need to retry defendants convicted of felonies by nonunanimous verdicts whose cases are still pending on direct appeal. The dissent claims that this fact supplies the winning argument for retaining *Apodaca* because it has generated "enormous reliance interests" and overturning the case would provoke a "crushing" "tsunami" of follow-on litigation. The overstatement may be forgiven as intended for dramatic effect, but prior convictions in only two States are potentially affected by our judgment. Those States credibly claim that the number of nonunanimous felony convictions still on direct appeal are somewhere in the hundreds, and retrying or plea bargaining these cases will surely impose a cost. But new rules of criminal procedures usually do, often affecting significant numbers of pending cases across the whole country. Our decision here promises to cause less, and certainly nothing before us supports the dissent's surmise that it will cause wildly more, disruption than these other decisions.

2

The second and related reliance interest the dissent seizes upon involves the interest Louisiana and Oregon have in the security of their final criminal judgments. In light of our decision today, the dissent worries that defendants whose appeals are already complete might seek to challenge their nonunanimous convictions through collateral (*i.e.*, habeas) review.
But again the worries outstrip the facts. Under *Teague* v. *Lane*, newly recognized rules of criminal procedure do not normally apply in collateral review True, *Teague* left open the possibility of an exception for "watershed rules" "implicat[ing] the fundamental fairness [and accuracy] of the trial." But, as this language suggests, *Teague*'s test is a demanding one, so much so that this Court has yet to announce a new rule of criminal procedure capable of meeting it. And the test is demanding by design, expressly calibrated to address the reliance interests States have in the finality of their criminal judgments.
In the final accounting, the dissent's *stare decisis* arguments round to zero. We have an admittedly mistaken decision, on a constitutional issue, an outlier on the day it was decided, one that's become lonelier with time. In arguing otherwise, the dissent must elide the reliance the American people place in their constitutionally protected liberties, overplay the competing interests of two States, count some of those interests twice, and make no small amount of new precedent all its own.
Reversed.

Justice Sotomayor, concurring as to all but Part IV-A.

I agree with most of the Court's rationale, and so I join all but Part IV-A of its opinion. I write separately, however, to underscore three points. First, overruling precedent here is not only warranted, but compelled. Second, the interests at stake point far more clearly to that outcome than those in other recent cases. And finally, the racially biased origins of the Louisiana and Oregon laws uniquely matter here.

I

Both the majority and the dissent rightly emphasize that *stare decisis* "has been a fundamental part of our jurisprudence since the founding." Indeed, "[w]e generally adhere to our prior decisions, even if we question their soundness, because doing so 'promotes the evenhanded, predictable, and consistent development of legal principles, fosters reliance on judicial decisions, and contributes to the actual and perceived integrity of the judicial process.'"

But put simply, this is not a case where we cast aside precedent "simply because a majority of this Court now disagrees with" it. Rather, *Apodaca v. Oregon*, 406 U.S. 404, 92 S.Ct. 1628, 32 L.Ed.2d 184 (1972), was on shaky ground from the start. That was not because of the functionalist analysis of that Court's plurality: Reasonable minds have disagreed over time—and continue to disagree—about the best mode of constitutional interpretation. That the plurality in *Apodaca* used different interpretive tools from the majority here is not a reason on its own to discard precedent.

What matters instead is that, as the majority rightly stresses, *Apodaca* is a universe of one—an opinion uniquely irreconcilable with not just one, but two, strands of constitutional precedent well established both before and after the decision. The Court has long recognized that the Sixth Amendment requires unanimity. Five Justices in *Apodaca* itself disagreed with that plurality's contrary view of the Sixth Amendment. Justice Powell's theory of dual-track incorporation also fared no better: He recognized that his argument on that score came "late in the day."

Moreover, "[t]he force of *stare decisis* is at its nadir in cases concerning [criminal] procedur[e] rules that implicate fundamental constitutional protections." And the constitutional protection here ranks among the most essential: the right to put the State to its burden, in a jury trial that comports with the Sixth Amendment, before facing criminal punishment.

II

In contrast to the criminal-procedure context, "[c]onsiderations in favor of *stare decisis* are at their acme in cases involving property and contract rights." Despite that fact, the Court has recently overruled precedent where the Court's shift threatened vast regulatory and economic consequences. *Janus v. State, County, and Municipal Employees*, (noting that the Court's opinion called into question "thousands of ... contracts covering millions of workers"); see *South Dakota v. Wayfair, Inc.*, (noting the "legitimate" burdens that the Court's overruling of precedent would place on vendors who had started businesses in reliance on a previous decision).

This case, by contrast, threatens no broad upheaval of private economic rights. Particularly when compared to the interests of private parties who have structured their affairs in reliance on our decisions, the States' interests here in avoiding a modest number of retrials—emphasized at such length by the dissent—are much less weighty.

Justice Kavanaugh concurring in part.

I agree with the Court that the time has come to overrule *Apodaca*. I therefore join the introduction and Parts I, II-A, III, and IV-B-1 of the Court's persuasive and important opinion. I write separately to explain my view of how *stare decisis* applies to this case.

I

The legal doctrine of *stare decisis* derives from the Latin maxim *"stare decisis et non quieta movere,"* which means to stand by the thing decided and not disturb the calm. The doctrine reflects respect for the accumulated wisdom of judges who have previously tried to solve the same problem. In 1765, Blackstone—"the preeminent authority on English law for the founding generation," *Alden v. Maine*, 527 U.S. 706, 715, 119 S.Ct. 2240, 144 L.Ed.2d 636 (1999)—wrote that "it is an established rule to abide by former precedents," to "keep the scale of justice even and steady, and not liable to waver with every new judge's opinion." 1 W. Blackstone, Commentaries on the Laws of England 69 (1765). The Framers of our Constitution understood that the doctrine of *stare decisis* is part of the "judicial Power" and rooted in Article III of the Constitution. Writing in Federalist 78, Alexander Hamilton emphasized the importance of *stare decisis*: To "avoid an arbitrary discretion in the courts, it is indispensable" that federal judges "should be bound down by strict rules and precedents, which serve to define and point out their duty in every particular case that comes before them." The Federalist No. 78, p. 529 (J. Cooke ed. 1961). In the words of THE CHIEF JUSTICE, *stare decisis'* "greatest purpose is to serve a constitutional ideal—the rule of law." *Citizens United v. Federal Election Comm'n.*

This Court has repeatedly explained that *stare decisis* "promotes the evenhanded, predictable, and consistent development of legal principles, fosters reliance on judicial decisions, and contributes to the actual and perceived integrity of the judicial process." *Payne v. Tennessee.* The doctrine "permits society to presume that bedrock principles are founded in the law rather than in the proclivities of individuals, and thereby contributes to the integrity of our constitutional system of government, both in appearance and in fact." *Vasquez v. Hillery*, 474 U.S. 254, 265–266, 106 S.Ct. 617, 88 L.Ed.2d 598 (1986).

The doctrine of *stare decisis* does not mean, of course, that the Court should never overrule erroneous precedents. All Justices now on this Court agree that it is sometimes appropriate for the Court to overrule erroneous decisions. Indeed, in just the last few Terms, every current Member of this Court has voted to overrule multiple constitutional precedents. See, *e.g.*, *Knick v. Township of Scott*, 588 U.S. ——, 139 S.Ct. 2162, 204 L.Ed.2d 558 (2019); *Franchise Tax Bd. of Cal. v. Hyatt*, 587 U.S. ——, 139 S.Ct. 1485, 203 L.Ed.2d 768 (2019); *Janus v. State, County, and Municipal Employees*, 585 U.S. ——, 138 S.Ct. 2448, 201 L.Ed.2d 924 (2018); *Hurst* v. *Florida*, 577 U.S. ——, 136 S.Ct. 616, 193 L.Ed.2d 504 (2016); *Obergefell v. Hodges*, 576 U.S. 644, 135 S.Ct. 2584, 192 L.Ed.2d 609 (2015); *Johnson v. United States*, 576 U.S. 591, 135 S.Ct. 2551, 192 L.Ed.2d 569 (2015); *Alleyne v. United States*, 570 U.S. 99, 133 S.Ct. 2151, 186 L.Ed.2d 314 (2013); see also Baude,

Precedent and Discretion, 2020 S. Ct. Rev. 1, 4 (forthcoming) ("Nobody on the Court believes in absolute stare decisis").
Historically, moreover, some of the Court's most notable and consequential decisions have entailed overruling precedent. See, e.g., *Obergefell v. Hodges*, 576 U.S. 644, 135 S.Ct. 2584, 192 L.Ed.2d 609 (2015); *Citizens United v. Federal Election Comm'n*, 558 U.S. 310, 130 S.Ct. 876, 175 L.Ed.2d 753 (2010); *Montejo v. Louisiana*, 556 U.S. 778, 129 S.Ct. 2079, 173 L.Ed.2d 955 (2009); *Crawford v. Washington*, 541 U.S. 36, 124 S.Ct. 1354, 158 L.Ed.2d 177 (2004); *Lawrence v. Texas*, 539 U.S. 558, 123 S.Ct. 2472, 156 L.Ed.2d 508 (2003); *Ring v. Arizona*, 536 U.S. 584, 122 S.Ct. 2428, 153 L.Ed.2d 556 (2002); *Agostini v. Felton*, 521 U.S. 203, 117 S.Ct. 1997, 138 L.Ed.2d 391 (1997); *Seminole Tribe of Fla. v. Florida*, 517 U.S. 44, 116 S.Ct. 1114, 134 L.Ed.2d 252 (1996); *Planned Parenthood of Southeastern Pa. v. Casey*, 505 U.S. 833, 112 S.Ct. 2791, 120 L.Ed.2d 674 (1992); *Payne v. Tennessee*, 501 U.S. 808, 111 S.Ct. 2597, 115 L.Ed.2d 720 (1991); *Batson v. Kentucky*, 476 U.S. 79, 106 S.Ct. 1712, 90 L.Ed.2d 69 (1986); *Garcia v. San Antonio Metropolitan Transit Authority*, 469 U.S. 528, 105 S.Ct. 1005, 83 L.Ed.2d 1016 (1985); *Illinois v. Gates*, 462 U.S. 213, 103 S.Ct. 2317, 76 L.Ed.2d 527 (1983); *United States v. Scott*, 437 U.S. 82, 98 S.Ct. 2187, 57 L.Ed.2d 65 (1978); *Craig v. Boren*, 429 U.S. 190, 97 S.Ct. 451, 50 L.Ed.2d 397 (1976); *Taylor v. Louisiana*, 419 U.S. 522, 95 S.Ct. 692, 42 L.Ed.2d 690 (1975); *Brandenburg v. Ohio*, 395 U.S. 444, 89 S.Ct. 1827, 23 L.Ed.2d 430 (1969) (*per curiam*); *Katz v. United States*, 389 U.S. 347, 88 S.Ct. 507, 19 L.Ed.2d 576 (1967); *Miranda v. Arizona*, 384 U.S. 436, 86 S.Ct. 1602, 16 L.Ed.2d 694 (1966); *Malloy v. Hogan*, 378 U.S. 1, 84 S.Ct. 1489, 12 L.Ed.2d 653 (1964); *Wesberry v. Sanders*, 376 U.S. 1, 84 S.Ct. 526, 11 L.Ed.2d 481 (1964); *Gideon v. Wainwright*, 372 U.S. 335, 83 S.Ct. 792, 9 L.Ed.2d 799 (1963); *Baker v. Carr*, 369 U.S. 186, 82 S.Ct. 691, 7 L.Ed.2d 663 (1962); *Mapp v. Ohio*, 367 U.S. 643, 81 S.Ct. 1684, 6 L.Ed.2d 1081 (1961); *Brown v. Board of Education*, 347 U.S. 483, 74 S.Ct. 686, 98 L.Ed. 873 (1954); *Smith v. Allwright*, 321 U.S. 649, 64 S.Ct. 757, 88 L.Ed. 987 (1944); *West Virginia Bd. of Ed. v. Barnette*, 319 U.S. 624, 63 S.Ct. 1178, 87 L.Ed. 1628 (1943); *United States v. Darby*, 312 U.S. 100, 61 S.Ct. 451, 85 L.Ed. 609 (1941); *Erie R. Co. v. Tompkins*, 304 U.S. 64, 58 S.Ct. 817, 82 L.Ed. 1188 (1938); *West Coast Hotel Co. v. Parrish*, 300 U.S. 379, 57 S.Ct. 578, 81 L.Ed. 703 (1937).
The lengthy and extraordinary list of landmark cases that overruled precedent includes the single most important and greatest decision in this Court's history, *Brown v. Board of Education*, which repudiated the separate but equal doctrine of *Plessy v. Ferguson*, 163 U.S. 537, 16 S.Ct. 1138, 41 L.Ed. 256 (1896).
As those many examples demonstrate, the doctrine of *stare decisis* does not dictate, and no one seriously maintains, that the Court should *never* overrule erroneous precedent. As the Court has often stated and repeats today, *stare decisis* is not an "inexorable command."
On the other hand, as Justice Jackson explained, just "because one should avoid Scylla is no reason for crashing into Charybdis." Jackson, Decisional Law and Stare Decisis, 30 A. B. A. J. 334 (1944). So no one advocates that the Court should *always* overrule erroneous precedent.
Rather, applying the doctrine of *stare decisis*, this Court ordinarily adheres to precedent, but *sometimes* overrules precedent. The difficult question, then, is when to overrule an erroneous precedent.
In statutory cases, *stare decisis* is comparatively strict, as history shows and the Court has often stated. That is because Congress and the President can alter a stat-

utory precedent by enacting new legislation. To be sure, enacting new legislation requires finding room in a crowded legislative docket and securing the agreement of the House, the Senate (in effect, 60 Senators), and the President. Both by design and as a matter of fact, enacting new legislation is difficult—and far more difficult than the Court's cases sometimes seem to assume. Nonetheless, the Court has ordinarily left the updating or correction of erroneous statutory precedents to the legislative process. See, *e.g., Kimble v. Marvel Entertainment, LLC*, 576 U.S. 446, 456–457, 135 S.Ct. 2401, 192 L.Ed.2d 463 (2015); *Patterson v. McLean Credit Union*, 491 U.S. 164, 172–173, 109 S.Ct. 2363, 105 L.Ed.2d 132 (1989); *Flood v. Kuhn*, 407 U.S. 258, 283–284, 92 S.Ct. 2099, 32 L.Ed.2d 728 (1972). The principle that "it is more important that the applicable rule of law be settled than that it be settled right" is "commonly true even where the error is a matter of serious concern, *provided correction can be had by legislation.*" *Burnet v. Coronado Oil & Gas Co.*, 285 U.S. 393, 406, 52 S.Ct. 443, 76 L.Ed. 815 (1932) (Brandeis, J., dissenting) (emphasis added).

In constitutional cases, by contrast, the Court has repeatedly said—and says again today—that the doctrine of *stare decisis* is not as "inflexible." *Burnet*, 285 U.S. at 406, 52 S.Ct. 443 (Brandeis, J., dissenting); *Payne*, 501 U.S. at 828, 111 S.Ct. 2597; *Scott*, 437 U.S. at 101, 98 S.Ct. 2187. The reason is straightforward: As Justice O'Connor once wrote for the Court, *stare decisis* is not as strict "when we interpret the Constitution because our interpretation can be altered only by constitutional amendment or by overruling our prior decisions." *Agostini*, 521 U.S. at 235, 117 S.Ct. 1997. The Court therefore "must balance the importance of having consti-tutional questions *decided* against the importance of having them *decided right.*" *Citizens United*, 558 U.S. at 378, 130 S.Ct. 876 (ROBERTS, C. J., concurring). It follows "that in the unusual circumstance when fidelity to any particular precedent does more to damage this constitutional ideal than to advance it, we must be more willing to depart from that precedent." *Ibid.* In his canonical opinion in *Burnet*, Justice Brandeis described the Court's practice with respect to *stare decisis* in con-stitutional cases in a way that was accurate then and remains accurate now: In "cases involving the Federal Constitution, where correction through legislative action is practically impossible, this Court has often overruled its earlier decisions." 285 U.S. at 406–407, 52 S.Ct. 443 (dissenting opinion).

In particular, to overrule a constitutional precedent, the Court requires something "over and above the belief that the precedent was wrongly decided." *Allen*, 589 U.S., at ——, 140 S.Ct., at 1003 (internal quotation marks omitted). As Justice Scalia put it, the doctrine of *stare decisis* always requires "reasons that go beyond mere demonstration that the overruled opinion was wrong," for "otherwise the doc-trine would be no doctrine at all." *Hubbard v. United States*, 514 U.S. 695, 716, 115 S.Ct. 1754, 131 L.Ed.2d 779 (1995) (opinion concurring in part and concurring in judgment). To overrule, the Court demands a special justification or strong grounds. But the "special justification" or "strong grounds" formulation elides a key ques-tion: What constitutes a special justification or strong grounds? In other words, in deciding whether to overrule an erroneous constitutional decision, how does the Court know when to overrule and when to stand pat?

As the Court has exercised the "judicial Power" over time, the Court has identified various *stare decisis* factors. In articulating and applying those factors, the Court has, to borrow James Madison's words, sought to liquidate and ascertain the meaning of the Article III "judicial Power" with respect to precedent. The Federalist No. 37, at 236.

The *stare decisis* factors identified by the Court in its past cases include:

- the quality of the precedent's reasoning;
- the precedent's consistency and coherence with previous or subsequent decisions;
- changed law since the prior decision;
- changed facts since the prior decision;
- the workability of the precedent;
- the reliance interests of those who have relied on the precedent; and
- the age of the precedent.

But the Court has articulated and applied those various individual factors without establishing any consistent methodology or roadmap for how to analyze all of the factors taken together. And in my view, that muddle poses a problem for the rule of law and for this Court, as the Court attempts to apply *stare decisis* principles in a neutral and consistent manner.

As I read the Court's cases on precedent, those varied and somewhat elastic *stare decisis* factors fold into three broad considerations that, in my view, can help guide the inquiry and help determine what constitutes a "special justification" or "strong grounds" to overrule a prior constitutional decision.

First, is the prior decision not just wrong, but grievously or egregiously wrong? A garden-variety error or disagreement does not suffice to overrule. In the view of the Court that is considering whether to overrule, the precedent must be egregiously wrong as a matter of law in order for the Court to overrule it. In conducting that inquiry, the Court may examine the quality of the precedent's reasoning, consistency and coherence with other decisions, changed law, changed facts, and workability, among other factors. A case may be egregiously wrong when decided, see, *e.g.*, *Korematsu v. United States*, 323 U.S. 214, 65 S.Ct. 193, 89 L.Ed. 194 (1944); *Plessy v. Ferguson*, 163 U.S. 537, 16 S.Ct. 1138, 41 L.Ed. 256 (1896), or may be unmasked as egregiously wrong based on later legal or factual understandings or developments, see, *e.g.*, *Nevada v. Hall*, 440 U.S. 410, 99 S.Ct. 1182, 59 L.Ed.2d 416 (1979), or both.

Second, has the prior decision caused significant negative jurisprudential or real-world consequences? In conducting that inquiry, the Court may consider jurisprudential consequences (some of which are also relevant to the first inquiry), such as workability, as well as consistency and coherence with other decisions, among other factors. Importantly, the Court may also scrutinize the precedent's real-world effects on the citizenry, not just its effects on the law and the legal system. See, *e.g.*, *Brown v. Board of Education*, 347 U.S. at 494–495, 74 S.Ct. 686; *Barnette*, 319 U.S. at 630–642, 63 S.Ct. 1178; see also *Payne*, 501 U.S. at 825–827, 111 S.Ct. 2597.

Third, would overruling the prior decision unduly upset reliance interests? This consideration focuses on the legitimate expectations of those who have reasonably relied on the precedent. In conducting that inquiry, the Court may examine a variety of reliance interests and the age of the precedent, among other factors.

In short, the first consideration requires inquiry into how wrong the precedent is as a matter of law. The second and third considerations together demand, in Justice Jackson's words, a "sober appraisal of the disadvantages of the innovation as well as those of the questioned case, a weighing of practical effects of one against the other." Jackson, 30 A. B. A. J., at 334.

Those three considerations together provide a structured methodology and roadmap for determining whether to overrule an erroneous constitutional precedent. The three considerations correspond to the Court's historical practice and encompass the various individual factors that the Court has applied over the years as part of the *stare decisis* calculus. And they are consistent with the Founding understanding and, for example, Blackstone's shorthand description that overruling is warranted when (and only when) a precedent is "manifestly absurd or unjust." 1 Blackstone, Commentaries on the Laws of England, at 70.

Taken together, those three considerations set a high (but not insurmountable) bar for overruling a precedent, and they therefore limit the number of overrulings and maintain stability in the law. Those three considerations also constrain judicial discretion in deciding when to overrule an erroneous precedent. To be sure, applying those considerations is not a purely mechanical exercise, and I do not claim otherwise. I suggest only that those three considerations may better structure how to consider the many traditional *stare decisis* factors.

It is inevitable that judges of good faith applying the *stare decisis* considerations will sometimes disagree about when to overrule an erroneous constitutional precedent, as the Court does in this case. To begin with, judges may disagree about whether a prior decision is wrong in the first place—and importantly, that disagreement is sometimes the *real* dispute when judges joust over *stare decisis*. But even when judges agree that a prior decision is wrong, they may disagree about whether the decision is so egregiously wrong as to justify an overruling. Judges may likewise disagree about the severity of the jurisprudential or real-world consequences caused by the erroneous decision and, therefore, whether the decision is worth overruling. In that regard, some judges may think that the negative consequences can be addressed by narrowing the precedent (or just living with it) rather than outright overruling it. Judges may also disagree about how to measure the relevant reliance interests that might be affected by an overruling. And on top of all of that, judges may also disagree about how to weigh and balance all of those competing considerations in a given case.

This case illustrates that point. No Member of the Court contends that the result in *Apodaca* is correct. But the Members of the Court vehemently disagree about whether to overrule *Apodaca*.

II

Applying the three broad *stare decisis* considerations to this case, I agree with the Court's decision to overrule *Apodaca*.

First, *Apodaca* is egregiously wrong. The original meaning and this Court's precedents establish that the Sixth Amendment requires a unanimous jury.

Second, *Apodaca* causes significant negative consequences. It is true that *Apodaca* is workable. But *Apodaca* sanctions the conviction at trial or by guilty plea of some defendants who might not be convicted under the proper constitutional rule (although exactly how many is of course unknowable). That consequence has traditionally supplied some support for overruling an egregiously wrong criminal-procedure precedent.

Third, overruling *Apodaca* would not unduly upset reliance interests. Only Louisiana and Oregon employ non-unanimous juries in criminal cases. To be sure, in those two States, the Court's decision today will invalidate some non-unanimous convictions where the issue is preserved and the case is still on direct review. But that consequence almost always ensues when a criminal-procedure precedent that favors the government is overruled. And here, at least, I would "count that a small price to pay for the uprooting of this weed."

Except for the effects on that limited class of direct review cases, it will be relatively easy going forward for Louisiana and Oregon to transition to the unanimous jury rule that the other 48 States and the federal courts use. Indeed, in 2018, Louisiana amended its constitution to require jury unanimity in criminal trials for crimes committed on or after January 1, 2019, meaning that the transition is already well under way in Louisiana.

Justice ALITO, with whom THE CHIEF JUSTICE joins, and with whom Justice KAGAN joins as to all but Part III-D, dissenting.

The doctrine of *stare decisis* gets rough treatment in today's decision. Lowering the bar for overruling our precedents, a badly fractured majority casts aside an important and long-established decision with little regard for the enormous reliance the decision has engendered. If the majority's approach is not just a way to dispose of this one case, the decision marks an important turn.

III

A

Stare decisis has been a fundamental part of our jurisprudence since the founding, and it is an important doctrine. But, as we have said many times, it is not an "inexorable command." There are circumstances when past decisions must be overturned, but we begin with the presumption that we will follow precedent, and therefore when the Court decides to overrule, it has an obligation to provide an explanation for its decision.

This is imperative because the Court should have a body of *neutral* principles on the question of overruling precedent. The doctrine should not be transformed into a tool that favors particular outcomes.

June Medical Services L. L. C. v. Russo, 140 S.Ct. 2103 (2020)

Chief Justice Roberts, concurring in the judgment.

In July 2013, Texas enacted a law requiring a physician performing an abortion to have "active admitting privileges at a hospital ... located not further than 30 miles from the location at which the abortion is performed." Tex. Health & Safety Code Ann. § 171.0031(a)(1)(A) (West Cum. Supp. 2019). The law caused the number of facilities providing abortions to drop in half. In *Whole Woman's Health v.*

Hellerstedt, 579 U.S. 5, 136 S.Ct. 2292, 195 L.Ed.2d 665 (2016), the Court concluded that Texas's admitting privileges requirement "places a substantial obstacle in the path of women seeking a previability abortion" and therefore violated the Due Process Clause of the Fourteenth Amendment. *Id.*, at ——, 136 S.Ct. (slip op., at 2) (citing *Planned Parenthood of Southeastern Pa. v. Casey*, 505 U.S. 833, 878, 112 S.Ct. 2791, 120 L.Ed.2d 674 (1992) (plurality opinion)).

I joined the dissent in *Whole Woman's Health* and continue to believe that the case was wrongly decided. The question today however is not whether *Whole Woman's Health* was right or wrong, but whether to adhere to it in deciding the present case. See *Moore v. Texas*, 586 U.S. ——, ——, 139 S.Ct. 666, 203 L.Ed.2d 1 (2019) (ROBERTS, C. J., concurring) (slip op., at 1).

Today's case is a challenge from several abortion clinics and providers to a Louisiana law nearly identical to the Texas law struck down four years ago in *Whole Woman's Health*. Just like the Texas law, the Louisiana law requires physicians performing abortions to have "active admitting privileges at a hospital ... located not further than thirty miles from the location at which the abortion is performed." La. Rev. Stat. Ann. § 40:1061.10(A)(2)(a) (West Cum. Supp. 2020). Following a six-day bench trial, the District Court found that Louisiana's law would "result in a drastic reduction in the number and geographic distribution of abortion providers." *June Medical Services LLC v. Kliebert*, 250 F.Supp.3d 27, 87 (MD La. 2017). The law would reduce the number of clinics from three to "one, or at most two," and the number of physicians providing abortions from five to "one, or at most two," and "therefore cripple women's ability to have an abortion in Louisiana."

The legal doctrine of *stare decisis* requires us, absent special circumstances, to treat like cases alike. The Louisiana law imposes a burden on access to abortion just as severe as that imposed by the Texas law, for the same reasons. Therefore Louisiana's law cannot stand under our precedents.

I

Stare decisis ("to stand by things decided") is the legal term for fidelity to precedent. Black's Law Dictionary 1696 (11th ed. 2019). It has long been "an established rule to abide by former precedents, where the same points come again in litigation; as well to keep the scale of justice even and steady, and not liable to waver with every new judge's opinion." 1 W. Blackstone, Commentaries on the Laws of England 69 (1765). This principle is grounded in a basic humility that recognizes today's legal issues are often not so different from the questions of yesterday and that we are not the first ones to try to answer them. Because the "private stock of reason ... in each man is small, ... individuals would do better to avail themselves of the general bank and capital of nations and of ages." 3 E. Burke, Reflections on the Revolution in France 110 (1790).

Adherence to precedent is necessary to "avoid an arbitrary discretion in the courts." The Federalist No. 78, p. 529 (J. Cooke ed. 1961) (A. Hamilton). The constraint of precedent distinguishes the judicial "method and philosophy from those of the political and legislative process." Jackson, Decisional Law and Stare Decisis, 30 A. B. A. J. 334 (1944).

The doctrine also brings pragmatic benefits. Respect for precedent "promotes the evenhanded, predictable, and consistent development of legal principles, fosters reliance on judicial decisions, and contributes to the actual and perceived integrity of the judicial process." *Payne v. Tennessee*, 501 U.S. 808, 827, 111 S.Ct. 2597, 115 L.Ed.2d 720 (1991). It is the "means by which we ensure that the law will not merely change erratically, but will develop in a principled and intelligible fashion." *Vasquez v. Hillery*, 474 U.S. 254, 265, 106 S.Ct. 617, 88 L.Ed.2d 598 (1986). In that way, "*stare decisis* is an old friend of the common lawyer." *Jackson, supra*, at 334, 73 S.Ct. 1031.

Stare decisis is not an "inexorable command." *Ramos v. Louisiana*, 590 U.S. ——, ——, 140 S.Ct. 1390, 206 L.Ed.2d 583 (2020) (slip op., at 20) (internal quotation marks omitted). But for precedent to mean anything, the doctrine must give way only to a rationale that goes beyond whether the case was decided correctly. The Court accordingly considers additional factors before overruling a precedent, such as its administrability, its fit with subsequent factual and legal developments, and the reliance interests that the precedent has engendered. See *Janus v. State, County, and Municipal Employees*, 585 U.S. ——, —— – ——, 138 S.Ct. 2448, 201 L.Ed.2d 924 (2018) (slip op., at 34–35).

Stare decisis principles also determine how we handle a decision that itself departed from the cases that came before it. In those instances, "[r]emaining true to an 'intrinsically sounder' doctrine established in prior cases better serves the values of *stare decisis* than would following" the recent departure. *Adarand Constructors, Inc. v. Peña*, 515 U.S. 200, 231, 115 S.Ct. 2097, 132 L.Ed.2d 158 (1995) (plurality opinion). *Stare decisis* is pragmatic and contextual, not "a mechanical formula of adherence to the latest decision." *Helvering v. Hallock*, 309 U.S. 106, 119, 60 S.Ct. 444, 84 L.Ed. 604 (1940).

Index